THE TEACHING OF PRIMARY SCIENCE: POLICY & PRACTICE

THE TEACHING OF PRIMARY SCIENCE: POLICY & PRACTICE

Colin Richards and
Derek Holford

(22) **The Falmer Press**
A member of the Taylor & Francis Group
London and New York

ISBN 0 905273 34 6 limp
0 905273 35 4 cased

First published 1983

Jacket design by Leonard Williams

Typeset in Bembo by
Imago/Graphicraft Limited
Printed by Taylor and Francis (Printers) Ltd
Basingstoke, England
for
The Falmer Press
Falmer House
Barcombe
Lewes, Sussex
BN8 5DL

Contents

Contents

Editors' Preface

In retrospect 1978 may well be seen as a decisive year in the development of primary science, at least in England. Before then there had been a number of uncoordinated initiatives – individual curriculum development projects, courses, publications and, in particular, pioneering work by individual teachers in classes scattered up and down the country. Science was regarded by many teachers as a possible addition to the primary curriculum but scarcely an essential one. The HMI Primary Survey published in 1978 countered this view and provided a very significant reassessment of the place of science in the curriculum. No longer was science seen as interesting but rather peripheral; it was seen as having a place in every child's primary education. After 1978 many initiatives were taken at national, local authority and school levels to reinforce that viewpoint and make science an actuality for primary pupils.

Prior to 1978 books had been published in the area of primary science but they had been concerned either to argue the case for the inclusion of science or to recommend specific approaches; none had provided an overall view of developments. After 1978 leading figures in primary science were concerned to capitalize on the impetus created by the HMI Primary Survey, and, appropriately, their writing reflected their own particular interests or initiatives concerned with the professional development of teachers and students. No detailed overall analysis of recent developments was published. This book provides the first detailed analysis and assessment of the development of primary science prior to and following the Primary Survey.

The book is intended for two main audiences: pre-service students who need background knowledge to give meaning and context to the more immediately practical skills and ideas they are acquiring through workshops and school experience; and teachers in service, either preparing specifically to take responsibility for fostering the policy and practice of science in their schools, or seeking more generally to deepen their understanding of the primary curriculum as part of their professional development.

In a compact, accessible and, hopefully, readable form the book draws together a considerable number of original contributions along with some of the best of previously published material by leading authorities. Key issues central to contemporary policy and practice are identified, set in context and interrelated for readers. Quite deliberately, the book provides a variety of viewpoints about these key issues. No one philosophy or approach is assumed to have a monopoly of truth or reasonableness; no set of detailed prescriptions is offered. Rather, the book seeks to inform, rather than supersede, readers' own judgement.

Colin Richards and Derek Holford
Leicester, May 1983

Acknowledgements

The publishers are grateful to the following for permission to reproduce copyright material:

The Controller of Her Majesty's Stationery Office for extracts from *Primary Education in England: A Survey by HM Inspectors of Schools (1978)* and *Trends in Education*, 12, 1968;

The Editor and Publishers of *The Times Educational Supplement* for Black. P. (1980) 'Why hasn't it worked?' 3 October 1980.

The Editor and Publishers of *Education 3–13* for Kerr, J. and Engel, E. (1980) 'Can science be taught in primary schools?', 8, 1; Squires, A. (1980) 'What is science for primary school children?', 8, 1; Richards, R. (1980) 'Children learning through science: A progress report, 8, 2; Holford, D. (1981) 'Nuffield Combined Science: Teams for the seventies, themes for the eighties?' 9, 1; Ashton, A. (1980) 'Balloons, solar energy and dyes: An approach to primary science', 8, 2; Evans, P. (1980) 'Science: Pure or applied?' 8, 1; Wetton, M. (1980) 'Science in a school of social priority', 8, 1;

The Editor and Publishers of *School Science Review* for Harlen, W. (1978) 'Does content matter in primary science?', 59.

The British Association for the Advancement of Science for Isaacs, N. (1962) 'The case for bringing science into the primary school'.

Foreword

It is one thing to say that primary schools should offer science as part of their curriculum. It is another to say of what the science should consist and how the teaching of it should be arranged across the school and within the teaching group.

The view expressed in the HMI survey of primary education, published in 1978, found widespread support: primary schools should offer more science than they did at the time of the survey. The contributors to this book take much further the discussion about what should be taught and how. They also raise important questions about how the teaching of science might be made more widespread and how what is done can be evaluated.

There continues to be a need for informed discussion on these topics so that action taken in schools and in support of teachers is well tailored to the needs of the children, the teachers, and the community. It has to be remembered that science in primary schools can only be justified on the ground that it is essential to the general education of the pupils, whether or not they will become professional scientists.

This book should help the movement forward and I am pleased to have been asked to write this foreword to it.

Norman Thomas CBE
formerly Chief Inspector for Primary
   and Middle Schools
May, 1983

PART I

Introduction

1 The Primary Curriculum and Primary Science

Colin Richards

Context and Contest

Primary, as opposed to elementary, education is a comparatively recent development within the educational system of England and Wales. As a stage of education, it was formally established by the 1944 Education Act, though it had been government policy since 1928 to establish schools specifically for children of this age-group. During its short history, primary education has had to contend with a number of formidable problems: the legacy of the elementary school tradition with its relatively narrow, instrumental approach focussing on the three Rs; the selective role assigned to primary schools and symbolized by the 11+ examination; the vast expansion followed by spectacular contraction in the number of children of primary school age; and the inability of the sector to attract resources on a scale comparable to secondary and higher education. Despite these difficulties in the way of realizing a genuine *primary* education, it has established itself as a distinct, and in some ways distinctive, sector and has influenced both the development of middle schools and, to a lesser extent, the early years of secondary education. Partly because of its comparatively recent origin and its frenetic development, overall appreciations of its achievements and shortcomings have not been plentiful. The Plowden Report (1967) provided one such appreciation; the HMI Primary Survey (1978) another. In part, this book attempts a further appreciation but one which focusses on science, only one facet of the primary curriculum.

As far as this chapter is concerned, the curriculum can be regarded as comprising those patterns of educational experience or courses of study provided or nurtured by teachers in primary schools. The curriculum is a major (though not the only) means through which children are introduced to *valued* skills, interests, attitudes, concepts and knowledge. However, within our society and its teaching profession there is disagreement over what is to be 'valued', and the curriculum inevitably reflects that conflict. As Blyth (1978) remarks, 'Everybody agrees that curriculum matters. That is probably the extent of agreement about curriculum' (p. 25). The 'contested' nature of the primary curriculum needs to be emphasized. In this country there is no one universally held view as to what constitutes an appropriate curriculum for primary children; there is no one set of meanings which all interested parties believe should be conveyed as the primary curriculum. There are disagreements about the range of the primary curriculum, about the bases on which it should be planned and implemented, and about its appropriateness and effectiveness. As far as science is concerned, its place within the primary curriculum is also 'contested', as is the nature of primary science itself. This chapter seeks to outline the nature of some of the contestations surrounding the primary curriculum in general and primary science in particular through discussing a number of issues of current concern. The issues themselves are discussed in greater depth in relation to primary science by other contributors to this book.

Range

The range of the curriculum has been an important and controversial issue ever since the introduction of schooling. 'How wide should the curriculum be?' is an especially pertinent question at the present time when falling rolls, cuts in educational expenditure and the consequent loss of staff and material resources threaten the preservation of the existing curriculum in some primary schools and even more so in some middle schools.

It is possible to argue that the curriculum is too wide and could profitably be narrowed. Columnists in certain daily newspapers and other Black Paper sympathizers want a concentration on the 'basics' (reading, writing and cyphering). Others with less extreme views query whether science or physical education or religious education need to be provided as part of the formal curriculum for all pupils in maintained primary schools. It is, of course, possible to argue the reverse – that the present curriculum is often too narrowly conceived, and its range should be extended. From this perspective, extension might take one of three forms. Firstly, new subjects or areas could be incorporated into the existing curriculum: a period of health education a week for junior children? A time each week when every class is taught science? Secondly, new strands could be added to existing work: a topic a year with a science bias for all children? The provision for children to make things that work (simple technology) in addition to their normal craft activities? Thirdly, the primary curriculum could be infused by more general perspectives: the application of science or micro-electronics in a variety of curricular areas?

It is important to note that arguments for increasing or decreasing curriculum range are advanced on shaky evidence. Chapter six of the HMI Primary Survey does provide some evidence on the extent to which certain activities appeared in the classes inspected, but no overall description or analysis of the range of the primary curriculum is available. Whatever the actual range, a recent statement of government guidance on the curriculum (*The School Curriculum*, 1981) does argue that science should have a place in every child's primary education:

> all pupils should be involved in practical as well as theoretical work in elementary science.... Primary schools should provide more effective science teaching. Children should be given more opportunities for work which progressively develops their knowledge; it is equally

important to introduce them to the skills and processes of science, including observation, experiment and prediction (p. 11).

This viewpoint is reinforced by the consultative document, *Science Education in Schools*, issued in June 1982, and the recently published discussion paper *Science in Primary Schools* (DES, 1983).

The range of primary science itself and the relative emphasis to be placed on particular aspects of work have also been 'contested'. Here, as elsewhere in the primary curriculum, there have been attempts to widen the scope of the work and thereby to increase the demands on schools and teachers (see Chapter 2). The study of living things in the form of nature study has long been a component of the curriculum for children below the age of 12; the Hadow Report (1931) stressed its importance along with the first-hand study of some elements of simple astronomy and 'a rudimentary study of some outstanding physical facts, such as the working of the mariner's compass' (p. 100). In the thirty years following Hadow there was increasing advocacy for the inclusion of elements of physical science, though the claims of astronomy (and the mariner's compass!) tended to be overlooked. By the early sixties, attempts were being made by some teachers to broaden the scope of 'nature study', as illustrated in Chapter 2. Recently, the claims of technology have been advanced as an element to complement science (as in *The School Curriculum*, 1981) or, less often, as an area in its own right, perhaps even replacing 'pure science' (Chapter 19). Though there has been increasing advocacy of physical science, the evidence presented in Chapter 4 suggests that work on the characteristics of living things is still by far and away the most important component of the science taught in primary classes. How far recent initiatives will increase the range of primary science remains problematic.

Structure

A second important general issue relates to the bases on which the primary curriculum and its component areas should be planned and implemented. What kind of 'structure' should it have? From what principles should this 'structure' be derived? During the last decade, there has been concern over the problem of 'structure', though compared with complaints about its absence, there have been far fewer attempts to spell out what this 'structure' should be.

Here, three senses of the term are distinguished and then related to primary science. In the first sense, the structure of the curriculum refers to the underlying bases used to select what it is that children should learn. Such bases may be one or more of the following: important general ideas or concepts, skills, processes, generalizations, areas of experience, children's interests, or items of valued subject matter. It is in relation to such bases that particular themes or activities are planned and particular experiences provided. The second sense of structure relates to the psychological principles which underlie the realization of the curriculum in the classroom, especially the view taken as to how children learn most effectively. Different views of learning have markedly different implications for the way children's work is sequenced and fostered by teachers. The third sense of structure relates to the way schools or classrooms are organized and managed as environments for teaching and learning. Here, the curriculum is structured if activities proceed smoothly, resources are readily available and space is adequately utilized.

Within primary science, bases for the choice of topics and activities have been fiercely debated during the last twenty years. Discussion has centred on a number of issues including the place of children's interests in the selection of themes and enquiries, but the most contentious has been concerned with the relative importance of process or content criteria in planning the work (see Chapter 7). One school of thought which has dominated discussion of primary science and which is represented in this book by contributors such as Wastnedge, Squires and Richards has stressed that work should be pursued primarily (but not exclusively) with scientific processes and attitudes in mind so that children can develop the abilities to observe, raise questions, propose enquiries to answer questions, experiment or investigate, find patterns in observations, reason systematically and logically, communicate findings and apply learning. An alternative viewpoint represented here by Redman, McClelland and Black and discussed elsewhere by Booth (1971, 1980) argues that activities should be planned primarily (but not exclusively) with major scientific ideas or concepts in mind so that children are able to use these conceptual tools (for example, 'energy', 'structure', 'adaptation') to make sense of many aspects of the world around them. Recently, partly through the work of the Assessment of Performance Unit (Chapter 9), generalizations have been advocated as criteria, along with others, to be used in the selection of topics or themes for science work (see Chapter 7). It is argued that generalizations such as 'Living things depend on each other in various ways' provide a framework for selecting activities and content but can be achieved in a variety of ways and with a range of subject matter.

In recent years, a consensus appears to be developing, illustrated, for example, in the work of the Learning through Science Project (Chapter 15), the HMI Science Committee (DES, 1983), the Assessment of Performance Unit (Chapter 9) and the Scottish Committee on Environmental Studies in the Primary School (Chapter 23). On this view, processes, generalizations and concepts are all seen as important criteria for the selection of activities; general areas from which scientific activities are to be selected include the study of living things, the immediate environment, energy, and the nature of materials; children's interests are seen as very important but not absolutely paramount in the development of the work. Within this overall stance, process criteria are still pre-eminent but not nearly to the same degree as in the orthodoxy of ten years ago. Advocacy of the importance of concepts and generalizations is gaining ground. Perhaps, as Parker-Jelly suggests (Chapter 14), future work in primary science 'will have a greater concern for concepts than that shown by Science 5–13 and the two projects (Progress in Learning Science and Learning through Science) it has generated' (p. 153). Future concern may relate both to the underlying concepts which activities aim to develop and, as Kerr and Engel's contribution (Chapter 5) argues, to children's own understandings and ways of thinking about scientific concepts.

In contrast to the controversy over process and content in planning primary science, there has been near unanimity amongst English educationists regarding the psychological principles which underlie the learning of primary science. The basic Piagetian view of children's learning and development has been generally accepted, though some writers such as Isaacs (Chapter 10) have reinterpreted this to some extent in the light of observations of children engaged in concrete problem-solving situations arising directly from their own experiences and interests. Piaget's view of learning is concisely summarized in paragraph 521 of the Plowden Report:

> One of its most important conclusions is that the great majority of primary school children can only learn efficiently from concrete situations as lived or described. From these situations, children acquire concepts in every area of the curriculum. According to Piaget, all learning calls for organization of material or of behaviour on the part of the learner, and the learner has to adapt himself and is altered in the process. Learning takes place through a continuous process of interaction between the learner and his environment which results in the building up of consistent and stable patterns of behaviour, physical and mental. Each new experience reorganizes, however slightly, the structure of the mind and contributes to the child's world picture.

From the psychological principles produced by Piaget and elaborated by Isaacs and others have been derived principles for primary science teaching centring on (i) the provision of a wide range of practical experience, (ii) the encouragement of children's problem-solving related directly to the world around them, and (iii) the importance of questions and enquiries generated by the children themselves.

Until very recently, the Piagetian basis for primary science teaching has gone virtually unchallenged. However, an alternative view is beginning to be heard. In Chapter 11 McClelland outlines a different theory based on the work of Ausubel, who has been particularly concerned with the psychology of meaningful *verbal* learning. Both Ausubel and McClelland argue for the importance of high-level concepts (for example, adaptation, energy conservation) which can guide the provision of experiences by teachers and the pursuit of enquiries by children. On this view of learning, the material is presented as a short set of statements at a high level (for example, 'Living things are adapted to their life style and environment'), followed by specific low-level instances used to develop their meaning. Initially, the general statements have little meaning and the concepts they express are vague, limited and possibly confused. Experience with the widest possible range of situations to which they apply clarifies and refines them to the point where they can take over the task of explaining and incorporating further examples (p. 116). The principles for teaching drawn from Ausubel's theory of learning are different (though not entirely so) from those advocated by writers such as Wastnedge, Richards and Squires, wedded to a Piagetian view of children's learning and development.

The importance of the third sense of structure is not contested by any of the contributors to the book and, therefore, requires little attention in this introductory chapter. The crowded nature of primary classrooms places a premium on effective organization in all areas of the curriculum, but especially in science where individual or small group work is often attempted. The work outlined in the contributions by Thornley, Ashton, Wetton and Evans would not have been possible without prior consideration of the management of time, resources and space. More than many other subjects, primary science requires the effective organization of resources at both school and classroom levels; the chapter by Collis provides valuable guidance on this.

Continuity

A third important general issue is that of continuity. Curriculum continuity is concerned with the degree to which activities carried out by children relate to, and build upon, their previous experience. For our purposes, three forms can be distinguished: (i) the continuity which children experience in any one class during the course of a school year; (ii) the continuity they experience as they move from class to class within the same school; and (iii) the continuity they experience as they move from one stage of schooling to the next. To achieve the first form, teachers need to have a clear idea of what they wish to achieve in a specific area of the curriculum, and need accurate knowledge of the work carried out by the class or groups within the class as the year proceeds. Major prerequisites for within-school and inter-school continuity include accurate knowledge of what goes on in the same school or in other schools, a degree of trust in the professional judgement and integrity of colleagues, and a measure of common agreement as to the basic structure of the subject where continuity is sought.

Within primary science continuity has not been a major concern until recently, partly because of the lack of science in many schools and the consequent priority of getting science of any kind off the ground. The HMI Primary Survey (Chapter 4) does not explicitly discuss the problem of continuity in science, but does stress that work in observational and experimental science was less well matched to children's capabilities than work in any other area of the curriculum, and does state that 'In only a very small minority of classes were activities requiring careful observation and recording developed beyond a superficial level' (para. 5.78).

Each of the primary science curriculum projects discussed in the section of the book entitled 'Approaches to Curriculum Development has contributed to the first prerequisite for within–class continuity, that is, has provided teachers with an understanding of what might be achieved with children of primary age. Only one, Progress in Learning Science, has focussed on helping teachers gather information about children's understandings and activities. One of its publications, *Raising Questions* (Harlen *et al.*, 1977), looks at ways of determining children's level of development in relation to particular skills, concepts and attitudes, and another, *Finding Answers* (Harlen *et al.*, 1977), discusses experiences which can be provided to develop these further.

Within-school continuity has been the focus of recent attention stimulated partly by the work of the Learning through Science Project (Chapter 15) and partly by the publication of documents such as *The School Curriculum* (DES, 1981) *Science in the Primary School* (DES, 1983) and *The Practical Curriculum* (Schools Council, 1981) which have emphasized the importance of continuity within schools as well as between phases. Both in England and Scotland, a recommended strategy has been the development of a policy for science argued out and implemented by the staff of each school. In his contribution to this book, Roy Richards outlines the approach to policy-making advocated by the Learning through Science Project; the Scottish Committee on Environmental Studies in the Primary School (1980) takes a similar view of policy:

> The policy should state the main objectives towards which the teachers at each stage in the school will be working and the types of science activity (perhaps also a suggested range of topics) most suited to the pupils at each stage and therefore most likely to achieve the objectives. Thus, as well as giving each teacher guidelines within which to work it will tell her the types of experience her pupils have already had and the more complex situations they will meet in the following year. The policy must indicate the extent to which the pupils' various skills are expected to develop as they progress through the school (p. 7).

Other aids to within-school continuity are science guidelines produced by many local education authorities, and commercially produced schemes containing teacher and pupil materials.

The issue of inter-school continuity has tended to be neglected in primary science partly because of the underdeveloped nature of the subject in many schools and partly because of the problems encountered more generally in primary-secondary liaison. However, there have been considerable efforts to secure continuity between middle and upper schools in areas where three-tier systems operate. In many cases, local education authority working parties have produced policy statements or guideline documents aimed at fostering inter-stage continuity; often, the use of the same schemes (for example, Nuffield Combined Science) has contributed to continuity of experience for pupils. Nevertheless, the first two prerequisites for inter-school continuity are not always met (see Stillman and Meychell, 1982).

Consistency

Since the mid-seventies there have been growing pressures for greater consistency and coherence in the education offered children. A string of DES publications from *Educating Our Children* (1977) to *The School Curriculum* (1981) bears witness to the concern at the diversity of practice that has emerged at both primary and secondary levels. In the primary context, the issue was highlighted in Chapter 6 of the HMI Primary Survey which reported considerable inconsistencies in the curricular activities undertaken in primary classes and argued that 'ways of providing a more consistent coverage for important aspects of the curriculum need to be examined' (para. 6.9, 1978). Developments relating to consistency are taking place at three levels. Through *The School Curriculum* and its follow-up, the DES is setting out a broad structure for the curriculum at national level; through the issue of curriculum guidelines and the closer monitoring of the work of the schools, many local education authorities are responding to DES initiatives and developing broad curriculum policies for their schools; through such means as self-evaluation procedures and curriculum reviews, some schools are appraising their curricula and assessing how consistent is their teaching.

Primary science has witnessed attempts at creating greater consistency at all three levels discussed in the previous paragraph (see DES, 1983). As Wastnedge's second contribution (Chapter 22) points out, since 1978 great efforts have been made nationally to establish science as a normal part of the curriculum in all primary schools. Local education authorities have issued documents on the teaching of primary science and instituted programmes of in-service training (see Chapter 22) in a parallel attempt to foster science in all their schools and to achieve a more consistent coverage of activities, once science has been established. At school level, the policy documents discussed in the previous section are intended to 'ensure effective and consistent coverage of science throughout the school' (Richards *et al.*, 1980, p. 8). However, the same three prerequisites apply for curriculum consistency as for continuity and are equally problematic. Both topics raise a number of difficult professional issues concerned with teacher autonomy, curriculum planning and implementation, school policy-making, and local and national responsibilities for curriculum decision-making.

Evaluation

Parallel with the concern for greater consistency in the curriculum have been public demands for the Department of Education and Science, local education authorities and schools themselves to appraise how worthwhile is the curriculum offered pupils at primary and secondary levels. The area of evaluation is a complex and contentious one, both theoretically and practically. To help provide an introductory overview of developments related to primary science, a number of simple distinctions can be made. Evaluation can be seen as comprising two major activities: the collection of information, and the making of judgements based on the application of criteria to that information. For our purposes, three foci for evaluation can be distinguished: the activities and achievements of individual children, the performance of large numbers of children, and the methods, resources and forms of organization used in schools. Various means can be used to collect information including the administration of tests of various sorts, the employment of observational techniques, the scrutiny of work completed or in process, and discussion with teachers and pupils.

Much has been written about the evaluation of primary science, mainly because of the work of Harlen, who has been closely associated with three curriculum development projects and with the first national assessment of children's performance in science. The activities and achievements of individual children are the focus of the publications produced by the Progress in Learning Science Project directed by Harlen (see Chapter 8). The project team argue that teachers need help in collecting information as to what children can already do in science and what ideas they have, as a basis for providing further experiences which will develop their skills and ideas. They suggest that teachers' observations made daily in the classroom as a result of interacting with pupils can be structured to yield the necessary information. To help in this process, the project produced checklists consisting of three statements describing children's behaviours at progressive levels of development for each of a number of skills, attitudes and concepts. These include skills such as raising questions and applying learning, concepts such as cause and effect and force, and attitudes such as perseverance and open-mindedness. Other check-lists of children's activities in science have been produced, including a thought-provoking one by Hull reproduced in *Learning through Science: Formulating a School Policy* (Richards *et al.*, 1980).

The second focus of evaluation, the assessment of performance of large numbers of children, is a relatively recent development as far as primary science is concerned. It was not until 1980 that the Assessment of Performance Unit carried out the first large-scale survey of performance in science by primary-aged children in England, Wales and Northern Ireland (Chapter 9). With its large random sample of 11,000 top juniors and its combination of pencil-and-paper and practical tests (the latter taken by 3500 pupils,) it assessed children's performance in five categories: (i) using symbolic representations, (ii) using apparatus and measuring instruments, (iii) using observation, (iv) interpretation and application, and (v) performance of investigations.★ Surveys will proceed on an annual basis until 1984. Data from the tests will provide information on the basis of which judgements can be made about the worthwhileness and effectiveness of primary science in the nation's schools.

Thirdly, teaching methods, resources and forms of organization used in primary classes have been foci for evaluation in each of the curriculum development projects discussed in the section 'Approaches to Curriculum Development', but few details of the procedures used have been released. The evaluation of Science 5–13, for example, included the use of a visitor's report from which provided information about the interaction of teachers, pupils, materials and organization in the classes working with the project, but this has not been published (Harlen, 1975). Summaries of schedules used by HMI in appraising work in primary classes (including science) are found in the appendices to the Primary Survey and can be used as starting points for the evaluation of methodology, resources and organization. Many local education authorities have produced school self-evaluation schemes which involve the gathering of data on a range of phenomena. Some of the questions on such schedules can be focussed on provision for primary science.

In Conclusion

This introductory chapter has attempted to isolate a number of issues – range, structure, continuity, consistency and evaluation – and has related these to the primary curriculum in general and to primary science in particular. As the contributions by Kerr, Whittaker, Allsop and others imply, establishing science as an accepted part of the primary curriculum and tackling the issues outlined in this chapter require a very significant commitment of resources and expertise to pre-service and in-service teacher education. This book is offered as a small contribution to work at both these levels.

★A sixth category, design of investigations, was assessed in 1981.

References

BLYTH, W. (1978) 'The curriculum in the middle years', *Education 3–13*, 6, 2.

BOOTH, N. (1971) 'Middle school science', *Trends in Education*, 24.

BOOTH, N. (1980) 'An approach to primary science', *Education 3–13*, 8, 1.

CENTRAL ADVISORY COUNCIL FOR EDUCATION (England) (1967) *Children and Their Primary Schools* (The Plowden Report), London, HMSO.

CONSULTATIVE COMMITTEE OF THE BOARD OF EDUCATION (1931) *The Primary School* (The Hadow Report), London, HMSO.

DES (1977) *Educating Our Children*, London, HMSO.

DES (1978) *Primary Education in England: A Survey by HM Inspectors of Schools* (The Primary Survey), London, HMSO (see Chapter 4 in this book).

DES/WELSH OFFICE (1981) *The School Curriculum*, London, HMSO.

DES/WELSH OFFICE (1982) *Science Education in Schools*, London, HMSO.

DES (1983) *Science in Primary Schools*, London, HMSO.

HARLEN, W. (1975) *Science 5–13. A Formative Evaluation*, Schools Council Research Studies, Macmillan Education.

HARLEN, W. *et al.* (1977) *Raising Questions*, Match and Mismatch, Edinburgh, Oliver and Boyd.

HARLEN, W. *et al.* (1977) *Finding Answers*, Match and Mismatch, Edinburgh, Oliver and Boyd.

RICHARDS, R. *et al.* (1980) *Learning through Science: Formulating a School Policy*, London, MacDonald Educational (see Chapter 15 in this book).

SCHOOLS COUNCIL (1981) *The Practical Curriculum*, London, Methuen Educational.

SCOTTISH COMMITTEE ON ENVIRONMENTAL STUDIES IN THE PRIMARY SCHOOL (1980) *Towards a Policy for Science in Scottish Primary Schools*, Committee on Primary Education.

STILLMAN, A. and MEYCHELL, K. (1982) *Transfer Procedures at 9 and at 13*, 'Research in Progress' Series, Windsor, NFER.

PART II

'Locating' Primary Science: Three Overviews

Introduction

Despite moves in some schools towards more collective decision-making by staff and towards the sharing of expertise and experience, teaching in primary schools is usually an isolated activity, though, paradoxically, directed towards, and involving, large numbers of other people. The isolation of the primary teacher symbolized by the closed classroom door, the blocking-off of open-plan areas and the close, often exclusive, identification of the teacher with 'his' or 'her' class is compounded by the relative immaturity of the children and their consequent inability to share the teacher's perspectives and problems and by the insistent nature of their demands, which leaves the teacher little time to reflect on his teaching as it occurs. The isolation of the primary teacher surrounded, often literally, by large numbers of demanding, developing human beings is a potent social–psychological factor with many ramifications. Only one is briefly examined in this introduction: the problem of 'location'.

In such a situation, how is the teacher to 'locate' his practice? How does what he does relate to the practice of his colleagues in the school? How does his practice relate to the collective practice of primary teachers nationwide? Are the problems and difficulties he faces shared by most others or simply the result of his own personal inadequacies or circumstances? The problem of location can also be considered in a temporal sense. How does his current teaching compare with his practice of three, five or ten years ago? How far does his development as a practitioner reflect his unique personal experience of the craft of teaching or how far does it relate to the changing context and content of primary education generally?

The isolation of the class teacher is matched, to a considerable extent, by the isolation of the individual school. The problem of location can be couched in similar terms for schools as for teachers.

Establishing a sense of personal or collective location is neither easy nor final but is a prerequisite for providing a sense of direction for future professional development. Neither the sense of location nor that of direction can be acquired while teachers are engaged hour-by-hour, minute-by-minute in the activities of teaching; both require a degree of detachment but equally both derive from, and require, extensive knowledge and experience of the complexities of primary teaching. This book in general, and this section in particular, provide material on which, hopefully, personal and collective senses of location and direction can be developed.

The publication of this book has prompted at least one practitioner to reflect on her practice and to locate it temporally. Conran's contribution, written specifically for the book, traces her personal development as a teacher of primary science from the 1950s to the present. Her autobiographical account reflects on issues of wider than personal concern, which are discussed elsewhere in the book: the enlargement of the range of primary science beyond nature study to include elements of physical science and, more recently, technology; the concern to introduce children to the processes and techniques of scientific enquiry; the growing understanding of the importance of children's 'proto-scientific' concepts; the vexed process/content dichotomy; and the more sophisticated conceptualization of the role of the teacher in developing children's learning in science. The chapter conveys a sense of the surprises, uncertainties and insecurities of a primary teacher starting with a well-established knowledge of natural history and confidence in teaching it but having to take on simultaneously new approaches (encouraging children to behave scientifically in addition to helping them acquire scientific knowledge) and new content (physical and technological as well as biological science). Her reflections on her experiences provide pointers for those wishing to influence teachers' professional development in primary science. 'Starting from where the children are' needs to be paralleled by 'starting from where the teachers are' (see Chapter 24.1); building on children's interests and strengths needs to be matched by building on teachers' knowledge and enthusiasms; providing gradually more demanding experiences matched to children's capacities needs to be paralleled by providing different paths of professional development geared to different levels of teachers' understanding, confidence and commitment in primary science (see Chapter 24.2).

Conran's personal perspective on developments in primary science is complemented by Black's more detached analysis of why some of the curriculum development projects discussed in Part V of the book have failed to make an impact, In Chapter 3 he suggests that this has been the result of a number of factors: the complexity and mass of material from which teachers have been able to choose, teachers' lack of knowledge and first-hand experience of science, the lack of adequate guidance on choice and level of activities to be provided, and the stress, amounting almost to an orthodoxy, on the processes and skills of concept-free science. He asserts the need for more direct guidance on content and advocates 'a strategy in which children's interests and their need for first-hand experience are still given first priority, but which also organizes problems and materials to channel interest and to ensure that some of the experiences provide a helpful challenge in a few particular concept areas' (p. 31). Viewed in this light, the failure of primary science so far to establish a place in the curriculum is less the result of indifference or downright opposition by class teachers and more the failure of other agencies to provide appropriate development strategies which take due account of the needs of most teachers for direct guidance and support. Black's analysis should prove comforting to those attempting to locate how and why their aspirations proved difficult to realize and should provide food for thought for those who are to set, and support, future aspirations for themselves or others.

The third chapter in this part is an extract from the HMI Primary Survey and provides a perspective of a rather different kind. It focusses, not primarily on how or why developments have taken place over time, but on the 'state' of primary science in the mid-seventies. It provides the reader with a means of comparing his current practice with the practice of a large number of teachers at a particular time in the recent past. It also provides a yardstick against which to assess personal and collective progress since the mid-seventies. The critique it offers is tersely summarized in its first paragraph:

> Few primary schools visited in the course of this survey had effective programmes for the teaching of science. There was a lack of appropriate equipment; insufficient attention was given to ensuring proper coverage of key scientific notions; the teaching of processes and skills such as observing, the formulating of hypotheses, experimenting and recording was often superficial. The work in observational and experimental science was less well matched to children's capabilities than work in any other area of the curriculum (p. 33).

As the first publicly accessible evaluation of primary education since the latter was established as a stage of schooling, the Primary Survey has been very influential in the discussion of policy and practice in primary education. In particular, as Chapter 22 points out, the survey's findings have prompted a great deal of activity in the area of primary science. Many of the recent developments discussed in this book have been a direct result of its measured but critical analysis. In many ways this book itself is a response, five years on, to the primary survey.

Between them, the three overviews presented here raise most of the important issues discussed in more detail later in the book. They help locate activities in primary science as part of the general attempt since the Second World War to develop a genuinely primary, as opposed to elementary, education for young children. To use Black's analogy introduced in his last paragraph, the authors of all three chapters believe that the 'feeble plant' of primary science needs not only light, air and water, but also fertilizer and stakes to support its growth. Feeble it may be, but one other point is agreed. The plant *is* trying to establish itself in an appropriate place; primary children should have the opportunity to be introduced to the skills, concepts and attitudes associated with scientific enquiry.

2   Primary Science 1950–82: A Personal View

Jean Conran

In 1963, the School Nature Study Union, with its motto, 'To see and admire; not harm or destroy', became the School Natural Science Society. Members that year were asked for exhibits, ' . . . not only of the traditional Nature Study and Natural History kind but also of the new work with Physical Sciences being done in primary schools'. This represented a change of image to present to schools at the threshold of a period of unprecedented curriculum development, research and evaluation, with advocacy of new teaching styles and a greater variety of subject matter. For many of us working in primary education, the 1960s heralded the end of a period of rather lonely concentration on the three Rs, accompanied by variable and idiosyncratic inputs of work from other areas of the curriculum.

While teaching in the 1950s, I had exploited my interest in natural history, cultivated during my training at the Froebel Institute in the late 1940s. From our first week at the college, we had been plunged into pond dipping, aquarium keeping, gardening, the mapping and study of trees, a fungus foray, badger watching, a dawn chorus of birds and the recording of weekly visits to Richmond Park. As I watched my first dragonfly emerge at 2 a.m., saw my first badger cubs, learned to distinguish sparrows from greenfinches, watched corn being harvested in the Park and searched in ponds for evidence of life-styles so different from my own, I imbibed the Froebelian ethos of personal involvement and first-hand experience, the development of skills and encouragement of individuality.

When I began teaching in an urban primary school in the 1950s, I initially taught 'everything' to 8- and 9-year-olds, but engaged in exchanges with colleagues: 'Will you take my history if I take your nature?' In those days of fifty children per class, an extra teacher was not unusual so, observing my tendency to accumulate nature and children, the headmistress gave me a small, empty room and a blank timetable and asked me to introduce the whole school to 'Nature Study'. At that time teaching was characterized by large numbers of ability-streamed children packed in rooms filled to capacity with immovable desks and remarkably little else in the way of resources, apart from sets of books. Standing in a modern classroom, it is difficult to recapture a situation in which I was allowed one pencil per term per child, one box of wax crayons per four children, one packet of coldwater paste and six tins of powder paint per term, one sheet of sugar paper per child per week and a box of plasticine shared with the class next door. Our single rubber was tied to teacher's desk and our handful of rulers was kept in a drawer.

Junk and pastry modelling, newspaper painting and collage, finger painting, stick printing, home-made equipment, work cards on the backs of cereal boxes, puppets made from potatoes or matchboxes, orange-box furniture and general DIY expertise were born of necessity as much as from educational principle. Perhaps nature study enjoyed a heyday not only because of inherited traditions* but because the environment provided a free, prolific and stimulating resource. This accessibility of natural objects may have contributed to a later absence of endeavour in building up more varied resources for science. At the time, my only request was for drawing books and boxes of pencil crayons. My first request today would be for a set of sturdy magnifiers.

We started the year with a 'Seaside Room'. Ready beforehand were displays of shells, pebbles and sand; aquaria with live crabs and sea anemones; seaweeds; boxes and tables for collections made during the summer holidays; drawing materials, paper for labelling and selection of named specimens, reference books and pictures. We then followed the seasons with an ever-changing set of exhibits, a growing family of resident plants and animals, and a flow of temporary visitors brought in by the children. They marvelled at the unfamiliar and became confident in handling and caring for the familiar. Work extended beyond the classroom to the school grounds and open areas in the surrounding council estate. Animals and plants were kept at home and books were purchased or borrowed from the library. Research was undertaken into cats and dogs. Diaries were kept. Expeditions to parks, museums and zoos were made on Saturdays, and the children brought along parents, siblings and friends. I spent two hours per week in each classroom, was in the Nature Room before school and at playtimes, and ran a weekly club. Class teachers could introduce relevant activities to follow up interests aroused and together we could organize expeditions.

The Nature Room had a special appeal for children with learning, social and emotional difficulties. Basic skills could be practised and extended in a context which had relevance, and some children initially found it easier to form a relationship with a guinea pig than with a peer. The sharing of a common enthusiasm with children of varying age groups could lead to new and unexpected friendships. A 7-year-old bringing in a caterpillar would be helped by an 11-year-old to identify and house it. One child suggested we needed a new hamster cage, another got Dad to make it. Peter decided that Squeaker needed a wife and brought some of his pocket money to start a fund for one. Groups of children developed an increasing sense of responsibility and collaborated in activity producing such notices as 'Closed for Cleaning', 'Mouse Hurt', 'Be Quite – Persys Having Babies' [sic].

Drawing, colouring, painting and plasticine modelling; the making of

---

* I was not aware at the time that I was responding to deep roots and long traditions. The nature study of the twentieth century has, to a remarkable extent, been the outcome of events in the last century, documented by David Layton (1973) *Science for the People: The Origins of the School Science Curriculum in England*, Allen and Unwin.

individual or group books, charts or displays; the arrangement and labelling of collections or records; the matching of observations against statements in books; games involving exploring, handling, sorting, comparing, contrasting, identifying and classifying – these were all encouraged. It is interesting, with hindsight, to consider to what extent these activities met the aims and objectives of the Schools Council Science 5–13 Project. I was engaged in familiarizing children with the natural world and was particularly concerned with developing interests, attitudes and aesthetic awareness; with observing, exploring and appreciating (to some extent) patterns and relationships; with acquiring knowledge and with developing ability to communicate in a variety of fairly conventional ways. Questions were encouraged but tended to be those amenable to answer by direct observation rather than by controlled investigation. I paid little conscious attention to encouragement of prediction, testing, hypothesizing, experimenting, interpreting findings critically, developing logical thinking or generally fostering a scientific approach to problems. We saw the world as an interesting place to discover and explore rather than as a series of problems to be identified and solved. Children interacting actively with reality were bound to develop some enquiry skills but in those days we were unaware of the coming shift in emphasis towards children behaving scientifically and much was left to intuition and chance.

I enjoyed my semi-specialist role for only two terms; increasing numbers created an extra class and I was back for the next half-decade integrating the experiences I had gained into the full curriculum. So responsive had I found these children to the enthusiasm an 'expert' can bring to her work that I produced an article (Conran, 1956), recommending a temporary period of specialization for teachers in rotation, each promoting in the school an interest in his or her particular area of expertise and interest. Teachers often take on curriculum responsibilities now beyond the confines of their own classrooms, but in the 1950s it was rare except in the case of music and games.

Throughout the 1950s, nature tables, nature diaries, weather charts and, to a lesser extent, nature walks were commonplace. The following extract, describing work in an urban infant school, conveys the tenor of what many teachers were doing at that time.

> The work centres round the Class Nature Table and Weather Chart.... At first, the chart can be a simple set of pictures with a moveable pointer ... further up the school, the chart can take the form of a calendar for the month ... by the time the children are seven years old they can also keep a temperature and wind chart. Class Nature diaries or Nature scrap books of all kinds are also made ... collections are started ... we have endeavoured to fulfil a need by keeping pets in school ... seeds, such as mustard and cress, grass, peas and beans, germinate on blotting paper or in jam jars ... in winter time, just as much pleasure is derived from the lacy patterns made by the bare trees against the sky, the shape and markings on twigs and buds, the ice in the gutter, and the pigeons and sparrows in the street.... When we find our first snowdrop in the school garden, or the first coltsfoot on the bombed site, out comes our wild flower stand and we begin the flower chart for the year.... About this time

we get some frog spawn, and another tank is added to the class nature table (Bush, 1956).

Similar activities continued into junior classes and one of the weaknesses of science at that time, apart from the narrowness of its content base, was the absence of progression. These children did progress from matching pictures with weather to measuring temperature and recording wind but there is no evidence of guidance towards more advanced analysis of weather records or towards understanding of underlying concepts (relating, for example, to air, water and heat). We accepted progression at an individual pace in mathematics, language and reading but failed to perceive the progressive nature of scientific development and the contribution this makes to a child's overall intellectual development. Our own education had emphasized the learning of content and we were inexperienced in the processes of science and unfamiliar with many underlying concepts. We had not heard of the work of Jean Piaget.

It took many years for Piaget's work to pervade our educational system to a point where an entire curriculum development project, Science 5–13, related its materials to Piagetian stages of development (see Chapter 14). After the critical reception of Piaget's first publications in Britain between 1926 and 1930, the intervention of the war and the random flow of translations of his later works and the difficulty experienced in understanding and accepting his ideas led to a considerable hiatus in the process of diffusion. The 1950s saw publication in Britain of interpretations of Piaget for teachers and some training colleges began to disseminate his findings, particularly in the field of mathematics, but there was little observable impact in schools. This state of affairs came to an end in this country with publication of the Plowden Report in 1967. Primary teachers were here quite explicitly asked to consider the issues raised by Piagetian research.

> [Piaget's] work has important implications for teachers; one of its most important conclusions is that the great majority of primary school children can only learn efficiently from concrete situations.... Piaget's observations support the belief that children have a natural urge to explore and discover.... that ... is self-perpetuating (CAC, 1967).

Basically, the Plowden Report welcomed the support Piaget seemed to be giving to 'progressive education' and to 'discovery learning'.

Piaget's ideas, filtering down to teachers slowly through teachers' centres, curriculum development projects, and courses in the 'new mathematics', forced us eventually to ask, 'Can this really be so?', and the subsequent rush for plasticine and tall/thin, short/fat jars may have seemed naive to some, but helped to give a new dimension to the term 'child-centred education'. We not only had to accept the child as the main architect of his own intellectual growth but had to ask, 'What *can* he learn?' rather than, 'What *should* he learn?'. After years of obsession with quantitative measurement and assessment (IQ, 11+, number of right answers), Piaget turned our attention to qualitative assessment of the processes of thought and degree of success and failure, an approach of greater diagnostic value to the practising teacher. It is generally accepted now that children's thinking is not simply scaled down adult thinking; it is qualitatively different. This came as something of a shock to primary teachers brought up on the writings of Susan Isaacs and believing in the main that, like the 2- to 10-year-olds in her Malting House School, '. . . if one treated children . . . as intelligent beings, eager to learn and understand . . . there was very little in the way of progressive learning and understanding that they could not master'. Piaget's child 'just did not seem to correspond to all we knew about those children whom we thought we knew best' (Isaacs, 1955). The implications of this for science education in general and my practice in particular permeated slowly.

How did those of us in primary schools, entering the 1960s in the main as 'intuitive' and rather limited teachers of science in the form of nature study, come to take on board the physical sciences? What influences came to bear upon us to produce changes in attitude and approach? The 1960s developed into a decade of extroversion, expansion, development and high hope. Teachers who had been ploughing somewhat lonely furrows and creating pockets of scientific excellence scattered in characteristic, uncoordinated, British fashion, became more aware of what was going on in other classrooms and in other schools. Major curriculum development projects led to the setting up of teachers' centres for discussion and evaluation of pilot studies; in-service training grew in response to teachers' need for help in meeting new demands; architects designed schools which encouraged team work; increasing affluence led to immense increase in material resources. Teachers were encouraged to bring their children out of the classroom on organized visits; increasing numbers of museums, zoos and other places of interest appointed education officers (often qualified teachers); pioneer organizations like the Council for the Promotion of Field Studies (catering for older pupils) were joined by LEAs setting up field centres for their own children; National Nature Week in 1963 stimulated the creation of nature trails aiding interpretation of the countryside; national and local organizations extended help to teachers in many forms. Added to these resources were those of radio and television.

It was into this expanding field of teacher support that I moved in the 1960s, managing the Children's Centre (for children up to 13 years of age) at the Natural History Museum in South Kensington, writing and broadcasting occasional programmes in the BBC's 'Nature' series for 8- to 10-year-olds, organizing fieldwork and writing nature trails for primary schools. Inspectors in schools were being transformed into advisers with corresponding changes in role and in teachers' attitudes towards them. But attitudes changed slowly and even with the help of wardens appointed to the increasing number of teachers' centres, there were too few 'non-threatening' people available to whom teachers could turn for the kinds of help they were beginning to feel and acknowledge they needed.

The Children's Centre had opened in 1948 in collaboration with London County Council. Under a full-time teacher the Centre set out to encourage teachers and children to visit the museum regularly and to use it effectively for personal research and enrichment. Teachers were helped to integrate series of visits into their normal school work and were encouraged to support first-hand examination of museum material by field visits. For example, studies of water birds in the galleries were followed by walks up to the Round Pond in Kensington Gardens. Interests were initiated and sustained; new working habits involving first-hand material were developed. Support was provided for teachers in areas where they lacked confidence. Yet these services tended to be taken up and exploited to the full only by those teachers who were most outgoing and confident in the first instance. Then, as now, the extensive educational facilities of museums benefited only a small proportion of primary children in any sustained way. Economic factors were not the only ones operating here. Organization, staffing levels, management of children inside and outside the classroom and the availability of time all contributed, but underlying these practical considerations were difficulties teachers experienced in moving away from conventional classroom approaches to learning.

At the Natural History Museum I catered for enthusiastic followers of the BBC's 'How Things Began' series. This developed a depth of interest and expertise in geology and evolution which I seldom see today, because most current series are miscellaneous and do not sustain interest in one topic long enough to develop the intensity of interest which leads to sustained investigation. During the sixties I contributed scripts to 'Nature', radio's most successful primary series (in terms of audience numbers and longevity). Unfortunately, development was discouraged by the lack of continuity between programmes and too seldom did a programme lead children to observation of real plants and animals or to any activity other than listening, answering questions, drawing or writing. The programmes tended to reinforce the vicarious approach to nature study which the Plowden Report criticized in 1967.

More successful in this respect was Harry Armstrong's 'Junior Science'. His programmes depended on his personality and were radio's first attempt to introduce the physical sciences to primary children. He introduced new approaches which are still used today, asking children, for example, to carry out activities while the broadcast was in progress. He launched schools into science where there had been none before and effectively demanded a practical approach, with detailed notes to guide teachers and children. In the mid-sixties Nuffield Junior Science (see Chapter 13) introduced science which was new in content and methodology and within this new climate of opinion was born a radical new series entitled 'Discovery' which, using less familiar topics such as 'Bridges' and 'Kites and Flight', involved children in activity during the broadcast but also left many unanswered questions for later investigation. 'Discovery' was highly praised for its adherence to then current educational ideals, but the producer found that the teachers who remained faithful to the series were those already dedicated to the teaching of primary science as a practical, investigative subject. (In contrast to 'Discovery', current programmes, on both radio and television, are less demanding, employ relatively familiar material, and tend to be more didactic and less dependent on lengthy written notes for the teacher's guidance.)

How then shall I characterize the late 1960s and the 1970s? Diffusion to classrooms of the novel Plowden and Nuffield Junior Science ideas of 1967 was slow (see Chapter 13); later project teams came to appreciate that new ideas and materials required a great deal of dissemination if they were to have an impact on practice (see Chapter 14). For those of us to whom the message came (and the evidence of the 1978 HMI report suggests this was to a minority), Nuffield Junior Science represented the ideal of good primary science teaching, but its complete acceptance of an open-ended approach daunted those of us who were inexperienced in the processes of a science, in the physical sciences and in helping children to devise investigations to answer their own questions. We had not yet learned to ask and answer our own questions. Encouraged and supported, however, by the subsequent flow of Science 5–13 books, with their more specific guidance on content, activities, aims and objectives, we attempted to recapture H.E. Armstrong's 'art of making children discover things for themselves'. We turned out nature tables into interest or discovery tables, with a wider range of objects, including not only plants, bones and hamsters but magnets, batteries, toy cars, old clocks and tuning forks. We placed the children 'as far as possible in the attitude of the discoverer' and used methods which involved 'their finding out instead of being merely told things' (Armstrong, 1898). We tried not to have too many prescriptive work cards lying around and encouraged the children to ask questions. It must have been disheartening for the pioneers of Nuffield Junior Science and Science 5–13 to read in the HMI report that in less than one class in thirty was there evidence of investigations which had been initiated as a result of questions asked by the children (see Chapter 4).

Apart from the practical difficulties of too few or inappropriate resources and too many inexperienced, though enthusiastic, children, simultaneously approaching an inexperienced teacher (who had not been given a meccano or train set, tool kit or motorbike as a child) for help of a practical, manipulative or technical kind, we floundered a bit because so many of the children's questions, 'Why is the sky blue?'; 'Why does the moon follow me about?', did not seem amenable to answer by simple investigation, though I improved my skill in diversionary questions, 'But is the sky always blue?'. Their questions seemed to demand explanation rather than investigation. It was to deeper, more theoretical questions that my mind then turned. I only gradually, with the help of such writers as Nathan Isaacs (Chapter 10), gained better understanding of the nature of children's 'why' questions. According to Isaacs, children's curiosity about the world around them leads to information-seeking questions. Causal questions seeking explanation as well as information arise, from reality conflicting with expectation, from observation clashing with existing schemes of thought. There is a parallel with Piaget's ideas; from an early age children begin the process of building up internal working models of the world and match these to reality, assimilating new examples and accommodating to anomalies. When reality clashes with expectation, children pick on 'why' questions to evoke their at-a-loss state and signal for adult help. In this way, Isaacs argues, children come close to 'the very spirit and attitude of the scientist' (Hitchfield, 1980).

This proto-science of children is akin to 'scientists' science'. Theories are creative acts of the imagination by which scientists provide plausible models to fit ('explain') observable phenomena and these are accepted for the time being by consensus of view within the scientific community. Are such theories amenable to simple 'discovery' by children? There is no evidence to suggest that first-hand observation and experience lead automatically to the theoretical systems which represent the current consensus of view as to the explanations underlying observable phenomena. Theories are not static, observable, discoverable truths, but dynamic, evolving, creative ideas. 'Children's science' progresses along similar lines. Young children, for example, commonly predict that a stone will sink 'because it is heavy'. Sooner or later, this simple 'theory', that heavy things sink and light things float, is challenged by an anomaly, perhaps a heavy tree trunk floating and a grain of sand sinking. A new 'theory' may develop – wooden things float but stones sink. The child is now paying attention to what the objects are made of. On another occasion, he finds that a sinking lump of plasticine can be made to float when transformed into a boat. His 'theories' now focus on shape. The problem for the young child is not that he cannot pay attention to each of these items of knowledge or experience in turn but that he finds it difficult to pay attention to them all simultaneously. As he matures, he increases his ability to make connections between different pieces of knowledge and to resolve discrepancies. I felt I made an important step forward as a teacher when I began to perceive learning in the primary school as concerned not only with provision of experience of the 'real world', of innumerable and diverse, concrete and first-hand examples of all kinds of concepts and areas of knowledge, but also concerned with helping children to construct for themselves alternative models of the world, 'proto-type theories or hypotheses', and to check these against as much reality as one could bring them into contact with.

With other teachers, I also had to re-examine what we meant by 'discovery learning'. A philosophy which encouraged children to 'make their own discoveries' pervaded the 1960s curriculum development projects in science. At the primary level, the Plowden Committee (1967) claimed that the treatment of science 'may be summarized in the phrase "learning by discovery" ... Initial curiosity, often stimulated by the environment the teacher provides, leads to questions and to a consideration of what questions it is sensible to ask and how to find the answers'. However, not even H.E. Armstrong, in his famous 1898 report, believed that children could find out everything for themselves. He recognized the mediating role of the teacher in structuring the environment and selecting resources. A teacher is making profound value judgements when, as recommended by the Plowden Committee, she contrives within the school an environment for children's learning. The experiences and resources she selects or rejects for the children's attention and the responses and questions from the children that she accepts as valid and relevant or rejects are a reflection of her own assumptions about what is or is not worthwhile and of her assessment of what is appropriate for a particular group of children. Rather than discovering new things for themselves, it can be argued that they are encouraged to share the teacher's perception of the situation, particularly in relation to the inferences which can be drawn from observations.

An example can serve to illustrate the point. In the introduction to the Schools Council Science 5–13 Project, we read,

> ... the teacher made sure that there would be opportunity to notice and explore fresh and exciting features. This time they walked through some dense parts of the wood and, also, through large green clearings which, in itself, encouraged the children to question why there were green spaces, why certain trees had fallen, why some trees were taller than others, how much taller they were and why it was so

much wetter under the trees than in the clearings (Ennever and Harlen, 1972).

It is questionable whether, *in itself*, this situation led the children to seek the kinds of explanation suggested. From what basis, other than prior experience, could they make inferences of the kind implied in the questions? This extract goes on to belie its own words and to describe what any good teacher would probably do in similar circumstances.

> Evidently the teacher had thought in some detail about the potential which this occasion would hold for adding to the children's experience.... This did not mean ... that she had decided exactly what the children should collect and observe, rather it meant that the children discovered things which they might have otherwise missed.

The teacher was using her knowledge and her perception of the situation to decide what it might be fruitful for the children 'to discover' and, by the probably unconscious way in which she accepted or rejected the children's observations and questions, she led them largely to share her perception of what was significant. This does not totally preclude accommodating to unexpected discoveries by the children but does imply the positive role for teachers, in inducting children into scientific methods and in helping them to organize what could be an unmanageable number of disparate observations, which the HMIs advocated in their report. For a time, the prevailing climate of opinion, favouring an anti-authoritarian, child-centred approach to learning, over-emphasized the notion of the child as an independent discoverer and, I believe, produced a measure of uncertainty in teachers. I felt inadequate when children (and later students) placed in a stimulating environment failed to 'discover' satisfactorily and felt guilty when I gave them too much structured help.

Some of the learning experiences I now promote, as part of my current work in primary teacher education, are not so very different in kind from those described earlier. We go to ponds, waste ground and museums, we study trees and woodlands, we keep plants and animals and we generally engage in interaction with an environment which now includes physical and technological, as well as biological, material. The greatest changes are in attitude and approach, in objectives and expectations and in the range of activities and methods of recording and communicating. In the 1950s, we looked at the ivy climbing up the tree and wondered how it managed to hang on and why its leaves were so variable in shape. We recognized the first question as amenable to answer by direct observation but the second as more intractable. Our response to the latter was more likely to be, 'Let's see what the experts in the books have to say', than, 'Is there an investigation we can set up to find out?' Fewer solutions are now sought in books in the first instance; there is more emphasis on formulating a wider range of questions which can be answered by reference to reality, by collection of one's own empirical data. Observation ('Our hamster feels cold to the touch and is stretched on his side with his eyes shut') is more clearly differentiated from inference ('Our hamster is dead') – an important example, since, in my early days of teaching, my 8-year-olds and I nearly buried our unexpectedly hibernating hamster! Predictions are encouraged before testing, and alternative hypotheses are deliberately sought.

I have, in fact, accepted that primary science should include development of skills in the processes and techniques of scientific enquiry. I continue, however, to value interesting content, which is rich in potential for learning, as the means by which a predisposition to learn is created in children and as the means by which children gain access to worthwhile knowledge. Content relates not only to specific topics and materials of interest to children, but also to important underlying concepts such as those identified by the DES Assessment of Performance Unit as appropriate for development during the primary years of schooling (APU, 1981). The ivy climbing up the tree becomes an example of the interdependence of living things in addition to having its own immediate interest. This transferable concept is reinforced when sticklebacks are seen to be dependent upon water fleas for food and hermit crabs are seen to be dependent upon sea snails for a protective shell.

During the last decade, I have been able to extend my work in science to include the physical sciences (up to a point) but it has taken some time to build up confidence in this area and I started from the firm base of reasonably successful work with children in an area in which I had both interest and some confidence, that is, in nature study. Was it perhaps a mistake in the 1960s and 1970s to have expected the predominantly female and biologically-orientated primary school teaching force *simultaneously* to take on both new approaches (behaving scientifically in addition to acquiring scientific knowledge) *and* new content (physical and technological in addition to biological science)? Would primary science have developed more rapidly if teachers had been encouraged in the first instance *either* to accept nature study as 'proper science' and suitable for developing in children an enquiring mind and a scientific approach to problems (as Thomas Henry Huxley had claimed for it more than a hundred years ago) *or* to expand their content base to include the physical sciences as a development of topics already studied? A study of pond animals, for example, leads easily to studies of the properties of water; studies of fruit and seed dispersal lead to investigations of flight and the properties of air. Could more teachers have coped had they not been asked to tackle new methodology and new content simultaneously?

However, that moment has passed. Just as the BBC has responded in its school broadcasts to recognized problems by reducing the demand for mediation and selection by the non-specialist teacher, so, too, are current publications of pupil materials, at both local level (e.g., West Sussex 'Science Horizons') and national level (e.g., Schools Council 'Learning through Science Project'), reducing the pressure on teachers to make frequent decisions relating simultaneously to both content and methodology. Many of us are uneasy about this large-scale production of pupil materials which are mainly in the form of work cards and, insensitively used, could negate the aims and objectives of Nuffield Junior Science and Science 5–13. But they come in response to genuinely felt needs for more structured help, and it is too early to evaluate their impact. There is some evidence that the 1980s, with stronger encouragement from the DES and more initiatives at local level in appointing teachers with posts of responsibility for science and in formulating LEA or school policies for science education, may be the decade when science comes at last to be accepted as a normal part of the primary school curriculum and the excellent work which has always existed in some schools spreads to a wider population.

References

ASSESSMENT OF PERFORMANCE UNIT (1981) *Science in Schools: Age 11,* Report No. 1, London, HMSO (see Chapter 9 of this book).

ARMSTRONG, H. (1898) *The Heuristic Method of Teaching or the Art of Making Children Discover Things for Themselves*, Special Reports on Educational Subjects, Board of Education.

BUSH, A. (1956) 'Nature study in an urban infants' school', *School Nature Study*, 203.

CENTRAL ADVISORY COUNCIL FOR EDUCATION (ENGLAND) (1967) *Children and Their Primary Schools,* (The Plowden Report), London, HMSO.

CONRAN, R., (1956) 'Specialisation in the primary school', *The Link*, 46.

ENNEVER, L. and HARLEN, W. (1972) *With Objectives in Mind*, London, MacDonald Educational.

HITCHFIELD, E. (1980) 'Early scientific trends in children: A tribute to the work of Nathan Isaacs', *Education 3–13*, 8, 2.

ISAACS, N. (1955) *Piaget and Progressive Education,* National Froebel Foundation (see Chapter 10 of this book).

3   Why Hasn't It Worked? *

Paul Black

In the 1978 Primary Survey, the Inspectorate presented a bleak picture of primary science. In their view, serious and effective work was achieved in only 10 per cent of schools. Elsewhere, much of the effort was superficial and the teaching in science was less well matched to the capabilities of pupils than in any other curriculum area. Few headteachers appeared to recognize that science could make a significant contribution to the development of young children (see Chapter 4).

This contrasts sadly with the hopes of curriculum reform in the 1960s. Primary science teaching was due for reform, having resisted criticism over many years: in 1913 Henry Armstrong had said of nature study that 'Nature too seldom comes into the work and too often study is the last thing thought of'.

The Nuffield Junior Science Project expressed the following belief in the natural power of children to learn: 'Children's practical problem solving is essentially a scientific way of working, so that the task in school is not one of teaching science to children, but rather of utilizing the children's own scientific way of working as a potent educational tool' and '. . . their own questions seem to be the most significant and to result most often in careful investigations' (Wastnedge, 1967). So the project's books gave general advice on how to follow children's leads and how to provide resources to support this strategy; facts, concepts, content were ruled out of order.

The project's successor, Science 5–13, built on this work, but differed in giving teachers a definite framework in the form of a set of over 150 behavioural objectives, divided into three neo-Piagetian levels (Ennever and Harlen, 1972). These were not to determine a syllabus – the child's motivation and the need for learning to be rooted in experience were still paramount. The objectives were to guide the provision of opportunities for learning and to form a basis for monitoring individuals' progress. The project also provided a set of more than twenty-five books, each giving guidance, and examples of children's work, on a particular theme. This material was interpreted and analyzed throughout in terms of the detailed objectives which the proposed activities might serve (see Chapter 14).

* From *The Times Educational Supplement*, 3 October 1980.

29

Both of these projects were based on the view that the essentials of scientific work lay in the processes of careful observation, perception of patterns, formation of hypotheses and design of experimental tests. Scientific concepts were inappropriate as a framework for curriculum design because they were too abstract and too little related to children's interests. At the same time, it was emphasized that science is a unique source of intellectual stimulus, being the area in which observation and thinking skills have to be based on direct experience. It was hoped that such work could play a distinctive part in an integrated curriculum where any one pupil investigation could lead to activity in science, art, writing, craft and other skills.

Two further projects succeeded these. Progress in Learning Science (Harlen, 1977) concentrated on the appraisal of the progress of individual children by a scheme based on the developmental objectives of Science 5–13. The other Learning Through Science is still in progress (Richards, 1980 and Chapter 15 of this book).

These four major projects, added to many smaller and local initiatives and to the normal efforts of authors and publishers, have influenced only a minority of schools. Yet if the materials produced have failed, it seems that they fell at the first hurdle – that of convincing teachers to take them seriously. A survey has shown that Science 5–13 has only been studied seriously in 30 per cent of schools and is being used by 22 per cent while the corresponding figures for Nuffield Junior Science are 20 per cent and 7 per cent respectively.

Primary teachers almost certainly lack confidence to take up the new philosophy. Muriel Whittaker (1980) has pointed out that most primary teachers probably have a strong aversion to physical sciences, which they last experienced in secondary schools where the didactic and factual approach left them with no experience of the type of work now required. Open-ended activity in which a teacher has to encourage particular skills by careful guidance of the pupils' own interests requires some knowledge, or confidence to learn, about many topics and some first-hand experience of the skills involved. Most primary teachers have neither. When the schemes of work they are offered have a complex rationale, offer a wealth of materials, but leave choice of the specific activities and decisions about level and pace to them, it may not be surprising if the challenge is refused (see Chapter 14).

While it is clear that active help for primary teachers is a first priority, it cannot be assumed that the only problem is to help them to use the ideas and materials that exist. These materials themselves raise several problems.

One such problem concerns the view that science is organized common-sense, arriving at its theories by intelligent induction. The practitioner works within and through a complex framework of concepts and it took the genius of Galileo and Newton, in defiance of the commonsense of generations, to establish such concepts for mechanics.

It is, of course, true that these abstract concepts are beyond the powers of young children and that to channel work towards them risks loss of enthu-siasm and meaningless rote learning. But the problems illustrated by the mechanics example will not go away: research with children is now estab-lishing in this area, as in many others, that they construct their own conceptual schemes to cope with the problems of understanding nature, and that these, like those of every scientist up to the sixteenth century, are a real barrier to the scientific understanding.

What then is to be made of the plea to encourage children to develop and rely on their own ideas? It is not now obvious, *a priori*, that the best route for developing understanding of science up to age 11 is to concentrate exclusively on the process skills of concept-free science.

Arguments for adjusting the policy about content in primary science were put forward recently by several authors, notably Professor Kerr (1980 and Chapter 5 of this book) in the Spring 1980 number of *Education 3–13*. Norman Booth recalled another project of the sixties, the Oxford Primary Science Project (see Chapter 12). This offered a scheme which, although based on children's activities, wanted these planned to serve four broad themes – energy, structure, chance and life. This too failed, and perhaps one reason was the gap between the grand conceptual design and the activities of which children were capable. Wynne Harlen (1978 and Chapter 7 in this book) proposed a more modest list of content drawing on her experience in the Science 5–13 and Progress in Learning Science projects. Her article reviewed the arguments for and against some content aims, and concluded that while the process aims must come first, the children's activity had to be about something and it might as well be arranged to cover some common broad themes.

Others have argued that children ought to begin to have access to those ideas which have helped scientists to make sense of the natural world. It is also evident that if children's own interests have to be a prime source for activity, then some interests, such as space travel or nuclear energy, may need a degree of reliance on secondary evidence that is fully acceptable in other areas (such as history) for 10-year-olds.

If these various arguments have force, they would lead to a strategy in which children's interests and their needs for first-hand experiences are still given first priority, but which also organize problems and materials to channel interest and to ensure that some of the experiences provide a helpful challenge in a few particular concept areas.

Such a strategy would have an effect on another aspect which also needs reconsideration, that of providing materials for pupils and more and more direct guidance for teachers. The experience of the superb work which can be produced when children's own initiatives are guided by the best teachers has led many to the view that any planned provision will be an obstacle to excellence. However, without such provision, teachers can only be given vague advice, and the demands, for decision, anticipation and preparation, become too great.

The recently published series on Teaching Primary Science (produced by the College Curriculum Science Studies Project under John Bird) has tried to provide firmer guidance giving advice and samples on producing work cards for children and clearer background information for teachers with each of its themes, while also providing a short list of objectives to guide the activity, chosen from the schedule of Science 5–13.

Such designed activity can make the teaching task more manageable, partly because contrived experience raises problems which can more easily be guided to fruitful work than many that appear in the complex world of the natural environment. However, the strategy for choosing such activities will have to take account of a further factor that has been largely ignored hitherto. The science of most successful primary teachers has been pure science. If it had been technology, their philosophy and emphasis might have been different and the work of mechanical and electrical construction might have invaded the classroom (see Chapter 19).

Many and strenuous efforts are now being made to support and promote primary science. But those tending the feeble plant face the dilemma: does it need just light, air and water, does it need artificial fertilizer, or should we pull it up again and have another look at the roots?

References

BIRD, J. (Ed.) (1975–78) *Teaching Primary Science,* London, MacDonald Educational.

BOOTH, N. (1980) 'An approach to primary science', *Education 3–13,* 8, 1, pp. 23–7.

ENNEVER, L. and HARLEN, W. (1972) *With Objectives in Mind,* London, MacDonald Educational (see Chapter 14 of this book).

HARLEN, W et al., (1977) *Match and Mismatch,* London, Oliver and Boyd.

HARLEN, W. (1978) 'Does content matter in primary science?', *School Science Review,* 59, 209, pp. 614–25 (Chapter 7 in this volume).

KERR J. and ENGEL E. (1980) 'Should science be taught in primary schools?', *Education 3–13,* 8, 1, pp. 4–8 (see Chapter 5 of this book).

RICHARDS, R. et al. (1980) *Learning through Science: Formulating a School Policy with an Index to Science 5–13,* London, MacDonald Educational (see also Chapter 15 in this book).

WASTNEDGE, R. et al. (1967) *Teachers' Guide I,* Nuffield Junior Science, London, Collins (see also Chapter 13 in this book).

WHITTAKER, M. (1980) 'They're only playing – the problem of primary science', *School Science Review,* 61, 216, pp. 556–60 (see also Chapter 24.2).

4   *The Content of the Primary Curriculum: Science*★

Her Majesty's Inspectors of Schools

5.66   Few primary schools visited in the course of this survey had effective programmes for the teaching of science. There was a lack of appropriate equipment; insufficient attention was given to ensuring proper coverage of key scientific notions; the teaching of processes and skills such as observing, the formulating of hypotheses, experimenting and recording was often superficial. The work in observational and experimental science was less well matched to children's capabilities than work in any other area of the curriculum.

5.67   Heads' statements showed that the degree to which programmes of work in science had been thought out varied considerably from school to school. A number of heads referred to the importance of developing children's powers of observation, and to the responsibility of schools to encourage enquiry and curiosity. One wrote that his intention was to encourage in the children an attitude of wonder and enquiry so that these may become a lasting part of their life and outlook and to assist children's desire to communicate and construct; and help them to gain an insight into the happenings of everyday life.

5.68   Some heads also mentioned the scientific subject matter they considered children should study; for example, practical work in nature study, plant and animal life, and an introduction to a study of the environment. Another head wrote: The children should be able to perceive relationships and pose hypotheses to be tested through experiments, to be discarded if found untenable; they should become acquainted with the evolution and meta-morphosis of animals; learn the simple properties of air and water; and understand how simple machines work.

5.69   Science is a way of understanding the physical and biological world. However, the general impression given by heads' statements was that only a small minority recognized the important contribution which science could

★ From Des (1978) *Primary Education in England: A Survey by HM Inspectors of Schools,* London, HMSO, pp. 58–63.

make to children's intellectual development. Although some science was attempted in a majority of classes, the work was developed seriously in only just over one class in ten, either as a study in its own right, or in relation to other topics being studied. The attention given to science did not vary greatly with the age of the children.

5.70   In science it is essential that children should develop observational skills and begin to recognize similarities and differences. The study of living and non-living things can stimulate children to ask the sort of questions which can lead, with careful guidance, to the formulation of hypotheses and the devising of experiments to test them.

5.71   In about two-thirds of all the classes a nature table or 'interest' table was kept, where objects such as pieces of wood, sea shells, building materials, old clocks or radios were collected and displayed. In a similar number of classes plants were either grown in school or brought in for study. About half the classes kept small mammals such as hamsters or gerbils and a similar proportion undertook some work arising from outdoor activities such as a nature walk, a visit to a local park or the study of a local habitat such as a canal or pond.

5.72   Unfortunately, although children in a fair proportion of the classes were introduced to plants, animals and objects intended to stimulate scientific enquiry, in very few classes were opportunities taken to teach children how to make careful observations or to plan and carry out investigations of a scientific nature. For example, collections of autumn leaves were commonly used for decorative purposes or to stimulate work with pattern and colour; they were seldom used to help children to recognize similarities and differences in formation, such as the different forms of multiple leaf in ash and horse-chestnut trees, or notions of stability and change in living things.

5.73   In about two-fifths of the classes some use was made of television broadcasts for the teaching of science, but radio was used in less than one class in ten. In some classes a particular television or radio broadcast was selected to fit in with a topic the class was studying, and in others part of a term's work was planned around a series of programmes. Used in these ways, television and radio broadcasting made a valuable contribution to the work in science and it is surprising that, in a subject where many teachers lacked confidence in their own abilities, more use was not made of this resource to support the work in science.

5.74   Textbooks or assignment cards were used to initiate work in science in only about a fifth of all the classes, although their use increased with the age of the children. At the 11-year-old level about a quarter of the classes made use of assignment cards and a similar proportion worked with textbooks. The discriminating use of carefully chosen textbooks or assignment cards can help to sustain work in science if their use is carefully planned to supplement a programme of work; more use of this resource to support a particular line of scientific enquiry could have been made. Considerable use was made of reference books in nearly two-thirds of the 7-year-old classes and four out of five of the 11-year-old classes. However, in only about a fifth of the classes were reference books well used to support first hand observation or experimental work or to develop sustained work on a particular topic.

5.75 Children's interests arising from their life at home, outside school or on holiday sometimes provide starting points for work in science. There was some evidence in about two-fifths of the classes that work had arisen in this way, although the potential of such work was seldom exploited. Children may collect shells, pebbles or fir cones; may wonder why aeroplanes stay in the air or how a canal lock works; may become interested in the behaviour and characteristics of animals or immersed in the details of the latest space exploration reported on television. There is a wealth of experience for teachers to draw on, and most children are willing to bring things to school and discuss their enthusiasm in class.

5.76 Although four-fifths of all classes had access to some resources for their work in science, the provision was generally inadequate. Simple equipment for measuring, observing and discriminating, for example, thermometers, hand lenses, tuning forks, and materials such as batteries, bulbs and wire for work with electricity, can be assembled easily but were rarely seen to be available in the classroom. Older children were only marginally better catered for than the younger children in this respect.

Content

5.77 In interpreting the findings relating to the content and quality of children's work in science it has to be kept in mind that there was no evidence of such work in nearly a fifth of all the classes. In those classes where work in science was undertaken, about half had touched on topics which contributed to children's understanding of the characteristics of living things and to notions of stability and change in living organisms. Fewer classes gave attention to reproduction, growth and development in plants and animals. Sources of energy were considered in about half of the 11-year-old classes but rarely by the younger children.

5.78 In only half the 11-year-old classes and about a third of the 7- and 9-year-old classes were children prompted to look for and identify significant patterns, for example, the way leaves are arranged on a twig, patterns of bird migration, the way materials react to heat or light, or the arrangement of colours in a rainbow, and the way light behaves when it is reflected, casts shadows or is dispersed into its component parts. Such topics can be developed without specialized facilities, using simple materials such as twigs, water, salt or mirrors or simply carrying out observations in a natural habitat. In only a very small minority of classes were activities requiring careful observation and accurate recording developed beyond a superficial level and in less than one class in thirty was there evidence of investigations which had been initiated as a result of questions asked by the children.

5.79   In those classes where efforts were made to introduce children to science as both a body of organized knowledge and an experimental process the emphasis tended to be placed on work relating to plants and animals. This probably reflects the fact that rather more teachers were knowledgeable in the field of biology than in the physical sciences, although some were able to extend the work to take account of physical as well as biological aspects. For example, in one 9-year-old class the teacher had arranged a visit to a bird sanctuary. The preparatory work involved drawing children's attention to the characteristics of different species of birds which would assist in their identification, examining the construction of birds' nests and relating the materials used and the method of construction to the size of the bird and the shape of the beak. At a later stage the children constructed a bird table and went on to collect bird droppings; they placed them in sterilized seed compost and witnessed the germination of seeds which had been carried by the birds. In an 11-year-old class where germination was being studied, the children were growing plants under different conditions and recording their findings in a systematic way. They were being encouraged to make predictions and generalize from their findings; the teacher was also able to introduce the notion of the need for a control sample.

5.80   Another school had its own small area of woodland in part of a nearby Forestry Commission plantation. The children in the 11-year-old class had planted seedlings and were carrying out systematic observations of their growth. They also made careful comparisons of other plants and animals found on open ground, on the fringes, and in the centre of the woodland. This included the observation and identification of living things found under stones and logs and on the trees. In the course of these activities the children designed and constructed clinometers and other instruments to enable them to measure dimensions such as the height and girth of the trees and the spread of the branches. The children had learned to distinguish hard and soft timber and had employed a rigorous technique for comparing the hardness of woods by dropping a weight from a standard height on to a nail in the wood. The children were knowledgeable about the kinds of wood appropriate to different forms of manufacturing, for example, paper and matchsticks, and the types used in the construction of different household articles.

5.81   Studies relating specifically to man-made artefacts or mechanical actions were comparatively rare, although one 9-year-old class had paid a visit to a working water mill. During the visit the children made notes and drawings and, on their return to school, were able to construct a working model to illustrate the action they had observed at the mill. Subsequently the children looked at other applications of the mechanics of a chain of cogwheels including the gears of a bicycle, the action of an alarm clock and a rotary food whisk. The study of mechanical artefacts supported by constructional activities is an aspect of the work in science which is seldom exploited and which could usefully be developed at the primary stage.

Comment

5.82   During the past few years considerable efforts have been made to stimulate and support science teaching in primary schools. There have been curriculum development projects at national level and in some areas local authority advisers and teachers' centres have been very active. Guidance about the kind of science which is suitable for young children, its place in the curriculum and teaching methods is readily available in the publications of the Schools Council, the Nuffield Foundation, the Department of Education and Science and elsewhere. Yet the progress of science teaching in primary schools has been disappointing; the ideas and materials produced by curriculum development projects have had little impact in the majority of schools.

5.83   The most severe obstacle to the improvement of science in the primary school is that many existing teachers lack a working knowledge of elementary science appropriate to children of this age. This results in some teachers being so short of confidence in their own abilities that they make no attempt to include science in the curriculum. In other cases, teachers make this attempt but the work which results is superficial since the teachers themselves may be unsure about where a particular investigation or topic in science could lead.

5.84   Making good the lack of science expertise among existing teachers is a complex matter but the careful deployment of those teachers who do have a background of study in science is a straightforward step that should be taken. Such teachers should be encouraged to use their expertise to the full, as class and specialist teachers, to bring about an improvement in the standards children achieve in science. Teachers with a particular responsibility for science need to be supported fully by heads and advisers and where necessary receive further in-service training, particularly courses which are designed to help them to further their own knowledge of science. The planned acquisition and use of resources for science teaching would also contribute to a general improvement of the work in this area. In addition, more attention should be given to the ways in which initial training courses can best equip new teachers to undertake the teaching of science whether as a class teacher, as a science consultant, or as a specialist in the primary school.

PART III

Key Questions

Introduction

From one perspective Chapters 5 to 9 encompass four phases of curriculum design: analysis of the current situation in primary science teaching, the formulation of goals accordingly, the planning of programmes which translate these goals into the content to be taught and finally evaluation of the progress made. First, Kerr and Engel analyze the 'situation' which pertains in schools and training institutions, noting some features which presently inhibit what can be achieved there and also some recent developments in science education that might assist the redefinition of goals for primary science. In Chapter 6, Squires, based on her considerable experience of local curriculum development, describes what in her view is the essential purpose of teaching science to young children, that it should introduce them to scientific ways of investigating the physical world. She considers scientific investigation at this level to be divisible into discrete processes such as observation and question–posing, and argues that children's journey towards more sophisticated understanding of scientific phenomena occurs through the stepwise enrichment of their personal experience allied to reflective thinking about this experience.

Programme planning would logically follow, the third phase of curriculum design, for the implication of Squires' chapter is that processes and progression should feature prominently among criteria which determine the choice of course content. But just how important among selection criteria are these? Is course content to be chosen on the grounds that it provides opportunity to foster processes of the kind Squires describes and to be taught with a suitable notion of progression in mind such as Bruner's spiral curriculum might provide? Content then merely becomes the vehicle for experiencing the processes of scientific enquiry. Harlen, in Chapter 7, argues that course content is more important than that and she proceeds to offer content guidelines which delineate the key ideas in science that she feels children should have been exposed to at particular ages.

Information is not yet available on the consequences of implementing the kinds of programme taught in schools that would fit Harlen's guidelines. Certainly the idea of mapping content in terms of basic concepts underpins the national surveys of school science from the Assessment of Performance Unit, one of which is reviewed by Harlen in Chapter 9; also the guidelines for primary science which several LEAs have now produced.[1] From these and other published sources content guidelines have begun to infiltrate schools.

Viewed in historical terms the function envisaged for evaluation in curriculum design has gradually become more flexible and, in particular, less wedded to learning outcomes. In Chapter 8 Davis fleshes out one role for evaluation, the monitoring of pupils' progress during classroom transactions. As someone who has held a responsibility post for primary science he is well able to bring a practitioner's understanding to the design of schemes for recording children's acquisition of attitudes, skills and concepts. But what of children's demonstrable capabilities at the end of their primary schooling? In Chapter 9 Harlen sets out the procedures and results of the APU's national survey of science attainment. Clearly the procedures described by both Davis and Harlen are intended to lead to reconstruction of the curriculum in the light of the evaluative evidence which has accrued of pupils' response to it.

From this first perspective then, the authors in this Part propose rationales for key curricular features of primary science as they would wish it to be taught. As preamble to a second perspective note that these authors are all in positions of influence over those whose practices they seek to affect. Collectively they exert that influence through teacher training, research, published curriculum guidelines, evaluation at national level, LEA advisory services and school management. From a second perspective then, the authors engage in the task of mediating theory and practice by bringing to practitioners' attention approaches to primary science valued currently by the community of researchers, developers and like-minded people and which they regard as being feasible for practitioners to adopt.

From a primary teacher's point of view only certain parts of their papers may seem initially of significance. No doubt many will be helped by Squires' answer to the question, 'What is primary science?', for a defensible rationale is offered to those who like the rest of us failed to find an answer in their own schooldays. However, considerations such as the clear specification of goals, the production of schemes of work reflecting the thinking in curriculum guidelines, and the systematic recording of scientific attainments are not among the early concerns of teachers inexperienced in primary science.

Should a sense of deficiency, then, pervade consideration of teachers' current levels of understanding and modes of operation? Are the issues the mediators raise worth attending to? Certainly the question, 'What should the goal of primary science be?' is worth addressing for if it is to succeed in schools this will be as much through changing the image of science in teachers' minds as providing good resource material to get them off the ground. Too often primary staff carry an image of science as high-status knowledge that is difficult for children to access and an image of the science teacher far distanced from their self-image as primary teachers. He (!) is seen as occupying a remote world comprising laboratories, apparatus and safety hazards. What Squires offers us is accessible science, a science which partly circumvents the question, 'How will I know the answers to the children's questions in order to plan with them their investigations?' Instead, an approach to teaching through science conceived as processes gives scope for starting with simple activities to foster skills such as observation. Investigation is seen as a worthwhile end in itself, offering opportunity to acquire through practice valued skills – for example, in deciding what is and what is not a fair test – rather than it being judged in terms of the validity of the outcomes it yields. Moreover, the divisibility of science processes into discrete entities and the separation of these from content give the flexibility that teachers may feel they need in planning plus an effective way of screening classroom activities for relevance.

So maybe the process versus content debate that Kerr and Engel turn their minds to need not concern the primary teacher. The simpler processes of science can certainly be inculcated into children's minds. Yet consider the risks of producing curricula which favour the biological at the expense of the physical sciences as grist for the process mill, given the limited academic knowledge of physics, especially, among primary teachers. Might not skills so essential to gaining scientific understanding such as inference and hypothesis-testing be neglected? Noting Kerr and Engel's reference to the strength of children's common belief patterns, it seems probable that science 'processes' strongly interact with children's existing beliefs and that a hypothetico-deductive approach, one based on the testing of reasoned hunches, comes closer to children's thinking and the nature of scientific enquiry. Clearly the debate *does* impinge crucially on the decision of how teachers should map the curriculum for teaching purposes. Considerations of this kind have influenced the developers of recently marketed curriculum materials packages at both primary and secondary levels. The 'Look' scheme, for example, provides a mapping of science activities for 7 to 11s in terms of both process and concepts.

Given limited subject knowledge and an approach to planning that is somewhat intuitive, favouring child-centredness among criteria for content selection, imaginative science teaching may nevertheless result. But currently some kinds of knowledge are felt to be more equal than others. In other words, as Harlen argues here, there may be core ideas in science which reflect important cultural understandings that all pupils ought to be exposed to before entering their secondary schools. If one accepts this argument, then concern for structure, progression and continuity will feature among the criteria used to devise content guidelines and specific schemes of work. Maybe staff themselves should collaborate within schools to produce guidelines of the kind Harlen proposes, and then as Ward has done[2] suggest classroom activities through which these can be implemented.

Interestingly, data from the HMI Primary Survey indicated that roughly twice as many schools had schemes of work for mathematics and language as had these for science[3]. The difficulty of primary teachers taking on board an approach which predetermines content, however loosely, is recognized by Harlen. On the one hand it implies neither the theory-centredness of planning by objectives nor the rigidity of a syllabus. But it does seem to imply some formalization of planning procedures for if teachers are to map out in schemes of work the basic concepts they intend to cover over several lessons presumably they should aim to include the kinds of activities and resources that will support the teaching of these effectively and the means by which progress towards more sophisticated understanding is to be logged.

Turning to the question of what roles evaluation should serve, again there is contrast between what practitioners do and what the author (Davis) would have them do. According to Clift's extensive survey[4] schools frequently record such things as social and personal characteristics which influence children's learning, their specific learning difficulties, their levels of attainment on reading and mathematics schemes and in basic skills. The report regrets the limited time available for recording pupils' progress and the lack of interest in some secondary schools in using the results. Not surprisingly record-keeping is not a priority in primary schools. Again is this partly a matter of image? Its associations are maybe with marks and grades, success and failure in secondary school examinations rather than it being seen as a tool for the teacher. Those who argue, as Davis does, that opportunity must be found for monitoring pupils' progress face a clientele needing reassurance that they are capable of teaching and monitoring concurrently. Nevertheless, the science teacher clearly does need some efficient means of checking up on the progress made by children in order to produce a good match between each child and the tasks set in lessons and to assist the decision on when to intervene in learning. Clift advocates freeing primary teachers from non-teaching and supervisory duties in order to give them more time for record-keeping.

Thus far it has been assumed that control of what is taught in primary schools rests in teachers' hands and that it is they who must be influenced and assisted for innovation to occur. Yet the production of curriculum guidelines by some LEAs suggests that accountability to audiences outside the school for the quality of the science curriculum will increasingly influence what is taught. Within the schools, provision of career incentives such as posts of responsibility and the level of resource support, both of which crucially influence the quality of science taught, lie with the management team.

Turning to accountability on a national scale the uncertainties of the APU's monitoring of science attainment are legion, not least the level of political commitment to continuing its funding. Harlen is sensibly cautious when interpreting results of the first survey but in due course when progress in children's performance levels is seen, or is seen to be lacking, survey findings may be drawn upon more vigorously by policy-makers in schools and LEAs and by those who have a powerful guidance function such as HMIs. The APU's results would then play a more significant part in arguments for primary science to have a greater share of scarce resources such as finance, time and suitably qualified staff. A current problem, however, is the apparent lack of effective dissemination of findings to teachers.

If science is to take on the mantle of being an essential ingredient of every child's experience in schools, once its novelty diminishes it will need a defensible rationale to face competition from other subjects for its time and the capacity to update this rationale in response to changing circumstances. The desire for technologically and socially relevant science in schools and current advocacy for the inclusion of more opportunities for children to design and make will not leave primary science untouched and will influence the reshaping of its goals. Questions such as, 'What kind of science should we teach *now*?', 'What kind of content best serves us *now*?' and 'What functions should evaluation serve *now*?' will remain. The chapters here provide both an overview of current answers to these questions and examples of attempts to link theory and practice.

Notes

1 Examples are: SQUIRES, A. (1980) The Middle Years Science Curriculum Project, *Core Intentions for Science in the Middle Years*, Leeds City Council Department of Education; and DARK, H.G.N. *et al.* (1981) *Lancashire Looks at ... Science in the Primary School*, Lancashire County Council.
2 WARD, A. (1981) 'Guidelines for early primary science education (5–10 years) – concepts and lesson contents', *School Science Review*, 62, 220, pp. 540–5; WARD, A. (1980) 'Guidelines for later primary science education (to ages 11–12) – concepts and lesson contents', *School Science Review*, 64, 226, pp. 31–7.
3 DES (1978) *Primary Education in England*, London, HMSO, 40.
4 CLIFT, P., WEINER, G. and WILSON, E. (1981) *Record Keeping in Primary Schools*, Macmillan.

5   Can Science Be Taught in Primary Schools? *

Jack Kerr and Elizabeth Engel

A positive answer to the question posed in the title of this chapter is conceded at the outset, but a detailed response must surely depend on the resolution of a number of problems. First, what precisely do we mean by primary science? Has the approach as represented by the Nuffield Junior Science and Science 5–13 Projects resulted in more scientific investigations in classrooms? Is the time appropriate to re-examine the current orthodoxy which lays so much more emphasis on ways of behaving scientifically than on science itself? At the 5-11-year stage, should the case for a more ordered and deliberate introduction of essential scientific concepts be given further thought? Do we know how children learn to behave in scientific ways? How adequate is the provision for the preparation of primary school teachers, at both initial and post-experience stages, to cope with scientific activities in their classrooms? Attention must be focussed on these important questions if planned scientific experiences are to become accessible to young children.

Although we believe it is essential to provide opportunities for children of all ages to enjoy scientific experiences, translation of this conviction into practice is known to be far from simple. And the dichotomy (which has always been a dichotomy in theory only) between, at the one extreme, science as a means of acquiring skills and attitudes characteristic of the discipline and, at the other, science as learning information has not necessarily provided us with a useful framework for practice. Wynne Harlen (1978) has analyzed the alternative approaches to primary science and attempts to find some guidelines for avoiding the errors of both extreme positions. The questions we have posed need to be re-examined, but perhaps a de-emphasis of the processes/content polarization and a conscious avoidance of extreme views of science may provide a more useful context for this re-examination.

Assessment of Progress in Primary Science

Judged on the basis of published material alone, the reader might conclude that the past twenty year period has been one of unusual progress and innovation.

* From *Education 3–13*, 8, 1, 1980, pp. 4–8.

Apart from the mass of commercially-produced books, kits and resources of all kinds, since 1964 at least six project teams in Britain alone have been actively developing curricular materials for teachers to stimulate and support scientific activities and experiences with young children. Many reports have been published by the Association for Science Education, the Department of Education and Science, the British Association and other bodies. The Interim Report of the Schools Council's Impact and Take-Up Project (1978) suggests that in quantitative terms the outcome of all this activity has been disappointing. The Nuffield Junior Science Project materials were familiar (that is, 'read parts or know well') in only 18 per cent of a random sample of 279 primary schools. According to the headteachers, 13 per cent of schools in the sample were using the materials but only 7 per cent of the teachers agreed that they were doing so. The Science 5–13 Project was known to 30 per cent of the same sample, 36 per cent of the headteachers claiming the books were used, as against 22 per cent of their teachers. Science 5–13 books were actually seen by members of the project team in 50 per cent of the schools visited. It is interesting that when about 600 teachers were asked which national curriculum project was 'best known', Science 5–13 ranked very highly – fourth out of 107 projects listed. In Ashton's study (1975) based on data collected in 1969–72, 1513 teachers rated seventy-two aims of primary education in order of importance. That the child should 'know some basic scientific procedures and concepts' was ranked 62nd; 'know basic facts of sex and reproduction' 63rd; and 'understand how the body works', 64th. Yet scientific activity in the classroom would be a powerful means of achieving other, more highly-ranked aims in Ashton's study. For example, 'to make reasoned judgements and choices' was 23rd in importance of the same seventy-two aims; 'a questioning attitude to his environment' ranked 24th; 'inventiveness and creativity', 30th; and 'to observe carefully, accurately, and with sensitivity', 37th. This discrepancy between the ranking of aims which specifically mention science and the ranking of more generally expressed aims which in fact describe important aspects of scientific (and, of course, other) activity, is interesting. It may be that many primary teachers simply do not recognize the particular contribution science could make to the achievement of aims which they themselves rank highly, or it may be that they would prefer to try to achieve these aims in non-scientific contexts in which they feel more comfortable. The most recent report on the state of science in primary education in England is based on a survey of 1127 classes in 542 schools by HM Inspectorate (1978). They found that the 'work in observational and experimental science was less well matched to children's capabilities than work in any other area of the curriculum ... only a small minority recognized the important contribution which science could make to children's intellectual development' ... and ... 'the ideas and materials produced by curriculum development projects have had little impact in the majority of schools' (Chapter 5, iv, p. 58).

In summary, the evidence suggests that many primary teachers are aware of the existence of important curricular developments in primary science, they rank highly objectives which science educators would recognize can be achieved through planned scientific activity, and yet there seems to be precious little scientific activity going on in our classrooms. Apart from inspired work by a minority of schools and teachers' centres, it is clear that our efforts to spread science teaching in primary schools over the past decade have been largely ineffective. Why is there so little visible progress? Is it simply that the pace of any educational change is always painfully slow? Are there any other reasons?

A Reassessment of Policy

Factors commonly thought to impede the improvement of science at the primary stage include: (i) the poor science background of teachers, resulting in lack of confidence to attempt work in science; (ii) failure of headteachers to recognize the potential contribution of science to the curriculum; and (iii) inadequate provision of simple apparatus and materials. These obstacles to change will be looked at later, but there may be a more fundamental reason why progress has been so slow.

The writings on child development of Isaacs, Dewey, Piaget and others had a powerful influence on most of us in the 1960s. The case for more openness, more activity and more concern for the individual child won over the Plowden Committee, whose work was in progress at the same time as the Nuffield Junior Science Project. This project team followed suit, and recommended that children should be allowed to investigate the environment by working at self-appointed tasks to develop skills of observing, questioning, exploring, interpreting findings and communicating, across the curriculum. The team argued that at this stage starting to *do* science was more important than science itself (see Chapter 13). The so-called 'process approach' to primary science had arrived. Few noticed the much-less publicized Oxford Primary Science Project supported by the Ministry of Education which produced its report in 1969, a little later than Nuffield Junior Science (Redman *et al.*, 1969) The Oxford group argued that it was impossible to ignore the fact that 'children will bring science into the school' and it was vital to include the contribution of science in the interpretation of the environment. Children must be given an understanding of some of the essential ideas used by scientists. Four main concept areas – energy, structure, chance and life – were explored by methods which were not *in fact* dissimilar to those recommended by the Nuffield group. But to no avail. The all-embracing child-centred philosophy dominated discussion about the whole of the primary curriculum, and generally precluded consideration of materials such as the Oxford project which delineated content areas for scientific exploration.

The process–content debate, referred to earlier, has been with us since the start of science teaching. It figured in varying degrees in Henry Armstrong's campaign for discovery methods a hundred years ago, the general science movement of the 1950s and all the Nuffield Science Teaching Projects. But at no time did we try to lay so much emphasis on process and attitude objectives as in recommendations for primary science a decade ago. This sophisticated orthodoxy – for this is what the process approach has become for teachers – was so deep-rooted that, until recently, few people were prepared to appear so heretical as to question it. Could it be that progress in primary science has been limited because the *general* principles controlling primary policy have been applied unbendingly in the case of science? In Harlen's paper (Chapter 7), she lists examples of 'guidelines to content' to meet the process criteria, but at the same time emphasizing that 'the content objectives must not be allowed to replace the process and attitude objectives'. The same shift to a more practical balance, albeit tentative, is detectable in the HMI report and, more overtly, in Norman Booth's article (1978). At present the content of primary science is left almost entirely to chance, a state of affairs which puts a considerable strain on conscientious teachers who lack sufficient background and experience of science. We conclude that if science *should* continue to be taught in primary schools, an adjustment of policy is desirable. Perhaps we should begin by forgetting all about the process-content dichotomy, and look more closely at how the child acquires scientific skills and attitudes as well as an understanding of essential concepts, and then at what the teacher is required to do about it.

Children's Scientific Ideas

The fact that learning depends on the learner successfully relating new experience to what is already known is crucial to all theories of cognitive development, and is an idea familiar to teachers. It follows that what a learner brings to a learning situation is of great importance. Irene Finch (1971) makes a very interesting distinction in this connection. She suggests that teachers of English show interest in children's own ideas and opinions, but by contrast, science teachers frequently give the impression that children's ideas are not worth much consideration beside those of great scientists. She goes on:

> But the English teacher is not, and cannot, be aiming at producing a class of Shakespeares, and we cannot be aiming at producing a class of scientists.... Somehow we must arrange for children to produce useful scientific ideas in our lessons, and to get credit and kudos for them (p. 407).

Many teachers would agree, and some science educators (e.g., Driver and Easley (1978) Deadman and Kelly (1978)) have suggested that there is a need to look more fundamentally and in detail at pupils' own understandings and ways of thinking about scientific ideas, and to use this information in planning teaching strategies. Thus the traditional curriculum/pupil model would be reversed; pupil understanding would be investigated *first* and then gradually incorporated into teaching and curricular planning. As with classical botany and zoology (on which the modern study of these subjects is founded), it may be that the first job is description and classification.

But is this any more than good teachers have always done? Good practice has always included listening carefully to individual children's ideas and then beginning from the vantage point of the learner's own experience. This is quite true, but we believe that research can provide valuable support for this approach.

There are indications from the small body of qualitative research into children's understandings that *common belief patterns* emerge. Frequently these patterns, which may be totally 'wrong' ideas or may represent a partial understanding, persist despite instruction. This seems to be particularly true for scientific notions which defy 'common sense'. (For example, the fact that all matter is made up of molecules and atoms, or the fact that sideways pressure at a given depth in a fluid is the same as downwards pressure.) Sometimes the alternative explanations offered by children are unanticipated, and even bizarre. Documentation of these common patterns of understanding in children of different ages (and, ideally, in the same children at different ages) should yield useful information on developmental trends and on individual pupil differences.

Two examples of investigations with young children may perhaps serve to illustrate the points made so far. Nussbaum and Novak (1976) interviewed fifty-two 7–8-year-olds in an attempt to elucidate their ideas on the 'earth' concept. The interviews, which included the use of models and drawings, began with a set of questions which included, 'How do *you* know that the earth is round? Which way do we have to look in order to see the earth? Why don't we see the earth as a ball?' etc. From analysis of the data, Nussbaum and Novak identified five common patterns of children's thinking about the earth, ranging from primitive notions of a flat earth with no concept of space to a notion of a spherical planet, surrounded by space and with things falling to the centre. They concluded that the problem of developing a conception of cosmic space is central in learning the earth concept, and yet this aspect is not emphasized by teachers or in textbooks. Similarly, they thought there was a need to explore ways of helping young children to understand that 'down' directions are towards the centre of the earth. Many children who 'know' that 'a person on the other side of the earth does not stand upside down, and does not fall off because gravity pulls him towards the earth' still do not completely comprehend the meaning of this statement.

Using a similar approach, Albert (1978) identified eleven 'thought patterns' which underlie the concept of heat found in children from 4 to 9 years. Just one of her findings will suffice as illustration. The adult conception of heat implies that cold, warm and hot are a single dimension. Albert found that the 4-, 5- and 6-year-olds in her sample did not consistently distinguish between 'hot' and 'warm', even though they used both terms. But at the age of 8 children began to distinguish clearly between 'hot' and 'warm', at the same time regarding them as different instances of the same dimension. They did this by reflecting on how *they* act on and react to objects at different temperatures. For example, Ron (age 9) pointed out: 'Like hot is sort of burn you, and warm is just feeling nice'. Teachers of older children will be aware that the idea of 'cold' as an entity, and a separate one from 'hot', is held quite frequently up to 15 years (and probably beyond!).

Many primary teachers would accept the need to take account of the learner's perspectives. If the approach outlined above could demonstrably identify difficult areas, isolate problems (perhaps ones which impede any further development of understanding) and suggest ways of overcoming them, teachers are likely to respond positively. Over-generalizations are no use – justice must be done to the rich variety of children's ideas.

To summarize, it has been suggested that descriptive studies of children's understandings could be accessible and very useful to teachers. If research can identify common belief patterns, some of the 'spade work' will have been done for teachers. These patterns would not be considered as 'norms' or 'stages', but would certainly alert teachers to the possible perspectives their pupils may bring to learning. A build-up of information from studies of this kind, one conceptual area at a time, is bound to be slow (but then most 'instant' educational solutions turn out to be ephemeral). The *application* of information gleaned from these studies must be investigated by classroom-based research, preferably by teachers themselves. One thing is quite clear. It is obvious that the requirement for primary teachers to be well-trained in science will become no less urgent if this approach is adopted.

Professional Training of Primary Teachers in Science

How adequate is the preparation of primary teachers at both initial and post-experience stages to meet the demand for scientific activities in their classrooms? As far as initial training is concerned, attention given to science is *less* than it was twenty years ago. A survey of thirty-six of the 109 training colleges in England and Wales was carried out in 1960 for use at a British Association conference on 'The Place of Science in Primary Education' the proceedings of which were published in 1962 (Perkins, 1962). At that time, about three-quarters of the students 'were getting some science instruction', 40 per cent of the colleges required all primary students to attend science courses, and 45 per cent allocated thirty hours or less for primary science. Two provided over 100 hours. This was thought by the delegates to be a highly unsatisfactory picture. What would they have thought about our present provision?

Since the introduction of BEd degree courses in colleges, the majority of students are given the most scanty professional training in science. Many are given none at all. The fact that the study of curricular areas other than English and mathematics usually operates on an options system is partly responsible for this deterioration. The preparation of primary teachers to cover all the areas of the curriculum has been a major problem for decades. Part of the intention of setting up separate Professional Studies Departments and Educational Studies Departments in the majority of training institutions was to enrich professional training and underline its importance. In fact, too often the consequence has been quite the opposite. Universities and the CNAA have imposed their views of what kind of knowledge is academically acceptable for the award of degrees, and the development of professionally-relevant courses (seen by the teaching profession to be necessary) has been neglected. McNamara and Desforges (1978) claim the time is ripe to abandon the disciplines of education at the initial training stage and develop 'the teaching of professional studies as an academically rigorous, practically useful, and scientifically productive activity' (p. 17). Through a project funded by The Nuffield Foundation, they aim to work out a more clearly-articulated rationale for professional studies, one which is informed by practical knowledge (which they call 'craft knowledge'). The project seeks to develop professional skills through the generation of classroom-based theories of instruction and teacher behaviour. The Science Teacher Education Project (Haysom and Sutton, 1974) was a move in this direction, that is, towards building theory from professional practice. Given the present pattern of teacher education programmes, the professional preparation of teachers is unlikely to be improved until the aims of these projects are taken seriously.

Opportunities for the further professional training of primary teachers in science, especially at teachers' centres, have been generously provided until the recent financial cuts. These courses and workshops have been actively supported by teachers. School-based courses, using the staff as the 'unit' rather than individual teachers, seem to be the most promising method of bringing about change (see Chapter 24).

Looking to the Future

It is clear that progress will depend on the tempering of theoretical 'ideals' (which are anyway rather subject to fashion) to take realistic account of practical constraints. Some of these constraints, such as the low level of scientific training of many primary teachers, may be very unpalatable. To ignore them is simply escapist. Sometimes the contrast between consultative reports from 'experts' and teachers' opinions is striking. In a recent evaluation of a health education course in some Sheffield primary schools, it was found that the project appealed to teachers precisely because it was prescriptive, in terms of content especially, and because it offered the necessary in-service training and resource back-up.

The recent shift from the practice of producing only teachers' materials for primary science to preparing materials for use by pupils is another example of a realistic response to practical constraints. Local curriculum development groups and commercial publishers have been turning out children's science work cards and assignment sheets for some time. The HMI report (p. 59) acknowledges that 'the discriminating use of carefully-chosen' pupil material can 'help to sustain work in science'. The Director of the most recent Schools Council project, 'Learning through Science', plans to produce pupil materials, although as a team they are wedded to the idea of getting children to show initiative and to devise some of their own methods of carrying out investigations (see Chapter 15).

Seemingly, these advisers perceive the danger of worksheets becoming the syllabus. We would agree with this view. It would be an extreme and totally retrograde step to finish up with a prescribed science course for primary schools. Even so, if we expect primary teachers to plan scientific activities for children, more understanding of children's scientific ideas is needed, more rigorous and relevant professional training in science for all primary teachers must be introduced, headteachers must be persuaded of its importance, and the resources for the children to engage in these activities must be provided.

References

ALBERT, E. (1978) 'Development of the concept of heat in children', in *Science Education*, 62, pp. 389–99.
ASHTON, P. *et al.* (1975) *The Aims of Primary Education: A Study of Teachers' Opinions*, Macmillan Schools Council Research Studies.

BOOTH, N. (1978) 'Science in the Middle Years', in *Education 3–13*, 6, 2, pp. 37–41.

DEADMAN, J.A. and KELLY, P.J. (1978) 'What do secondary school boys understand about evolution and heredity before they are taught the topics?', in *Journal of Biological Education*, 12, 1, pp. 7–15.

DRIVER, R. and EASLEY, J. (1978) 'Pupils and paradigms: A review of literature related to concept development in adolescent science students', in *Studies in Science Education*, 5, pp. 61–84.

FINCH, I.E. (1971) 'Selling science' in *School Science Review*, 53, pp. 405–10.

HARLEN, W. (1978) 'Does content matter in primary schools?', in *School Science Review*, 59, pp. 614–25, reprinted as Chapter 7 in this book.

HAYSOM, J.T. and SUTTON, C.R. (Eds) (1974), *Science. Teacher Education Project* publications, McGraw-Hill.

KERR, J.F. (1962) 'Training for learning through investigations', in PERKINS (Ed.), *The Place of Science in Primary Schools*, The British Association, pp. 33–44.

McNAMARA, D. and DESFORGES, C. (1978) 'The social sciences, teacher education and the objectification of craft knowledge', in *British Journal of Teacher Education*, 4, 1, pp. 17–36.

NUSSBAUM, J. and NOVAK, J.D. (1976) 'An assessment of children's concepts of the Earth utilising structured interviews', in *Science Education*, 60, pp. 535–50.

Primary Education in England: A Survey by HM Inspectors of Schools (1978), London, HMSO, see Chapter 4 in this book.

REDMAN, S., BRERETON, A. and BOYERS, P. (1969) *An Approach to Primary Science* (The Oxford Primary Science Project), Macmillan, see Chapter 12 in this book.

STEADMAN, S.D. *et al.* (1978) *An Enquiry into the Impact and Take-up of Schools Council Funded Activities*, Schools Council Publications.

6   *What Is Science for Primary School Children?* ★

Ann Squires

For a long time small numbers of enthusiasts have regarded science as an important, rewarding activity for young children. Recently there has been wide recognition of the place of science as an essential element in the primary curriculum. This article tries to provide both a justification for primary science and an introduction to the kind of science which can be fostered by non-specialist class teachers in primary schools.

One 10-year-old expressed her feeling for science like this:

> Science is to help you to find out about everything. You say what you think about things. You do experiments to find out if what you thought was right. You feel excited and curious to find out if you were right or not.

Her description conveys that sense of science as a way of making a direct, first-hand relationship with the physical world — a way of making the environment itself answer the questions we ask about it. Science is one of the ways which human beings have developed for relating to the physical world around them, and it offers natural and most fruitful ways of learning for children at the primary stage when they are dependent upon first-hand, concrete experiences. Science is concerned with exploring the materials, the forms of energy and the living things which make up the physical world. It amounts to getting to know these things, as we get to know people, by constant, ever-widening personal experience over many years. Getting to know the physical world means learning to ask good questions about it, learning how to set up experiments to 'trap' nature into answering your questions, and learning how to 'read' the answers the experiments give. In fact, it means building the kind of personal relationship with the things of the world which that 10-year-old obviously felt when she described her science. We should look to primary science to provide each pupil with the opportunities to develop such a feeling of involvement and competence in finding out.

We have already touched upon two aspects of what science has to offer to pupils: these are suggested by 'to find out about' and 'what you think about things' in the pupil's view of science. A diagram can express the way in which

★ From *Education 3–13*, 8, 1, 1980, pp. 9–12.

science is made up of investigating on the one hand and of the understandings gained on the other:

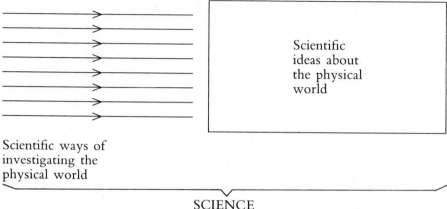

Scientific ideas about the physical world

Scientific ways of investigating the physical world

SCIENCE

We often describe the ways of working as 'scientific processes' and the scientific ideas as 'concepts' and it is sometimes suggested that it is the processes of science which are particularly appropriate to primary school children. But we must not neglect the development of a pupil's ideas about the world he experiences. Of course, the ideas a young child develops from his early scientific investigations will not be those of 'official' science; they will be simply 'first steps' towards accepted scientific ideas. In the sense of 'official' scientific ideas, the body of knowledge of science is not generally appropriate to younger children but the practices of thinking about experiences and of developing one's own ideas and conclusions from investigations are an essential part of science at any age. It is unfortunate that we have so often separated 'processes' from 'content' in thinking about science for young pupils (see Chapter 1). Much better simply to recognize that young pupils' developing ideas will not be those of secondary science but they are no less important for that! Young children will develop what we might call 'stepping-stone ideas' from which 'official' scientific ideas will later develop. If a teacher's emphasis in offering experiences is upon scientific ways of investigating and looking for patterns of events, pupils can be relied upon to develop ideas appropriate to themselves.

Scientific Ways of Investigating

We can best think about the processes of scientific investigation for younger children by considering a particular investigation such as one into bouncing balls. Pupils may well begin with a simple *observation* that 'Balls bounce better on the hard floor than they do on the carpet'. Or they may begin with a *question* like, 'What is the best surface for bouncing a ball upon?' Or they may begin with a *prediction* like, 'I think all the balls will bounce better, on the playground than they do on the grass' Their questions or predictions show that they suspect that this or that factor will affect the bounce.

Their plan is to arrange a series of experiments, or fair tests, so that they can check their ideas. They will collect evidence by *observing*, by *measuring* and by *recording* events so that they can 'read' what their tests are telling them about bouncing. They will take great care to *make the tests fair*, and their teacher will help them to see the ways in which their tests are not quite fair and help them to make it fairer. It would not be fair to let the ball drop from a greater height onto one of the surfaces; it would not be fair to use a 'better bouncer' on some surfaces. Children will see the sense of making it fair but they will sometimes need help in picking out 'unfair things' and in making things fairer. Scientists call this 'performing controlled experiments' but it is no more than making sure that we are not misled by having several things changing at the same time. If we are interested in the effect of different surfaces on bouncing then we vary the surfaces but keep everything else, such as the kind of ball and the height of bounce, the same.

Pupils will *measure* the height of bounces. They should not be satisfied with saying 'that surface made it bounce higher than the other one'. They may want to check their measurements in case something went wrong with one of them. Measuring is simply a more precise way of describing, which is very useful when the differences we see are quite small and when we are making a lot of observations. Measuring is a way of communicating to one another, and of reminding themselves, exactly how high each surface made the ball bounce.

Recording their observations and measurements is a very important part of the investigation. It allows children to see all the separate events in front of them at once. It helps them to see what the investigation is telling them about bouncing. It helps them perhaps in *sorting* surfaces into 'good for bouncing' and 'poor for bouncing'. Pupils will find bar-charts, graphs and tables very helpful when it comes to sorting and interpreting their evidence – far more helpful than sentences of description. But when it comes to pupils establishing and developing the ideas which grow from their experiences, there is no better way than *talking and writing about it in their own words*. Science work provides pupils with a splendid incentive for talking and writing (see Chapter 17). When children describe to one another, and to their teacher, what they are finding out about balls bouncing and what they think about it they are turning a purely practical experience into real learning. When Professor J.Z. Young gave the Reith Lectures in the 1960s he appreciated the key role of talking and writing for others and this is how he described his experience:

> When I was asked whether I would consider undertaking the Reith Lectures ... frankly, I did not consider that this would be a piece of research. The scientist does not usually think of the writing of books or the preparing of lectures as research ... I therefore sat down to use the time available more in the hope of making a summary than a discovery. But when I began to do this I came to realize the extent to which having to describe the results of one's thoughts to others is part of the process of discovery itself.

Throughout their investigation of surfaces for bouncing, children will try out their emerging ideas. They may say, 'It looks as though hard surfaces make the ball bounce higher and the springy surfaces make a smaller bounce.' Trying like this to put into words the patterns they see in their observations and measurements will help them to make sense of the evidence they collect. The important thing at the primary stage is that the patterns children see and the ideas they develop should be their own, expressed, in their own words, in talking or writing or perhaps by drawing or modelling.

The exciting thing about seeing patterns in evidence is that it makes children want to look for an explanation. *Attempting to explain* the patterns found is one of the more sophisticated aspects of scientific investigation. Young children will not try to explain in the abstract terms which a scientist would use. Scientists have developed very sophisticated explanations of what they find and their explanations are usually in terms of intangible things, like forces or atoms, which would hold no meaning for young children. Children will usually try to explain in the simple terms of cause and effect. Whereas a scientist would explain bouncing in terms of energy and elasticity a young child would perhaps suggest that a harder surface makes a ball bounce higher because it hits the ball harder. But, whatever the explanations, wanting to explain, and trying to provide an explanation which is satisfying, are very much a part of science for all but the youngest pupil. A teacher should not feel inadequate when he doesn't know a scientist's explanation for events, provided that he is encouraging his pupils to seek their own.

In summary, any scientific investigation would be likely to involve children in most of the processes or ways of working mentioned in relation to the bouncing balls investigation. Children would be:

(i)   observing (looking, listening, touching, smelling);

(ii)   asking the kind of question which can be answered by observations and fair tests;

(iii)   predicting what will happen from what they already think about things;

(iv)   planning fair tests for collecting evidence;

(v)   collecting evidence by observing and measuring;

(vi)   recording evidence in the form of descriptions, drawings, models, tables, charts or graphs;

(vii) sorting observations and measurements;

(viii) talking and writing in their own words about their experiences and their ideas;

(ix)   looking for patterns in their observations and measurements;

(x)   trying to explain the patterns they find in the evidence they collect.

This whole sequence of processes makes up an investigation and they should all work together as do all the separate processes involved in driving a car. Individually, each is rather uneventful and something rewarding happens only when they are all brought into effect together. No matter how skilled a pupil is in observing or measuring, if he is to get the sense of satisfaction and competence which science has to offer he will need to fit his skills into whole investigations. It is of course important to recognize that for very young pupils the experience of handling materials or living things will often be sufficient in itself and they may not be ready to engage in all the processes of science.

Most important of all, science work for young children should usually be a collaborative enterprise when pupils talk and work together to plan and carry out investigations and to develop shared ideas.

The teacher should be encouraging investigation rather than 'teaching science', and that should include:

(i) helping pupils to raise questions and to put questions into a form which can be answered by a fair test;

(ii) encouraging children to predict and say what they expect will happen;

(iii) prompting closer and more careful observations;

(iv) helping pupils to see ways in which their tests are not fair and ways in which these can be made fairer;

(v) encouraging pupils to measure whenever it is useful;

(vi) helping pupils to find the most helpful way of recording their evidence so that they can 'see the wood for the trees' – the patterns in their observations;

(vii) encouraging children to think about their experiences, to talk together and to describe and explain to others;

(viii) helping children to see the uses they can make of their findings.

In all of this the teacher is aided by children's natural inclination to explore the environment at first-hand but of course it has to be admitted that pupils who have not been regularly using these ways of working will have learnt *not* to question, *not* to observe, *not* to plan fair tests and the job of their teacher will be that much harder at first.

The Growth of Early Scientific Ideas

When young children are involved in scientific investigations they will inevitably be developing, testing and revising their own understandings of the natural and physical world; those understandings were earlier referred to as 'stepping-stone ideas'. Children are in reality making a journey from lack of understanding towards more sophisticated and accepted ways of thinking about their surroundings.

As an example, we might trace the journey towards the accepted understanding of density of a material. The steps towards understanding would not be taught – rather they would grow from the child's experiences – but they would perhaps follow a route like this:

1 'Big things are heavy and small things are light'
(Weight depends upon size)
↓

2 'Some big things are light and some small things are heavy'
(Weight depends upon size but also upon something else)
↓

3 'Certain materials like plastics are light and other materials like metals are usually heavy'
(Weight depends upon size and upon the material)
↓

4 'We can make a fair test of weight by weighing equal-sized pieces of different materials'
↓

5   'We can make a fair test by calculating the weight of 1cm^3 of each material'

$\downarrow$

6   'We call the weight of 1cm^3 of a material its density and to calculate density we divide the mass by the volume of a piece of material'

$\vdots$

N   'The density of a material is related to the characteristics of the atoms and molecules of which it is built up.'

Most children, during their primary education, would perhaps have travelled as far as 'we can make a fair test of weight by weighing equal-sized pieces of different materials.' Each child almost certainly begins by thinking that big things are heavy, and indeed, we often fall back to this idea even though we 'know' otherwise. But, as soon as he meets a large light piece of polystyrene and a small heavy piece of lead side by side, the pupil's too simple view will be challenged and he will be provoked into a more refined idea further along the journey even if his teacher is not directing his attention towards an idea of density. The point is, however, that this journey is the foundation upon which a formal understanding of density will be built. It is a journey which should not be by-passed or hurried and it is for this reason that the many experiences which primary science provides are so necessary.

The journey towards understanding is made possible for young children when they are given first-hand personal experiences to work upon. It is these experiences which the primary teacher should provide and which ensure sound understandings in the future. Think, for example, of that well-known centrifugal force trick in which someone swings a bucket of water over his head and none spills. We all 'know' that the water will not run out but it is those of us who have actually had the experience of doing it who do not expect to get wet!

Teaching primary science is a matter of providing experiences, and of encouraging pupils to investigate and to think about their investigations (see Chapter 13). Each pupil has to make his own journey, and this notion is well expressed by the 11-year-old who said: 'All you can do is to help me to do things. I'm the one who has to work it all out.' There is ample evidence to suggest that pupils' attitudes to science are fixed by the age of 13. We rely upon primary teachers to offer pupils a stimulating, rewarding and useful acquaintance with science which makes for a feeling of confidence and competence in dealing with their environment.

7 *Does Content Matter in Primary Science?* ★

Wynne Harlen

The reader expecting a straight answer to the question posed in the title should be warned that I do not intend to give one. To do so would in any case be foolish without first discussing the various factors on which an answer would depend; for instance, which parts of the primary age range are being considered, how the content would be chosen, by whom and in what form it would be expressed. The discussion of these factors seems more helpful than a simple answer, and indeed it does lead to an answer, but not a simple one.

To some it may seem surprising to question whether content matters, for if it is assumed that primary science is all about learning content then of course it matters what is learned. But an alternative view, which has held sway in many parts for the past fifteen years at least, is that primary science is not concerned with learning a certain content but with learning skills of enquiry, fostering attitudes and developing basic concepts. In this view the most useful content is any that interests the child or arouses his curiosity – whether it is finding out if food dyes affect the taste of homemade sweets, or how quickly snails can travel across different surfaces. According to this opinion, what is important is the way a problem or enquiry is tackled, not the knowledge that comes out of it.

What is attempted here is an examination of the reasons given in various circumstances for the importance or otherwise of choosing a certain content for primary science work. This seems best done by looking at the arguments given in various programmes or projects which have taken one or the other view. From these we can perhaps draw out the pros and cons of having a defined content and can find some guidelines for avoiding the errors of both extreme positions.

In Britain the main curriculum development projects in primary science have been the Nuffield Junior Science Project (1964–6) and the Schools Council Science 5–13 Project (1967–74) (Wastnedge, 1967). The move which gave rise to these began in the early 1960s when teachers attempting more than the traditional nature study in primary schools found support from Inspectors (Ministry of Education, 1961) and the Association for Science Education, which established a Primary Schools Committee in 1963. The Ministry of

★ From *School Science Review*, 59, 1978, pp. 614–25.

Education[1] and the Froebel Foundation[2] sponsored projects to study the development of scientific ideas in children, which overlapped with the Nuffield Junior Science Project. The ideas which all the groups working on these projects held in common were that for children to learn with understanding it was essential for them to have first-hand experience of manipulating objects and materials; they rejected any idea of a simplified version of the science taught in secondary schools, and stressed the importance of science as a way of working rather than a body of knowledge to be mastered. As such this blurred the distinction between science and other areas of the curriculum and an integrated approach to learning was advocated, removing subject boundaries and timetable limitations. Statements made in the Policy Statement prepared by the ASE's newly formed Primary Schools Science Committee clearly supported the emphasis upon *how* rather than *what* children should learn: 'At this level we are concerned more with the developing of an enquiring attitude of mind than with the learning of facts' and again 'at no time is the imparting of factual knowledge to be regarded as an end in itself' (ASE, 1963).

Echoes of this statement can be found in many parts of the Nuffield Junior Science Project (Wastnedge, 1967) and in the Science 5–13 units for teachers (1972–5). But since there has to be *some* content that the children study, what was the basis for selecting it? The Nuffield Junior project's answer was that the children should tackle problems of significance to them, their own problems, ones they find themselves, not those handed to them by others (see Chapter 13). Science 5–13 replied in similar vein: 'In general, children work best when trying to find answers to problems that they have themselves chosen to investigate' (Ennever and Harlen, 1972). With these convictions it was impossible for these projects to produce anything like a course, a list of experiments, or a programme of work. Instead they have produced guides for teachers, giving ideas and suggestions but leaving teachers to make their own selection from these to suit their own pupils. There are no pupil books and no kits of equipment, since these would necessarily restrict the freedom of pupils to work on problems of their own finding (see Chapter 14).

The main differences between the Nuffield project and Science 5–13 are that the latter provides background information for teachers about topics and activities described, gives an explicit statement of objectives, and provides a structure for building up skills and concepts progressively. The Nuffield project team held that stating objectives might needlessly set limits to the children's achievement rather than assist it, whereas Science 5–13 considered that the statement of objectives was necessary for teachers to guide children's work effectively. Many of the Science 5–13 objectives are clearly content-free and can be achieved through pursuing practical investigations in a very wide range of subjects, for example:

> Ability to predict the effect of certain changes through observation of similar changes;
> Ability to investigate variables and to discover effective ones;
> Ability to choose and use either arbitrary or standard units of measurement as appropriate.

Others, however, while not indicating particular activities, can only be achieved if certain kinds of materials are encountered and certain problems pursued. For instance some objectives relating to living things are:

Awareness of internal structure of living and non-living things;
Ability to construct and use keys for identification;
Knowledge of conditions which promote changes in living things.

The teacher is still left the choice about *which* living things are studied as an aid to achieving these objectives. The objectives are intended to be in the teacher's mind so that she can take any opportunities which arise to work towards them, and thus their statement does not conflict with the project's child-centred philosophy.

One exception to the British projects' whole-hearted embrace of process as opposed to content mastery was the Oxford Primary Science Project, which was supported by Ministry of Education funds from 1963 to 1967 (Redman *et al.*, 1969). This group started from a definition of four basic scientific ideas, energy, structure, life and chance, and then set out to find ways of helping children learn them (see Chapter 12). Thus they began from the subject matter, not from the child as the other British projects did. The project did not have much impact on primary science outside its trial schools.

The approach through considering *what* children should learn before *how* they should learn has much in common with some US elementary science projects, particularly the Science Curriculum Improvement Study (SCIS, 1970). SCIS defined content, process and attitude objectives, but the basic form of the programme was set by the content objectives. There were also four main scientific ideas determining the content of this programme: matter, energy, organism and ecosystem. The process objectives refer to the process of organizing the content – by property, reference frame, system and model – and not the processes of finding out – by observation, experiment and discerning patterns, etc. Nevertheless, the method of working involves practical investigation and first-hand experience and is structured to provide experience of exploration, invention, and discovery, described as the three stages in a child's learning cycle.

In order to enable children gradually to build up the basic scientific ideas identified by SCIS, the programme consists of units geared to each year of elementary school, each unit comprising workbooks for pupils, a teacher's guide and a kit of equipment. Though there are 'optional activities' the basic experience of science provided by the programme is of working through a carefully devised series of experiments, or watching demonstrations, and reporting observations or answering questions in a workbook.

There are many similarities between SCIS, taken as representative of programmes which prescribe a given content, and Science 5–13, which is typical of projects which do not provide a course to follow. They, and similar projects, acknowledge that young children must have *concrete* experiences to help their learning, that they must *see* for themselves, *do* for themselves and form their own ideas rather than memorize those provided by others. I do not wish to deny these similarities in focussing on one of the main points of difference, the question of selection of content. The questions to ask next are about why this difference exists and what are the advantages and disadvantages as seen from each side.

Wynne Harlen

The Case against a Common Content

Those who hold that the content of science activities for young children is less important than encouraging the skills and attitudes of enquiry and experiment give five main reasons for this view.

1 The strongest point is that some of the important aims of primary science cannot be achieved if children are constrained to work on particular problems or investigate phenomena in a given way. Aims relating to children's ability to raise questions and find out answers for themselves, pursue an investigation until they are satisfied – these are difficult to achieve if a programme is, in effect, telling children to be curious and enquiring only about the things presented to them.

2 Another point is a reflection of a general reaction against a fixed content in science, because ideas change and what is important to know today may not even be regarded as true, much less important, tomorrow. Rather, it is felt, it serves children better to equip them with skills of learning and finding out that will later enable them to master a variety of content as required.

3 A syllabus of work which is centrally devised does not cater for regional and local environmental variations; it thus often results in city children learning about things of the country which have no immediate relevance and interest for them, and *vice versa*.

4 If the content of science activities is determined by the programme being followed then it is difficult to integrate with work in other areas of the curriculum. This means that many opportunities to inculcate scientific attitudes or develop enquiry skills may be lost because of association of science with a certain content and not with the solution of any problems which occur.

5 The motivation for learning skills and developing concepts is very strong when children are working on what interests them, and it will not be the case that all are interested all the time in the content chosen by someone else. Thus much activity in a prescribed programme will be desultory, lacking purpose as far as the children can see and will not result in a grasp of the ideas intended. This will often happen even though teachers try their hardest to interest the children in the work. In contrast, the work which starts from children's interests, and itself develops new interests, will engage their mental powers more readily and result in a firmer learning (see Chapter 10).

Before looking at the points for the opposite case it is perhaps as well to acknowledge straightaway the disadvantages of the kind of approach implied in the case against a common content. We can see that, however attractive and worthwhile in theory, it is very difficult in practice to follow the interests of a whole class of children. Teaching in this way is extremely demanding and must be a style a teacher adopts throughout her work, otherwise it will not be effective in only one part of her teaching. Then it must be faced that some children never seem to be interested in anything sufficiently to want to investigate or experiment, and these pupils have to be given problems in any case. Another set of disadvantages arises from the problems children face if they have to move from one primary school to another, or even from class to class in the same school. Where teachers are responsible for the content, there may be repetition of experiences or large gaps left in building up certain ideas. This would not be a serious matter if teachers really were able to 'start from where each child is' but, as we have said, this makes great demands on a teacher's flexibility and not all feel able to allow children to take the lead in science, where they often feel insecure themselves about pursuing certain enquiries.

Most teachers who work in a child-centred way and take advantage of children's wide-ranging interests find they do in any case cover the content that would be included in any prescribed 'core'. But what of the children of those teachers who do not manage to do so? The argument goes that we cannot leave it to chance, but should make sure that all children have the opportunity to gain basic ideas that lay a foundation for a gradually more sophisticated understanding of their world.

The Case in Favour of a Common Content

1 A first point links with what has just been said. There are certain ideas and facts that scientists have to use and there is a body of knowledge which helps not only the scientist but would be of benefit to all who wish to be scientifically literate. Children need knowledge of some scientific ideas and facts to help them make sense of their world, just as do scientifically literate adults. It is therefore our duty in education to make sure that the children encounter the content from which they can gain this knowledge. What actually is the knowledge would be decided from experience of what is, and is not, useful to children at different stages.

2 A second argument uses a different criterion for selecting content. It begins from the same point, that is, from the ideas and facts which are needed by a scientifically literate adult. On the theory that the development of these ideas and mastery of facts depends upon the earlier grasp of ideas which are basic to them, and these in turn on yet more elementary ideas, then a case can be made for laying a foundation of basic ideas chosen so that they contribute to future understanding and knowledge. Thus, for instance, it could be claimed that knowledge of electrical conductors and insulators was important at a certain point, so that ideas which depend on this information can be developed.

3 Those who advocate or develop programmes with a prescribed content to be learned do not necessarily dismiss as less important the development of enquiry skills and certain attitudes. However, they point out that in order to encourage development of these skills and attitudes it is more effective to work on some kinds of problems than on others, and to use structured materials rather than unstructured ones. For instance, the number of variables in a problem chosen by a child may be so great that there is no chance of controlling them and the result may be dissatisfying. With structured equipment, however, the great degree of control can be built in and the investigation carried out satisfactorily.

The point is, therefore, that we can avoid too much failure and develop skills more easily by providing activities which have been carefully tried out and for which the right equipment is available.

4 It has been said that 'knowledge is control' in all fields, and so even in the primary school knowledge of their environment helps children to make sense of what is around them and to control it. But children are immature, and faced with such a multitude of things they could come to know what should they choose? Hence the argument that it is the duty of adults to pass on to children – in this case through experimental activities and investigations – the knowledge which is most likely to be of use to them.

5 Finally, some points of a more practical nature are often part of this case. One relates to teachers, and though the point is often wrapped up delicately, what it really says is that teachers are not able to see that children encounter a balanced content and so this has to be laid down for them. The second counters a possible objection to the first that it does not matter whether there is a balanced content in the primary years in any case because there is time in the secondary years to provide this balance. It suggests that in fact there is not enough time in the secondary years to build up the necessary body of knowledge and therefore this has to start earlier. In some cases this is true, for instance in developing countries, where compulsory schooling lasts only until the age of 13, or where early specialization cuts a number of pupils off from science after only two or three secondary years. However, true or not, the argument that primary education should make up for the deficiencies of secondary education cannot be pressed too far.

Again, we can easily see objections to some of the points of this case. The greatest is probably to the implied arrogance that we know what the 'best' content is to be. We do not know with any certainty what are the prerequisite ideas or facts which provide a basis for a particular concept to develop and thus we cannot, by analysis only, determine the content which at the primary level will lead to later more sophisticated notions. Even if we could do this, that content is unlikely to meet the other criteria, of being interesting to children and relevant to their understanding of what they see in their immediate surroundings.

Despite the advantages of structured activities which 'work', they lack flexibility and can bring a stagnation to science lessons. The same things are done each year, with the same apparatus, and because they do 'work' they may remain in use long after the knowledge which they yield has become unimportant or obtainable more readily in their ways. Moreover, the common content for all children generally means that they do the same things, regardless not only of differences in interest but also of differences in ability. The self-instructional programme is not necessarily the answer, since time for working is only one variable which affects learning; the presentation of the problem, the materials used, the amount and kind of help given are also important. In the end it may be that a variety of content is needed to get the same ideas over to different pupils and the virtues of a common content are lost.

Is There a Middle Way?

It is evident that there are advantages and disadvantages on both sides of this argument and the decision to take one course or another is often swayed by circumstances which lend greater weight to some points. Thus in England, where the ethos of primary education is child-centred and the decentralized system gives teachers freedom and responsibility for making decisions about children's learning, the circumstances favour a local choice of content. In countries where the system is centralized there is a tradition of accepting that many decisions are taken out of teachers' hands and thus less tendency to question the merits of a detailed programme of work being laid down.

It may be possible to find a compromise by looking at what happens in practice in the two situations. A teacher enjoying the freedom to decide the content for herself, and being very successful in promoting lively science in her class, nevertheless expressed a worry: 'I'm not asking for a list of things to be "covered", but since there is such a wide field of content I would like to know if it is better for the children if we took up one subject rather than another. We can go to the wood time after time and do really exciting work, but I sometimes wonder if this means they are missing out on other things.' Again a successful teacher using a structured programme: 'We go through the activities, many of which are intriguing and they all "work", but it is difficult to avoid a kind of dull routine creeping in. I feel that I am teaching them to use words in relation to the particular things we do but they don't have any real significance for the children. There we are, surrounded by things they are curious about, but we feel guilty if we don't "get back to the book".'

What seems to be required are content guidelines that are firm enough to ensure that children encounter the range of ideas and facts which are relevant to understanding their environment, yet are loose enough to enable teachers to use a variety of routes to arrive at them. It is the range of possibilities in relation to the meaning of 'content' that makes for difficulty in giving a straight answer to the question posed in the title of this chapter.

My position would be that if by content we mean things like 'observing how broad beans germinate', 'separating sand and salt from a mixture of the two', 'connecting light bulbs in series and in parallel', then the answer to the question would be 'no'. There is other content through which the important ideas which could come from these activities might also be arrived at. Thus, in this meaning of the word, whichever items of content are covered does not matter. However, if by content we mean a set of ideas, generalizations and facts which children should encounter, then the answer would be 'yes'. Among the many ideas which children *could* encounter there are some that they *should* encounter. We do not need to prescribe specific activities but we should make sure that these ideas are conveyed through *some* activities.

What I am suggesting are content objectives which can be treated in the same way as process and attitude objectives. When, for example, we wish to encourage powers of observation, or ability to identify variables, we do this not by giving specific exercises in these skills but by using observation and by looking for variables as part of any investigation. So with content objectives; we can express these as ideas and items of knowledge to be achieved not through one set of activities but potentially from any of a variety, none having a greater priority than others.

The form in which such guidelines are stated is critical; if too vague they would be useless, if too specific they could be restrictive. They should also, in their wording, convey the tentative nature of some of the 'facts' and ideas that children pick up, based on their limited experience. Many early ideas are incomplete or ill-defined and later have to be modified and refined as children's experience widens. It is this gradual change towards ideas of greater applicability and generalizability that constitutes their progress. Thus one should expect somewhat different ideas in relation to particular phenomena or explanations from a 9-year-old or an 11-year-old, and the guidelines should reflect this difference (see Chapter 6).

The conclusion here is an attempt to suggest examples of guidelines to content to meet the criteria just suggested. The items have been arrived at by asking the question: While children are investigating problems they find and developing scientific skills and attitudes, what is the core of generalizations that they should at the same time acquire?

The words 'at the same time' cannot be emphasized too much. The content objectives must not be allowed to replace the process and attitude objectives. So it is perhaps necessary to state explicitly that our central concern in primary science should be to develop the abilities to:

> observe, raise questions, propose enquiries to answer questions, experiment or investigate, find patterns in observations, reason systematically and logically, communicate findings, apply learning

and the attitudes of:

> curiosity, originality, cooperation, perseverance, openmindedness, self-criticism, responsibility, independence in thinking.

These aims must influence teachers' guidance of *how* children carry out their activities. In addition, what is suggested is that content guidelines influence decisions about *what* activities they carry out.

Although the answers suggested here, for 9–10-year-olds and 11–12-year-olds, are based on reflection and discussion with teachers over many years, nevertheless they constitute a personal statement and should be regarded as no more than an example. It is important that any set of guidelines should be produced by discussion between the teachers who are to use them and others with relevant expertise in the education of children. Any list should always be under review, for content in any form is only useful in so far as it helps the understanding of the world around at a particular time. In a rapidly changing world for our children our objectives must change accordingly, not lag behind as has happened in the recent past.

The following is a minimal statement and it is intended that the children's ideas should *include but not be restricted to these*. The statements are worded so as to avoid indicating that particular activities must be carried out or specific materials used. Thus the activities through which they come to form these ideas can be chosen to reflect the children's environment and interests.

Examples of Content Guidelines

By the age of 9 or 10 the ideas which children have should include the following:

About ourselves and other living things
- living things have the capability of reproducing themselves and this takes place in different ways in different plants and animals, but for each the pattern is the same in each generation;
- living things grow and develop, and this requires food;
- human beings must have certain kinds of food for growth, energy and to fight disease;
- human beings gain information about their surroundings through their senses; there are limits to the range and sensitivity of the sense organs, but these can be increased by using tools, or instruments.

About the physical surroundings
- patterns occur in weather conditions and cycles in the apparent movement of the sun and moon and in changes in plants in the immediate environment;
- the materials described as stone, wood, glass, plastic, metal, have certain sets of properties which help to identify them;
- there are definite differences in the way matter behaves when it is solid, liquid or gaseous;
- some substances dissolve in water very well, others only a little and some not at all;
- some substances float in water, others sink; substances which sink can be used to make things which float.

About forces, movement and energy
- to make anything move (or change the way it is moving) there has to be something pushing, pulling or twisting it;
- when a push or pull makes something move it requires energy which can come from various sources: food, fuel, electricity, a wound spring, etc.;
- all things are pulled down towards the earth; the amount of this pull is the weight of an object;
- the speed of an object means how far it moves in a certain time.

Basic concepts
- the length of an object remains the same when only its position is changed even though it may look different;
- the area is the amount of surface across the face of an object which is unaffected by moving or dividing up the surface;
- the capacity of a container is the amount of space within it which can be filled; the volume of an object is the amount of space it takes up;
- a quantity of matter which exists at a certain time will still exist at a later time either in the same form or in different forms;
- objects or events can be classified in several ways according to their features or characteristics;

– certain actions always have the same consequences and this relationship can often be used to predict the effect of changes.

By the age of 11 or 12 the ideas which children have should include the above together with the following:

About ourselves and other living things
– the basic life processes are growth, feeding, respiration, excretion, reproduction, sensitivity to the surroundings, and some mechanism for movement and support;
– there is a great variety in the way in which these life processes are carried out by different living things;
– in the human body organs are grouped into systems, each concerned with one of the main processes;
– energy is needed by all living things to support life processes; animals take in food, plants use the sun's energy to produce food they can use and store;
– living things depend on each other for their survival and all animals depend ultimately on plants for their food;
– living things have changed very gradually through time by the process of adaptation to various external conditions; the most successful animals at any time are those best adapted to the present conditions.

About the physical surroundings
– air fills the space around us and contains oxygen, which living things need;
– air contains water vapour, some of which condenses out in various conditions to give rain, dew, mist, snow, hail, ice or water;
– soil is composed of small fragments from rocks, air, water and decayed remains from living material which provide substances needed by growing plants; these substances have to be replenished to keep soil fertile;
– all non-living things are made from substances found in the earth; their supply is not endless, so they must not be wasted;
– pollution of the air, water or land by waste, smoke, or noise can harm both living and non-living things;
– the earth is one of nine planets so far known to be circling the sun, which is our source of heat and light energy;
– the moon circles the earth, reflecting light from the sun;
– melting or evaporating requires energy in the form of heat;
– a complete circuit of conducting material is needed for electricity to flow.

About forces, movement and energy
– a force is needed to accelerate or decelerate a thing which is moving or to change the direction of its movement;
– when an object is not moving (or moving at a constant speed) the forces acting on it are equal and opposite;
– all things which are moving have energy and when they slow down some of their energy is changed into another form;
– friction is a force which commonly opposes motion;
– energy is changed from one form to another in a variety of processes; it is never lost, but what disappears in one form reappears in another.

Basic concepts
- the total volume of an object is not changed by dividing it up or changing its shape;
- the process of measurement is the repeated comparison of a quantity with an agreed unit of the quantity; all measurements, however careful or fine, are inexact to some degree;
- all changes in objects or substances are caused by interaction with other substances or by adding or taking away energy.

Acknowledgement

I am grateful to Norman Booth (formerly Staff Inspector for Science DES) for helpful discussion and comments.

Notes

1 The DES supported the Oxford Primary Science Project. The project team produced *An Approach to Primary Science*, by S. REDMAN, A. BRERETON and P. BOYERS (Macmillan Educational, 1969). (See Chapter 12 in this book.)
2 The Froebel Foundation, supported by the British Association, ran a research project into scientific development in children, directed by Nathan Isaacs. A report, *Children Learning through Scientific Experience*, was published by the Froebel Foundation in 1966.

References

ASSOCIATION FOR SCIENCE EDUCATION (ASE) (1963) Policy Statement prepared by the Primary Schools Science Committee.
ENNEVER, L. and HARLEN, W. (1972) *With Objectives in Mind*, MacDonald Educational.
MINISTRY OF EDUCATION (1961) *Science in the Primary School*, London, HMSO.
REDMAN, S. *et al.* (1969) *An Approach to Primary Science*, Macmillan Educational.
Science Curriculum Improvement Study (1970) Rand McNally.
Science 5–13 (1972–5) units for teachers, MacDonald Educational.
WASTNEDGE, R. *et al.* (1967) *Teacher's Guide 1, Teacher's Guide 2, Animals and Plants, Apparatus*, Collins.

8   How Can Children's Progress in Science Be Monitored, Recorded and Evaluated?

Barry Davis

Introduction

Within primary science teaching, the area most neglected by schools and individual teachers is the monitoring, recording and evaluating of children's work. First of all let me define these terms as I see them.

Monitoring is looking at the activities offered to children and the attitudes, skills and concepts which are being formed so that a *record* can be made of progress and development. From this, *evaluation* of the children and teaching can take place.

1   Why Check Up?

A survey started in 1976 (Clift *et al.*, 1981) found that very few primary schools kept records of progress in science. In visiting a considerable number of schools recently, I also found there were very few records of pupil progress in science. With the increasing demands made upon a teacher's time, perhaps this is understandable. However, it shows that many teachers are not clear about why they should give time to science. This chapter attempts to provide some ideas about what to look for, and ways of carrying out these checks.
Monitoring can be carried out for the following reasons:

(i)   to assess the extent to which a balanced programme of science activities is provided;
(ii) to assist in the planning of future work, revision and reinforcement;
(iii) to try to determine the level of development of each child in the class;
(iv) to match the work to the pupils' level of development.

After checking up, teachers should have a clearer picture of the scientific experiences which they are offering within the class, and this should help to formulate aims and objectives in the teaching of science (referred to later). Checks can also avoid situations such as the one I came across recently. A newly appointed teacher had carefully planned a topic on food, only to find out too late that the children had worked with this topic in the previous term. No record of this had been available to her and the time and energy spent in preparation were wasted.

2 Finding Out What Children Are Doing

The easiest way of monitoring what children are doing is by observation. The Progress in Learning Project (Harlen *et al.*, 1977) picks out the following five aspects which can make a teacher aware of childrens' thinking.

(i)   *Dialogue*, when we and children freely exchange views, ideas, feel able to ask and answer questions, and listen to each other;

(ii) *Questioning*, when we ask 'open questions' to find out what children are thinking and feeling, questions which do not need a particular response such as, 'Why do you think these leaves have gone brown'?;

(iii) *Listening*, when we let children do most of the talking and do not break in with such comments as 'do you mean?';

(iv) *Watching actions and working processes*, when we observe children's behaviour and work patterns, for example, cooperation with others, responsibility and perseverance;

(v)   *Looking at children's work*, when we look at all the aspects of each child's communication, for example, art, writing and number work, we can get an indication of the difficulties experienced and the child's way of working.

As this information is gathered a teacher builds up an overall picture of each child. However, we must be aware of two dangers. The first is that our observations cannot be completely objective. Secondly, inferences can only be of value when made from observations over a time. Factors such as motivation, the behaviour of other children in the group and physical fitness, could radically alter our perception of each child on a particular day.

3 Recording

Observation does not necessarily lead to recording, but there are several reasons why we should keep records.

(i)   one cannot assume that progress is being made by the children;

(ii) we must not become complacent and assume we are offering the right experiences;

(iii) carrying information in one's head may leave the teacher confused about children's development and progress;

(iv) records properly kept and passed on will save the teacher of the next class or school from starting afresh.

However, there is no point in record-keeping for its own sake. Records must be used to be of value. I shall return to methods of recording later.

4   Evaluation

Having observed and recorded children's work, we then need to make judgements about the science programme, the children's progress and our own teaching. Before these judgements can be made, schools and teachers will need to consider why time should be given to science, and which experiences children should be given. The process of evaluation can only be attempted when a basis of aims and objectives has been established either by the school or the individual teacher. One book of the 'Science 5–13 Series' (Ennever and Harlen, 1972) looks at objectives, and there is further help at the end of each unit of the series.

What Are We Looking For?

It is now recognized that science education is concerned with a way of thinking and not primarily with the transmission of facts. The scientist is concerned with seeking information and making judgements, in order to arrive at a closer approximation to the truth.

In primary school we attempt to make progress towards a scientific way of thinking by involving children at increasingly greater depth. We try to get them to investigate in the following sequence:

(i)   making observations;
(ii)   recording these;
(iii) making generalizations on the basis of (a) and (b);
(iv)   designing investigations (experiments) to test these generalizations;
(v)   recording new observations;
(vi)   drawing conclusions.

This is generally called the *process* approach which can also be applied to investigations in other areas of the curriculum as well as science. 'Investigations' in this chapter is another word for 'experiments'. It does not mean, for example, looking up facts in a book. Scientific investigations are distinguished from all else by the need to set up experiments.

The level at which each child will be able to perform the sequence above will depend on the stage of development. In the infant school, children will start with observing and recording, moving on to investigations as they develop these skills. So much of the work we do in primary schools is based on observing and drawing conclusions that it is important that the children have the opportunity to develop this process approach in all areas of the curriculum, for investigations are just as likely to arise in maths, history or art as in a more scientific topic.

1   Guidelines

Many teachers lacking the confidence to include science in their classroom activities need some sort of guidance to give them a much greater sense of security and purpose. Being told to 'incorporate science in the curriculum' because 'not enough is being done' does not help to get science started. Guidance in the form of guidelines should state the school's interpretation of primary science, the reasons for teaching it, the experiences considered suitable for the children and how science is organized and evaluated. It will require considerable time and discussion for a whole staff to develop these. 'Science 5–13 Series' and the ASE primary publications (1974, 1976) give particular help with this.

It is generally agreed that the aims of primary science can be divided into three sections: the development of (i) attitudes; (ii) skills; (iii) concepts and knowledge.

Let us look more closely at these three groups of aims.

2   Attitudes and Skills

Which attitudes and skills are developed during *science* activities? If we wrote down our own lists I have no doubt that they would be similar to those produced by teachers in the Schools Council Progress in Learning Project. For younger children these attitudes were:

> curiosity, originality, perseverance, open-mindedness, self-criticism, responsibility, willingness to cooperate, independence;

and the skills of:

> observing, raising questions, exploring, problem-solving, finding patterns in observations, communicating verbally and non-verbally, applying learning and classifying.

As children grow older and become more experienced 'raising questions' and 'exploring' might become 'proposing enquiries, experimenting and investigating'. Developing 'critical reasoning' might also be added to this list.

3   General and Specific Skills

The skills which are developed through scientific investigations are both general and specific. The general skills are common to other areas of the curriculum; these are the skills such as observation, recording and communicating. The specific skills are more wholly science-based, such as the use of controls and identifying variables.

Children must first have the opportunity to develop general skills such as observation and exploring, for without these skills they cannot develop the more specific ones. As children build up these general skills we can start to put them into situations where they are required to develop the more specific skills. This development will come from asking children the right questions, such as, 'Is it a fair test?', and from encouraging them to set up experiments. In the later years of the primary school the specific skills must not completely replace the general skills for both will need to be developed together.

A recent list of skills based on the process approach has been developed (APU, 1981). This is more clearly defined and more specifically science-orientated than the previous one. The skills are divided into six categories:

(i) *Using symbolic representation:* children's ability to record and interpret information using graphs, tables and charts;

(ii) *Using apparatus and measuring instruments:* children's ability to handle simple measuring and science equipment, such as a ruler, tape measure, hand lens, thermometer, etc.;

(iii) *Using observations:* the selection and recording of observations, looking at similarities and differences using keys and interpreting observations;

(iv) *Interpretation and application:* seeing patterns and relationships in data, identifying assumptions and applying science concepts;

(v) *Designing investigations:* children's planning and investigations, recognizing variables and controlling them and being critical of their own proposals;

(vi) *Performing and investigating:* performing an investigation, planning, measuring and observing.

This list contains both general and specific skills and was produced by the Assessment of Performance Unit (APU) of the Department of Education and Science to monitor nationally a sample of children aged 11, 13, and 15 (see Chapter 9).

It is not possible to test our pupils' performance using the APU tests, nor would this be useful. If teachers had the test questions available so that children could be monitored there would be a danger of teaching skills just to achieve a good result in the test. However, these categories can be used to help identify the experiences which we should provide for our children.

At the upper junior age the APU categories are more appropriate than the earlier list of skills, since they help to direct attention towards specifically science-based skills. Since becoming involved in trials of APU tests, I have noticed that children are less successful at the science-based skills, not because they are beyond their capabilities but because we teachers are not so aware of them.

The first APU report for 11-year-olds (APU, 1981; see also Chapter 9) indicates that children are developing general skills but not those which are more specifically science-based. Harlen (1981) has noted that the better performance in general skills is probably attributable to the effectiveness of an active approach to teaching and learning in general in our primary schools.

To improve primary science we must focus more attention on the skills which are science-based. The most important are: recognition of patterns in observation; explanation of events using science-based concepts; use of controls in investigations; identifying variables; making predictions; checking results and planning experiments.

Recently two children in my class investigating how fruits lost weight as the water content evaporated, observed and accurately measured the change in weight. They came to conclusions consistent with what they had observed, but the results were not valid because they had not controlled the temperature of the fruits by putting them all in the same place. In discussion with me the children became aware of the mistakes they had made. They were able to use the general skills of measuring and observing, but needed more experience in the use of controls.

We need to monitor and evaluate our teaching to see if we are giving opportunities to develop the more complex skills. Children do not need a deep knowledge of science facts but they do require some understanding of the scientific process. The experience of good teachers of primary science indicates that quite young children are capable of following this process through, providing that the context is concrete, fairly simple, and related to topic and interest areas. Attention must still be paid to general attitudes and skills, as well as specific ones, throughout the later primary years. Both will need to be related to the level of each child's development.

4   Concepts

Science knowledge and facts cannot be ignored, although in the process approach they will be secondary to the development of attitudes and skills (see Chapter 1). Each teacher or school will need to consider which concepts the children might need to grasp. The list might include: volume; length; area; cause and effect; life-cycles/circuits; time; speed; energy; force.

The APU report shows that by 11 children are well able to apply concepts about the properties of living things and the environment to new situations, but find difficulty in explaining the reason behind a particular application. Is this because it is beyond the power of the age group to do so, or because we are not offering children the right quality of experience and prompting them to set up experiments?

5   Areas of Study: Topic or Specific Content?

The choice between a topic approach or a syllabus of specific content is one of the problem areas of primary science (see Chapter 1). My own view should already be clear. I favour the development of attitudes and skills through topic work. However, some teachers still prefer a syllabus approach for the following reasons:

(i)   they feel more secure with content lists and a supporting text;
(ii) set content allows skills and attitudes to develop in a proved and tested framework;
(iii) set content allows the teacher to develop a balanced programme of science activities;
(iv) children need to be taught content from which scientific knowledge can be gained as an early foundation which can be built upon;
(v)   children must be given a body of knowledge early in their school life as there may not be enough time or opportunity to do this at secondary schools;
(vi) adults are the best judges of the experiences and knowledge a child will require.

Those in favour of the topic approach think that a syllabus tends to:

(i)   discourage children from following their own interests and designing their own investigations;

(ii)   give less opportunity for individual interest;

(iii)   make it virtually impossible to provide a variety of experiences at the right level which are required by different children in a group; a child unable to understand becomes bored;

(iv)   increase pressure upon a child to conform and avoid questioning what is taught. The topic approach allows the child more opportunity to find out and question;

(v)   relate less easily to other areas of the curriculum.

There is however, a need for a compromise. Teachers, particularly those who are uncertain about science, need some guidance on the choice of activities for children, and the scientific investigations which can be extracted from different topics. One way of combining content and topic areas is to list those areas of scientific investigation which children might experience in different topics during their primary school years. One such list might be the following.

The environment (weather, water, soil/rocks, air, planets/sun/stars, conservation)	Light and colour Heat and energy
Materials (wood, plastic, metal, food, building, structures)	Ourselves
Moving things (flight, transport, friction, machines, floating and sinking, etc.)	Animals and plants
Magnetism and electricity	Sound and music

How Do We Go about It?

1   Recording Areas of Work

In schools using a thematic or topic approach it is necessary to record the lines of investigation taking place. A central record, either in the headteacher's office or the staffroom, would help to ensure that this was so, and that children were not merely retracing their steps if the same topic were used twice. This record would allow the headteacher to rectify omissions, coordinate themes in progress and maintain a balance of science with topics in other areas. In some schools records might be kept as a termly forecast but this does not account for children focussing on other aspects of a subject, or teachers over-estimating what they can cover. This may mean amendments at the end of a topic or term. It would, therefore, be better to record areas investigated at the end of a period by means of a flow diagram or a statement of general areas covered in each subject in relation to the topic as in the following example.

Topic	*Canals*
Maths	Volume, capacity, scale plans, measurement
Science	Floating/sinking, loading boats, properties of water, bridge/tunnel structures, porosity of materials – clay, sand, soil, rock, water plants and animals
Environmental	Development of canals, costume, horses and horse-drawn

	barges, canal and boat equipment, canal architecture, maps, mapwork local and national
Language	Factual and story work, discussions, play about a barge family
Visits	Stoke Bruerne Canal Museum, Edstone aqueduct, Oxford canal – lock, canal basin, cantilever bridge

At the same time each teacher should keep a record of what activities each child or group of children has experienced. One way of doing this would be to list and letter-code all the activities which the class has undertaken, and then on another sheet of paper list those activities each child has followed, by putting the code letters by the name. The two sheets could then be stapled together for easy reference, as in the following.

Activities Sheet

A Sorting different materials that float and sink; altered materials from sinking to floating (such as plasticine);
B Investigating which shapes move most easily in water; investigating the wash made by different shapes at different speeds;
C Loading marbles into different floating containers; trying this in different water solutions, for example, fresh water and salt water;
D Weighing objects in and out of water;
E Making a working model of a cantilever bridge and investigating the strength of different structures used for bridges and tunnels.

etc.

Record Sheet

CANALS

Name	Activities				
J. Brown	A	B	E	G	
M. Smith	A	B	C	E	H

Though this record is an outline it should prevent repetition of areas of study and particular activities. Floating and sinking may be repeated with the same group, but the work can then be at a greater depth or placed in a different context such as a study of a harbour or port.

Recording the type of investigation undertaken in different topic areas also allows us to evaluate the depth and width of experiences we are offering our children. This record can be matched against content guidelines by asking the questions: Have the children had the opportunity to see . . .?; or Have they had the experience of . . .?

2 Children's Development: The Idea of Matching

If the attitudes, skills and concepts are monitored and recorded, the results can then be used to match children's level of development to their experiences.

Matching means giving a child an experience which promotes some step forward in his development. Judging the amount of forward development is important; too big a step forward and mismatch is created. Given that the experiences offered to a child should be matched to his level of development, we must first ascertain that level. Before matching can take place a teacher needs to determine that level through careful observation of the attitudes and skills attained. Once this is determined, how important is the match? Without it problems arise in a number of ways. Children of limited ability will easily become frustrated and bored if the work they are given is beyond their capabilities at that time. When frustration and boredom set in, the child either gives up or becomes a nuisance. Conversely, children asked to do work well below their capabilities are likewise reduced to a state of boredom, frustration and underfunctioning. Attempts to match work to children's level of development will reduce these problems, although it is not an easy matter and complete matching is unattainable in practice.

A detailed study on this has been produced by the Progress in Learning Project. There are two books, *Raising Questions*, which looks at ways of determining a child's level of development, and *Finding Answers*, which looks at the experiences which one could use to match attitudes, skills and concepts for individual children. The material was developed for Inset and though best used in group discussion, it provides valuable information on how to attempt matching.

3   Recording Children's Development

Determining and recording a child's development and progress requires the teacher to monitor and then record the development of each attitude, skill or concept that is felt to be important. To record the twenty-four characteristics listed by the Progress in Learning Project for a class of thirty-two children, will require considerable time and thought and this must be balanced against classroom pressures. However, the method could be used to determine the level of development of several characteristics for one child, or the level of development of one characteristic for all the children in a class. This could be done on a four- or five-point scale. Each school or teacher would need to determine what stage of development each point represented. On a four-point scale it might be:

(A) no understanding;
(B) little understanding;
(C) quite good understanding;
(D) very good understanding.

In *Raising Questions* there are suggestions for ways of recording and a rating scale for each of the twenty-four characteristics (see pp. 52–8; 239–58). Richards *et al.* (1980) also has a short section which looks at ways of recording and evaluating children's work and development. Using a checklist of attitudes, skills and concepts is also an important way of checking that a child is developing all the attributes, and records will show up those areas where more experience needs to be offered, or where areas of investigation may be

Name: M. Smith

Attitudes/skills	A	B	C	D
Curiosity	√	√	√	
Open-mindedness	√	√		
Perseverance	√			
Cooperation	√	√		
Observation	√	√	√	
Use of controls	√			
Identifying variables	√			
Recording	√	√	√	

deficient in opportunities to develop certain skills. These kinds of records obviously require a teacher to give up valuable time to monitor and then record each child.

We must also use the information we have gathered about children and their experiences to evaluate the effectiveness of our teaching programme. The children's achievement or lack of it may be a reflection of our own performance. Are they failing to develop certain attitudes and skills because we are not offering the right experiences? By keeping records on a class basis we immediately get an overall picture of that group's development. On closer inspection the sort of questions which might arise could be: Are children of different abilities getting similar opportunities? Are boys and girls making similar progress? Are there any attributes which all the class appear to have not experienced or developed?

Summary

If science is to take its rightful place as an integral part of every primary school's curriculum, the work must be monitored and records made to assist evaluation. The extent to which this is done will vary according to each school or teacher's needs. I have tried to indicate what we should be looking for in terms of attitudes, skills and concepts which ought to be provided. The general skills will need to be developed before blending in the more specifically science-based skills. The point at which the more specific skills are introduced will depend on each child's stage of development. The attitudes, skills and concepts can best be developed by a process approach through topic work. However, there may need to be a compromise between a broad topic approach and a more rigid syllabus in the form of content or areas of investigation guidelines, describing what experiences children should meet in the primary school.

Although simple monitoring of children's attitudes and abilities may need no recording, good evaluation requires evidence. Topic and content areas need to be recorded for future reference to avoid duplication. Monitoring and recording also allows the teacher to ascertain the stage of development which each child has reached, so that a better match of work for the child is achieved. On the other hand, one can become obsessed with the need to record. Be clear about why you want to keep records and about the use to which they are going to be put, and make the methods of recording of value to you or the school within the constraints and pressures of the situation. Any extra work done will bring rewards in being able to enhance the children's development and progress as well as make you a more complete educator in science activities.

Acknowledgement

I am grateful to John Robards (Science Adviser, Oxfordshire LEA) for most helpful discussion and comments.

References

ASSESSMENT OF PERFORMANCE UNIT (1981) *Science in Schools Age 11: Report No. 1,* London, HMSO.

ASSOCIATION FOR SCIENCE EDUCATION (1974) *The Headteacher and Primary Science,* Science and Primary Education Paper No. 2.

ASSOCIATION FOR SCIENCE EDUCATION (1976) *A Post of Responsibility,* Science and Primary Education Paper No. 3.

CLIFT, P. *et al.* (1981) *Record Keeping in Primary Schools,* Macmillan Educational.

ENNEVER, L. and HARLEN, W. (1972) *With Objectives in Mind,* MacDonald Educational.

HARLEN, W. (1981) 'Some gloom, some satisfaction', in *The Times Educational Supplement,* 18 December.

HARLEN, W. *et al.* (1977) *Finding Answers,* Match and Mismatch, Oliver and Boyd.

HARLEN, W. *et al.* (1977) *Raising Questions,* Match and Mismatch, Oliver and Boyd.

RICHARDS, R. *et al.* (1980) *Learning through Science: Formulating a School Policy,* MacDonald Educational.

9 The Assessment of Performance Unit's Surveys of Science at Age 11: What Scientific Skills Do Children Have?

Wynne Harlen

The Survey Results in Outline

Two years after the publication of the HMI Primary Survey (see Chapter 4), reporting that few of their sample of primary schools in England had effective programmes for the teaching of science, the first survey of science performance of 10/11-year-olds was carried out on behalf of the APU. It could hardly be expected that much would have changed in these two years, so the results of the survey might well make rather depressing, and familiar, reading. The picture was not entirely gloomy, however. The children were assessed in a range of skills, some relating to the general process of enquiry which can take place in any area of the curriculum and some constituting the process skills of science, and there was an important difference in the performance in these two groups of skills.

The APU survey results (DES, 1981) showed that children were well able to use skills relating to observation and to interpretation of information given in graphical, tabular or symbolic form. They were also able to set about a practical problem in an appropriate way and with signs of real interest and they were successful in using simple measuring instruments accurately. These are, of course, the more general skills which are important in many areas of the curriculum as well as in science-based activities and the high level of performance found is probably attributable to the effectiveness of an active approach to teaching and learning in general in our primary schools. For skills more specifically related to science-based work, however, the picture was of generally lower performance. In such areas as recognition of patterns in observations, the explanation of events using basic science concepts, the use of controls in practical investigations and the critical examination of practical procedures, there was less room for satisfaction. It seems that whilst many of our children have a good *foundation* for scientific development laid by their primary school work, this is built upon only in the case of a minority.

Schools in the APU survey sample were asked to complete a questionnaire which asked about their provision for science activities in terms of human and financial resources, policy and organization of science in the curriculum. The questionnaire also gathered information about what the schools regarded as being of greatest importance in science activities, indicated by the priority given to certain goals and types of activity. The results relating to provision and organization reflected closely those found in the HMI Primary Survey, as might be expected. On average schools spent about 5 per cent of their time and 5 per cent of their capitation allowance (which worked out at around 60 pence per pupil per year) on science activities. About 10 per cent of teachers in the primary schools had taken science as a main course in their training and a further 7 per cent had taken one course in science. This leaves 83 per cent without any appreciable training in science. About half the schools said they included science as a specified part of the curriculum, and a further 10 per cent as a planned part of topic work, whilst the remaining 40 per cent had no policy or included science as it might arise from other topics. Just under one-third of schools in England had a post of responsibility for science (in Wales the proportion was 10 per cent and in Northern Ireland 1 per cent).

These results about provision were used in the analysis of findings to investigate any relationships between pupils' performance and science experience. In the first survey few firm relationships were found. This was partly because, despite 1100 schools being involved, the numbers in various subgroups formed according to types of school with certain kinds of organization for science, for instance, were small. But it was no doubt partly due to the complexity of factors which influence children's performance in school, some of which originate in the home background of the children rather than the school provision. Also, of course, it would be naive to think that spending more money, or a greater amount of time, on science would, of themselves, affect performance. It is the quality of children's experience which matters and this is extremely difficult, if not impossible, to quantify. The nearest indication of this obtained in the survey was the information about the goals and activities regarded as most important. However, discussion of this comes later, after looking in more detail at kinds of tests given to the children and at some of the results.

The Purpose and Methods of the Survey

In the introduction to the report of the first survey in science at age 11 (DES, 1981), the aim of the APU is stated as 'to produce and make generally available national pictures of pupil performance, not to report on the performance of individual children, schools or local education authorities.' The survey involved testing a random sample of approximately 11,000 pupils in 1100 schools in England, Wales and Northern Ireland. The pupils were aged 10.7 to 11.7 years and were in primary or middle schools at the time of testing. About 3500 children were given one of two kinds of practical tests, the administration of these involving visits to over 500 schools by teachers trained to give the tests. As the selection of schools and of pupils within them was sufficiently large and random it was possible to generalize results from the sample to the age groups as a whole. As in all the APU surveys, the information was collected in such a way that no individual LEAs, schools or pupils could be identified.

The survey in 1980 was the first of a series of similar surveys which are being carried out annually until 1984 and thereafter less frequently. A large bank of questions has been established and each year a random selection of questions is taken from this to make up the test packages. The writing of questions for age 11 is in the hands of a team at the Centre for Science and Mathematics Education at Chelsea College.

In planning the test questions every effort was made to ensure that what was assessed would reflect what teachers and others considered to be important in early science education. A process of consultation between the team developing the tests and many different groups took place between 1977 and the time of the survey. It was agreed that scientific development at age 11 was best interpreted widely, as something relating to many topics across the curriculum as well as to more specifically science-focussed activities. The attempt was made to produce tests which reflect a view of primary science as *a rational way of finding out about the world, involving development of willingness and ability to seek and use evidence; the gradual building of a framework of ideas which help to make sense of experience and the fostering of skills and attitudes necessary for investigation and experimentation.* If this could be done, it was felt that the results would be of help not only at the national level but to individual teachers who, whether or not they teach science as such, might reflect on the opportunities provided for scientific development in their own classes.

It represented a considerable challenge to produce tests meeting the above prescription but in a form that could be given to large numbers of children in schools scattered across the country. All the test material was developed from scratch to suit the constraints of the national survey. It was not possible to use some of the methods which teachers can use in assessing their own pupils to help in teaching – methods based on detailed observation of, and discussion with, children in a variety of situations over an extended time. But it must be remembered that the purpose was *not* to give information about individuals, such as teachers require for own assessment, but to give a more general picture of performance across the age group. For this purpose it was necessary to gather information in a formal and uniform manner so that results of children in different schools could be added together. Moreover it was possible to give a number of different tests, since it is not necessary in a survey of this kind for all pupils to take the same ones.

Test questions were developed to assess the main categories and sub-categories of science performance which are summarized in Table 1. Category 5 was not included in the 1980 survey but is part of subsequent surveys. The categories were designed to apply to the surveys at ages 13 and 15 (DES, 1982a and b) and not all sub-categories are appropriate at age 11. Those omitted for the primary children are enclosed in brackets. Three of these categories (1, 4 and 5) are assessed by written tests and the other three by practical tests.

Members of the team at Chelsea developing the tests for age 11 children were acutely aware of the difficulties, which could only be minimized but not

Table 1   Categories and Sub-Categories of Science Performance

Category	Major sub-categories	Minor sub-categories
1 Symbolic representation	Reading information from graphs, tables and charts Expressing information as graphs, tables and charts	(Using scientific symbols and conventions)
2 Use of apparatus and measuring instruments	Using measuring instruments (Estimating physical quantities)	(Following instructions for practical work)
3 Observation	Observing similarities and differences Interpreting observations	Using a branching key
4 Interpretation and application	Interpreting presented information Applying science concepts to make sense of new information	Distinguishing degrees of inference Generating alternative hypotheses
5 Design of investigations	Planning parts of investigations Planning entire investigations	Identifying or proposing testable statements (Using knowledge of experimental procedures)
6 Performance of investigations		

overcome, of producing written questions for young children. In the case of practical tests, however, it was possible to get closer to what children can actually do and observe at first hand, thus special importance is attached to these results. For all types of question, of course, it is important to consider the results in relation to the particular questions used and the form in which they were put to the children.

A Selection of Results

The following examples are a few only of the thirty questions described in detail in the report. About 150 questions were used in the survey, this being a selection from a computerized bank of about 750 questions which is being established. There is room here to illustrate only three of the categories, 3, 4 and 6.

The practical tests for the category 'Observation' were designed so that each pupil was able to make observations of certain objects, materials or events which were presented. For the question in the first example, pupils were

Figure 1

Material given
to pupils

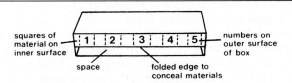

squares of material on inner surface

space

folded edge to conceal materials

numbers on outer surface of box

Question page

Inside the box behind each number there is a thin square which may be made of:

> glass
> metal
> wood
> leather
> rubber

Put your fingers in the box and feel the squares

(a) Decide which is *rubber*
Write down the number in front of the one you think is rubber:

[   ]

(b) How did you decide it was this one?

....
....
....
....

Comment

The tester showed the pupils how to put their fingers into the box through the space and touch the squares of material on the inside of the numbered surface. The tester then presented the question in the following words:

For this question you use your finger tips to feel the surfaces inside the box behind the numbers, like this. Stuck on the inside there are thin squares of five different things: glass, metal, wood, leather and rubber. By feeling them only (don't try to peep!) decide which one is rubber. When you have decided put down the number which is in front of the one you think is rubber. Then write down at (b) how you decided it was this one.

Mark scheme

(a) 5   *1 mark*

(b) One mark for each acceptable property to a maximum of   *2 marks*

Examples of acceptable properties:
> smooth
> soft/squashy
> spongy/bouncy
> can press into it

To be acceptable the property must be one which could distinguish rubber from the other materials.

Maximum = 3 marks

Mark distribution (n = 822)
Mean = 1.6

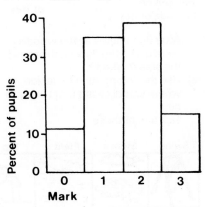

Source: DES, 1981, p. 58.

87

required to use the sense of touch by putting their fingers into the slit in a box (21 cm long) to feel the pieces of material glued inside. Figure 1, extracted from the report (p. 58), shows the question page on which the pupils wrote their answers, the instructions given by the tester, the mark scheme used and the distribution of marks. Almost 90 per cent of pupils gave a correct answer to part (a), the most common error being metal (chosen by 4 per cent). In part (b) 15 per cent of pupils mentioned two or more properties, 71 per cent mentioned one property and 5 per cent gave no answer to this part.

The general conclusions from a range of questions in this category were that pupils were well able to make observations, though they could identify differences between objects· or events more readily than similarities. In questions where objects had to be grouped together the level of performance was high in grouping objects correctly but much lower in explaining the basis of the classification. Performance was also low in describing observed events

Figure 2

Question page

Some a woodlice were put in the middle of a tray containing some wet soil and some dry soil. Half of the tray was then covered with a dark cloth.

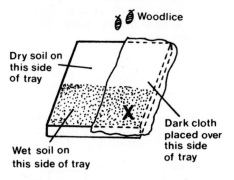

After 30 minutes all the woodlice were under the dark cloth around the area marked X.

(a) Use this information to decide where woodlice are most likely to be.

Tick one of these

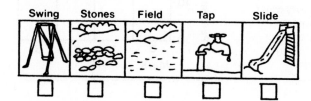

Comment

The question presents all the information required to answer it though it assumes certain everyday knowledge that woodlice are living things which can move about. The illustrations in part (a) contain relevant information and need to be examined carefully. For example, it is made clear that the tap could provide dampness but little shade, whilst the slide, not being on grass, could provide shade but not dampness. The stones are lying on grass and thus should provide both dampness and shade. However the mark scheme did allow for credit to be given if a pupil selected a place other than the stones *and* gave a good reason for doing so in part (b).

(b) Say why you think this is the most
likely place to find woodlice.
Because . . . .
. . . .
. . . .
. . . .
. . . .

Mark scheme			*Mark distribution (n = 1119)*
Response		*Marks*	Mean = 1.7

(a) Stones (or another which it is
argued in (b) is damp and dark) 1

(b) Answer consistent with
answer in (a) mentioning both
dampness and darkness
being provided for the
woodlice eg "Because under
stones it is damp and dark"
(Allow other factors as well
eg "damp, dark and cool
under stones.") 2

Mention only of damp or dark
with or without any other
factors. (Do not allow mark in
(a) for anything other than
"stones" if choice is justified
by providing only damp or
dark but not both eg "It is
dark under the slide" or
"Round the tap is damp.") 1

Irrelevant point or
inconsistent with choice in (a) 0

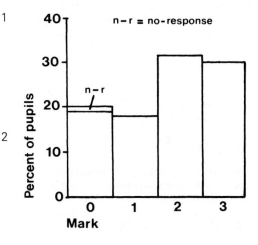

Maximum = 3 marks

Source: DES, 1981, p. 84.

---

in sequence. Simple patterns in observed events were identified and predictions made on the basis of patterns but children seem less able to give explanations of observed patterns.

The category 'Interpretation and application' was assessed by written tests. The example shown in Figure 2 was included in the questions for the sub-category 'Interpreting presented information'.

Just under three-quarters of the pupils chose the correct answer in part (a) but the performance in part (b) was at a lower level. What was found in general in this sub-category was that pupils could more easily use information than explain how they came to a conclusion based on the information. Several questions presented data in which patterns had to be identified and used. Only a small proportion of pupils described patterns or relationships in data in terms of general statements covering all the information. Patterns in data presented in numerical form were particularly difficult to identify.

In the sub-category 'Applying science concepts to make sense of new information' the emphasis was upon *applying* – no questions asked for straight recall of science knowledge or concepts. The example in Figure 3 was one where the results for each part are more interesting than the overall mark: 83 per cent gave the correct answer to part (a), the most common error being to choose snail C instead of A. For part (b) 44 per cent scored two marks and 54 per cent no marks. So only about half the pupils who could use the general idea of speed to answer the first part could also use the more precise concept of distance = speed × time in the second part.

The range of concepts to be applied in the questions in this sub-category was limited and had been discussed with groups of teachers. Results showed

Figure 3

Question page

How fast do snails go?

To find this out John and Pamela put four snails down next to each other and marked their trails.
They put a cross (X) where each snail had reached after 30 seconds.

Comment
Part (a) of this question requires the concept of what speed means but not necessarily how to calculate it. The concept that speed depends on the distance travelled in a certain time is sufficient to answer (a) correctly, but (b) requires the use of the quantitative relationship between distance, speed and time, albeit in a very simple application.

This question was unusual in this sub-category in requiring some manipulation of numbers.

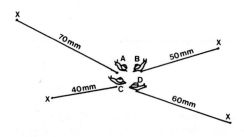

(a) Which snail went fastest?
....

(b) If snail C went on at the same
speed for another 15 seconds how
far would it go beyond X?
....

Mark scheme

Response	Mark
(a) Snail A	1
Multiple response or any other snail	0
(b) 20 mm	2
20 without units or correct answer expressed in another way eg 'half as far as 40 mm'.	1

Maximum = 3 marks

Mark distribution (n = 1019)
Mean = 1.7

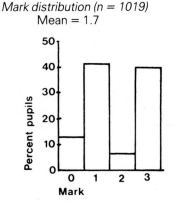

Source: DES, 1981, p. 96.

Figure 4

Question page

The drawing shows two fields next to each other, one freshy ploughed and one covered with grass. After a snow storm Jane could see more snow on the grass than on the ploughed field.

Before snow **After snow**

Grass   Ploughed   Grass   Ploughed

Think of two *different* reasons why Jane could see more snow on the grass. Write the first at (a) and the second at (b).

(a) If could be because . . . .
. . . .
. . . .
. . . .

(b) Or it could be because . . . .
. . . .
. . . .
. . . .

Source: DES, 1981, p. 107.

that performance in applying concepts concerning materials, living things and the environment was higher than for those relating to movement, forces, simple circuits and the transfer of energy in various forms. This was the only sub-category where the difference between boys and girls was, overall, statistically significant – and in favour of boys. (In category 1 girls were ahead of boys but not by a margin large enough to be statistically significant).

The minor sub-category which asked pupils to create hypotheses about possible reasons for given events is illustrated in Figure 4. For this type of question the marks are of less interest than the kinds of answers given by pupils. The answers showed flexibility in proposing alternative hypotheses but the reasons given often reflected a reluctance to try to explain events which might be observed in everyday life by using science concepts. In the example the two hypotheses given more often than any others were the same in the type of cause suggested but one mentioned only the grass and the other only the ploughed field. The former was that the snow rests on the blades of grass which therefore hold it up where it can be seen (14 per cent of responses) and the latter that the ploughed field has ridges or furrows into which the snow falls and cannot be seen (also 14 per cent).

Hypotheses based on the different surface characteristics of the field formed by far the main group of answers but some interesting ideas were included in the others. A small proportion mentioned that soil might soak up snow more than grass or that snow soaks into the earth without mentioning what happens on grass. Similar small proportions of answers mentioned that soil might be warmer than grass and so melt the snow or that the snow would melt, without suggesting why this would happen; other answers were that the soil would be wet and so melt the snow, that snow 'can't settle' on the soil without mentioning the grass, or that the grass would be pressed down to prevent the snow reaching the ground. Some 2 per cent of answers suggested that someone or something, often the wind, had removed the snow from one field; 3 per cent explained the observation in terms of more snow having fallen on one field than the other and 1 per cent were sure that it didn't happen – Jane was mistaken. Thirteen per cent of responses gave reasons in terms of the existence of the circumstances which were presented – that it was 'because of the grass' or 'because of the ploughing' – or were irrelevant in suggesting that the areas were different or 'the snow took time to settle'.

For the assessment of category 6, 'Performance of investigations', pupils were given three different practical investigations to carry out, taking about 50–60 minutes in all. Pupils were assessed individually and the testers used checklists to note down various points about what they did and how they reacted to the problem. The following extract from the report (pp. 144–6) outlines briefly the administration and results for one of the six different investigations. It concerned testing given samples of paper to decide which would be best for covering a book.

There was a large variety of materials supplied, more than the pupil needed for the three different tests he was asked to carry out, therefore he had to choose what he wanted to use. The materials supplied and the pupil's page were as follows:

Materials
Large sheets of 4 types of paper and
several small pieces cut from each:
  Brown paper
  Wallpaper
  Writing paper
  Sugar paper
Pieces of sandpaper, 10 cm square
Piece of stone
Hard & soft rubber
Scissors
Jar of water
Dropper
Paper towel
String, chalk, paper clip
Pencil, felt-tip pen
Book with wrap-round paper cover
Board (to do experiments on)

The tester used the book with a wrap-round paper cover to help present the problem. It was emphasized that the pupil was not going to make the cover (therefore size was not relevant) but just to find out which of the four kinds of paper would be best to use. The pupil was given two minutes to look at and feel the papers and to consider the function of the cover.

The materials which could be used for testing were introduced and the pupil told that he probably would not want all of them but should just take the ones he wanted. Despite this being said, there were a few pupils who felt obliged to use everything and indeed one managed to use everything on top of each other on each of the four papers! For those less willing to try anything or uncertain about how to start there was a hint given after four minutes to those who said they were stuck. This was to suggest that a book cover should protect a book if it accidentally gets wet, so the water could be used to see which would be best in that respect and then *'another thing is that it will be handled a lot and this will rub it and it mustn't wear through too quickly. You could try rubbing with something here'*. The pupils were told to think about it and try three different tests and were given an example to explain what a 'test' meant in this context. They were also told to give a heading or title for each test when they put down their results.

As the pupil carried out the tests, the tester observed whether the same treatment was given to the four papers in the same way and what results were obtained. Whether or not there was an attempt to control the amount of treatment was checked later in discussion. In the case of all the tests, there was a large difference between the number who said they had tried to treat all the papers in the same way and the number observed to actually keep the treatment the same, that is to give the same number of strokes with a rubber or put the same amount of water on each paper, etc. Nine out of ten of the pupils thought up and applied three tests which were different from each other. The care with which the pupil examined the result of each test was noted. A record was also made of the incidence of tests being repeated if the results were ambiguous and of the repetition of all tests as routine using fresh areas of paper.

Pupil's page (actual size: A4)

Paperback

> Test the papers in three different ways to find out which one would be the best to choose for covering a book.

a) Put the results of your three tests here:

Name of first test . . . .
Results: Wallpaper . . . .
        Writing paper . . . .
        Brown paper . . . .
        Sugar paper . . . .

Name of second test . . . .
Results: Wallpaper . . . .
        Writing paper . . . .
        Brown paper . . . .
        Sugar paper . . . .

Name of third test . . . .
Results: Wallpaper . . . .
        Writing paper . . . .
        Brown paper . . . .
        Sugar paper . . . .

b) From these tests the paper which could be best for covering a book would be

. . . .

In the discussion phase of the investigation, the tester asked the pupil about each test and noted whether the pupils' result was consistent with the evidence and whether the test had been suitably titled. The pupil was also asked to explain how he had arrived at his final decision at (b) so that it was possible to judge whether and how the results of the separate tests had been combined. Finally, the pupil was asked about changes which he might make if tackling this problem again.

The results for the items on the checklist shown in Table 2, reflect some general findings across all six investigations. A very large majority of children found an appropriate general way of tackling the problem, by applying similar

Table 2 Results for the Investigation on 'Paper' For all pupils in the sample (n = 559)	%	Boy/Girl differences %
Hint given	12	
First test: All papers given same kind of treatment	95	
Attempts to give same amount of treatment	58	
Amount of treatment actually controlled	23	B 20; G 26
Result consistent with evidence	77	
Second test: All papers given same kind of treatment (different from first)	93	
Attempts to give same amount of treatment	61	
Amoung of treatment actually controlled	26	
Result consistent with evidence	75	B 72; G 78
Third test: All papers given same kind of treatment (different from first and second)	82	
Attempts to give same amount of treatment	53	B 51; G 55
Amount of treatment actually controlled	24	
Result consistent with evidence	67	B 64; G 70
Fresh piece of paper (or unused area) used for each test	85	
Results closely examined in all cases	79	
Some tests repeated if results not clear (or all tests such that results are not ambiguous)	58	
All tests repeated as routine on different areas of paper	6	
Results noted after each test (no reminder)	84	B 82; G 87
Tests suitably titled (2 out of 3)	83	
Result noted at (b) without reminder	83	
Chooses tests well suited to problem	84	
Result at (b) consistent with separate results	79	
Justifies result at (b) quantitatively	50	B 53; G 48

Source: DES, 1981, p. 146.

tests to all four kinds of paper. More than four out of five pupils also recorded results in a suitable way on the pupil's paper (though rather fewer did this in other investigations where the papers were not laid out with dotted lines for writing on). When aspects of the performance which relate to a more specifically scientific approach to the problem were considered, however, the level of success was much lower. Only about a quarter of the pupils controlled the amount of treatment given in testing their papers; without this control the test is not a 'fair' one. Similarly low levels in controlling variables and fair testing were found in other investigations. Another common pattern was the very low incidence of repetition of observations or measurements as a routine check.

During the investigations information was gathered about three attitude-linked aspects of performance. The first concerned the general interest in the problem of willingness to become involved in the investigation. Only about 5 per cent of pupils were recorded as appearing 'bored, uninterested or scared', the remainder being equally divided between those willing to carry out the investigation but showing no special interest and those showing evidence of real interest and working intently and thoughtfully. The second attitude-linked behaviour was 'willingness to be critical of procedures used' and was judged during discussion with the tester after the investigation had been carried out. In this about 40 per cent were judged as being 'uncritical of procedures used' and a similar proportion were able to suggest alternative ways of tackling the investigation but still did not seem aware of the deficiencies in the procedures they had used. The remaining 20 per cent were those who 'showed awareness of variables which were not controlled, procedures which had turned out to be ineffective' or criticized other central factors relating to the investigation.

In the two investigations which involved handling living things the third attitude-linked assessment was made, concerning the care shown to these animals (snails and mealworms). Only a small proportion (2 per cent for snails and 6 per cent for mealworms) treated the animals as if they were inanimate and the large majority (85 per cent for snails and 62 per cent for mealworms) handled them with care and no dislike. Boys were rated noticeably higher than girls in this regard. About half the girls, but only a quarter of the boys, avoiding touching the mealworms.

Comment on the Survey Results

The results of a survey of this kind have to be interpreted carefully, partly because this was only the first of a series of similar surveys and on its own can only yield tentative findings. But another reason is that interpretation involves judgements about what performance levels could or should be and clearly depends on the expectations of those making such judgements. The scores and numbers, such as those quoted above, have little meaning in their own right. They tell that such-and-such a percentage gave a correct answer or made certain kinds of mistake, but they cannot pronounce on whether or not this is an acceptable state of affairs. A performance of 70 per cent on certain questions may be less satisfactory than a performance of 50 per cent on others if the former are judged to be easier or more important than the latter. It is open to the readers of the report to make such judgements and it is hoped that, at least among teachers and other educationists, the results will initiate debate from which proposals for improving science education at the primary level might be forthcoming.

Some of the findings which the report authors felt should feature in this debate relate to the goals and activities to which teachers gave priority. This information was mentioned earlier as being gathered in the questionnaire sent to all schools participating in the survey. Figure 5 shows the percentage of schools ticking each of twelve goals, when asked to select the five to which they attached most importance.

What becomes clear from these results is that the goals most embraced by schools are numbers, 4, 5, 6 and 8, which concern the attitudes and those cognitive goals which are shared by other areas of the curriculum. These are indeed as important to science as other activities, but those goals which more *specifically* related to a scientific approach are among those given low priority: 7

Figure 5   Goals of Science-Based Activities for 11-Year-Old Pupils

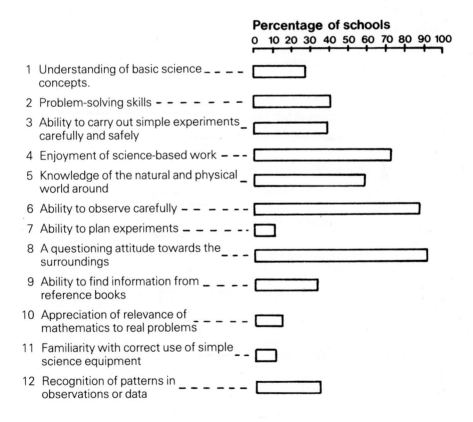

Source: DES, 1981, p. 37.

(the ability to plan experiments); 1 (understanding basic science concepts) and 12 (recognition of patterns in observations or data).

There is a marked similarity between the levels of performance of the

Figure 6 *Emphases in Science-Based Activities with 11-Year-Olds*

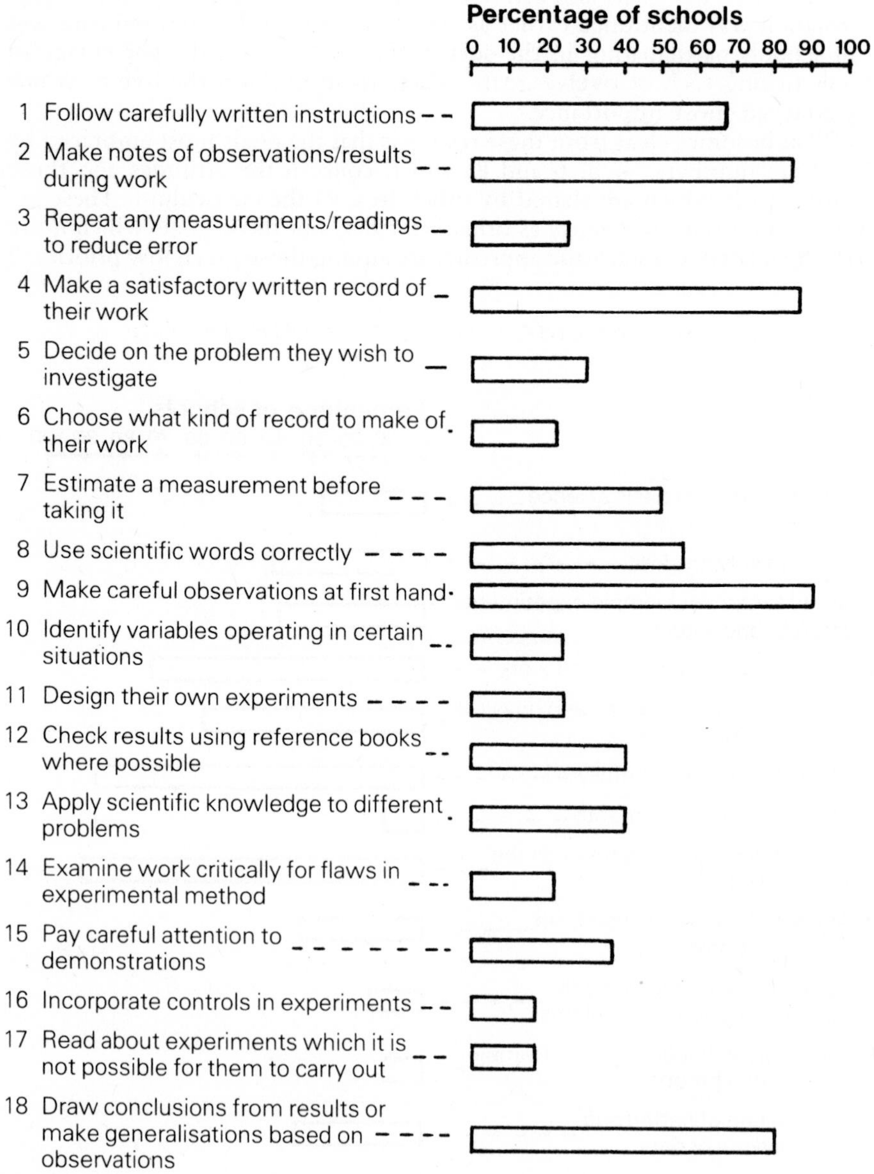

Source: DES, 1981, p. 41.

children in these things and the levels of priority accorded to them as goals. (Although the 1980 survey did not include the planning of investigations, this was included later and showed this area to be one where performance was particularly low.) The relationship between the teachers' view of what is most important and the children's performance was strengthened by looking at the emphasis given to various science-based activities. In this case teachers were asked to select the eight statements, from the eighteen given, which they regarded as most important. The results are shown in Figure 6.

Again the low priority given to 'incorporate controls in experiments', 'identify variables operating in certain situations', 'design their own experiments', 'repeat any measurements/readings to reduce error', 'examine work critically for flaws in experimental method', is seen to parallel the low performance of pupils in these areas.

There are various possible explanations for these findings. For example, it could be argued that the areas where performance is low are just very difficult and hence teachers avoid them. However, against this view is the evidence that children of this age *can* plan investigations, carry out 'fair tests' and become critical of procedures which omit necessary controls *if* they are given the opportunity. That such opportunity is not widely available was shown in the HMI survey: 'in very few classes were opportunities taken to teach children how to make careful observations or to plan and carry out investigations of a scientific nature' (DES, 1978, p. 59).

An alternative explanation is offered in one of the concluding paragraphs of the survey report:

> One interpretation which follows from this is that teachers may not be providing for scientific experience and the reason is to be found in their intentions rather than in the organisational structure or resources of the school. It is sad to note that the science processes undervalued by teachers were among those given prominence in the broad aims of Science 5/13 and in the Nuffield Junior Science Project. It is not then surprising that the essential nature of primary science as a process of enquiry has not been carried forward to any degree in the work of the pupils (DES, 1981, p. 178).

References

DES (1978) *Primary Education in England*, London, HMSO.
DES (1981) *Science in Schools Age 11: Report No. 1*, London, HMSO.
DES (1982a) *Science in Schools Age 13: Report No. 1*, London, HMSO.
DES (1982b) *Science in Schools Age 15: Report No. 1*, London, HMSO.

PART IV

Theories of Children's Learning

Introduction

The last section considered what should be taught in primary school science and the proper functions of evaluation. The guidance offered there was probably influenced by the authors' understanding of how children learn. Kerr and Engel drew specifically on research into children's scientific thinking. Squires had already written about the nature of the learning process[1] and Harlen had been evaluator of 'Science 5–13', a project strongly influenced by Piaget's theory of stages in intellectual maturation.

Isaacs' paper from 1963 (see Chapter 10) is also concerned with children's capacities to learn science. He argues that primary science is a logical and natural means of extending the proto-scientific reasoning skills 3- and 4-year-olds have developed before they begin formal schooling. He has in mind questions they pose about their everyday experiences, questions that indicate intentionality and so reveal their ability to generalize, seek a causal explanation, challenge given explanations, theorize and so on. Isaacs considers these probings to be real and significant preparation for school science.

In two respects Isaacs' paper relates to current debate in science education. First, in his recognition of the influence of pupils' existing learning on their teachability in new situations; second, in his preparedness to challenge the assumption that young children's capacities to learn science are very limited. This derived from Piaget's work. In essence, Piaget's position was that as maturation occurs, growth in capability can be described in terms of a limited number of systems which could be arranged in a hierarchical order of difficulty. Each person, he suggested, develops in sequence the mental capacity to handle the next, more difficult stage. The implication (for science teaching) of such a view is that children are not ready for certain kinds of teaching until sufficient intellectual development has occurred. Isaacs argues that a Piagetian orientation unnecessarily inhibits perceptions of the kinds of (science) learning which children are ready to engage in when they enter school.

More recently others have also criticized Piaget's stage theory of intellectual development. Driver and Easley reviewed studies which suggest that the ability to handle scientific concepts depends to a greater extent on specific abilities and prior knowledge than general levels of cognitive functioning.[2] They suggested that children develop autonomous 'frameworks' for conceptualizing their experience of the physical world, these being the product of their imaginative efforts to explain events and to abstract commonalities between these events. They drew attention to pupils' misperceptions in learning as an indication of the tenacity of their theories in the face of contrary evidence. Examples of theories commonly held by children are that heavier objects fall faster than lighter ones; clouds appear to move because the earth is rotating underneath them; vision is first conceived as the passage of light from the eye to the object. Such ideas do make sense at a superficial level of the child's own experience of the effect being studied. Often, too, they reflect the views of educated persons in previous centuries.

It is recognition of the conditioning influence of past experience on present actions that underpins an alternative approach to learning based on the work of David Ausubel, here described by McClelland. The basis of his argument is that concepts and memories are not kept in mind in random fashion but are organized into a structure. If a new piece of learning can be subsumed into the existing structure then it becomes meaningful to the learner. As such it can be used conjointly with other concepts held in mind in problem-solving situations. Assimilation is thus conceived as a dynamic, constructive process and accommodation (framework change) as an essential part of the acquisition of new ideas. Adopting this view, a fundamental criterion for selecting content for primary science would be to choose learning that is likely to be as meaningful as possible in that it was considered likely to interrelate well with existing knowledge in the learner's mind.

Recently McClelland has suggested that judgement of the suitability of a science task on an Ausubelian basis would have three differences to that of Piagetian analysis.[3] It would presume that children's performance would be strongly affected by the context in which the task was presented (as Donaldson's study of children working on Piagetian tasks revealed, for example)[4]; it would give consideration to the relevant organized knowledge to which the task could be related rather than to the inferred consistency of match between the intellectual difficulty of the task and a particular stage of cognitive operation; and it would stress the importance of choosing activities and concrete experiences not for their own sake but to give meaning through illustration to verbal statements of the principles to be learned.

What degree of validity do Piagetian studies retain? Whilst there is evidence to support the argument that prior knowledge and experience do have an effect on children's difficulties in handling a new concept it may also be that to a certain extent they have not yet developed sufficiently the mental capacity to cope. Certainly some recent large-scale surveys suggest that the Piagetian constructs hold up reasonably well within the domain of the physical sciences. Of no lesser significance given current interest to extend the proportion of physics, especially, taught in primary science programmes are Shayer's findings that only 40 per cent of 10-year-olds sampled were using late concrete operations fully in the science tasks he set and that the average age at which each Piagetian stage was attained was far higher than he tended to assume.[5]

Both the Ausubelian and Piagetian perspectives should continue to generate research findings of relevance to the primary science teacher. Several empirical studies of children's understanding, pursued along Ausubelian lines, aim to increase in due course the range of diagnostic tools available to teachers for probing children's personal constructs of knowledge, the way in which concepts are structured and interrelated in their minds. On the other hand, if a Piagetian view is substantially correct it might be possible to accelerate children's intellectual progress through the developmental stages by carefully designed interventionist science teaching. This, too, is a focus of current British research.

Notes

1 SQUIRES, A. (1976) *Study Series No. 6: Science in the Middle Years,* Association for Science Education.
2 DRIVER, R. and EASLEY, J. (1978) 'Pupils and paradigms: A review of literature related to concept development in adolescent science students', *Studies in Science Education,* 5, pp. 61–84.
3 MCCLELLAND, J.A.G. (1982) 'Ausubel's theory of learning and its application to introductory science, Part 1 Ausubel's theory of learning', *School Science Review,* 64, 226, pp. 157–61.
4 DONALDSON, M. (1978) *Children's Minds,* London, Fontana.
5 SHAYER, M. and ADEY, P. (1981) *Towards a Science of Science Teaching,* London, Heinemann Educational, pp. 8–9.

10 The Case for Bringing Science into the Primary School*

Nathan Isaacs

I believe that if we are to think usefully about 'science' in the primary school, we must first of all sort out with care the different things we currently mean by this term. When we ordinarily use it in the round, we are too apt to fuse its meanings together into a single vaguely grandiose whole. In fact, of course, *'a'* science always signifies a specific one, but when we talk of 'science' at large, we *ought* to mean one of two quite distinct though connected things. First, we may be referring to the unified sum of our separate sciences; that is, to all of them joined together as continuous parts of a single great structure: the present sum-total, in fact, of all our organized knowledge, understanding and vision of our natural world (including ourselves as members of it). In this sense of science it is self-evidently *not* something that we can dream of 'bringing' either into our primary schools, or our secondary ones, or anywhere else; no one can either 'learn' or be 'taught' more than some minute selective fraction of it.

Secondly, however, we also often want to refer to what *makes* science science; not now the product (so far), but the distinctive set of *processes*, the basic ways and means, which have brought it into being and are still developing it. Science here is the type of knowledge which we achieve by adopting a certain kind of approach; by pursuing certain methods; by accepting certain criteria; and by steadily continuing to focus all these on some particular set of features or subdivision of our world. The different specific sciences are thus the result of the successive application of this same procedure to one sector after another of our world.

I wish to suggest that here is a sense in which we *can* bring 'science' into the primary school, or rather help it to burgeon and develop there, and with genuinely valuable results. And not only so, but that sense underlies the whole case for incorporating it in *all* our education. When it comes to actual scientific knowledge, even professional scientists must usually be content, as I have said, with some fractional specialized area. Most of the rest of us can hardly hope for more than bare outlines, with perhaps just a section or two partly and sketchily filled in. What, however, we all need – and, as I shall try to show, *can* attain – is

---

* This is an edited version of a paper first published in Perkins W. (Ed.) (1962) *The Place of Science in Primary Education*, BAAS, pp. 4–22.

some grasp of the common root and core of the sciences, the overall key to what they are, aim at and achieve. The basic essentials of the methods that build up science (as distinct from all the auxiliary apparatus which they later gather round themselves) are not a late and sophisticated discovery of the human mind, but a crucial part of its initial equipment. They are put to vital use during the earliest years of every infant. They actually build up in his mind, tier upon tier, a first fundamental scheme of knowledge all new to him but *mainly dependable*, precisely in the sense that it can be safely acted upon and further built upon. Only at a subsequent stage, when the basic scheme is already established and in daily working operation, do these fundamental ways of learning tend to become overlaid and largely choked by other influences.

When our children enter the primary school the basic learning drives are as a rule still vigorously active. In other cultures lack of fresh stimuli is no doubt one main cause that leads to their withering away at a relatively early age. With us, however, new stimuli continually surge up all round the child; but all the conditions of formal schooling combine to act as a damping factor. In most children the basic active learning drives are mainly relegated to their out-of-school life, and very often survive only in a very superficial and limited form. In a minority they are later expressly reactivated in the course of a scientific training, but too frequently only within one segregated field.

It follows that if the foregoing is correct, we do not have to *bring* science, as here understood, into the primary school; our first decision has only to be not to shut it out. After that, however, if it is to make the right progress, we must take positive steps to encourage and help it and to bring it on. But before I come to that, let me give my grounds for my unlikely-sounding account of the facts.

Actually there is no difficulty about doing so; most of the *data* I have in mind are accepted commonplaces of child psychology, whilst the significance I want to assign to them has long been underlined by progressive educators (notably in our time by the late Susan Isaacs). It is the present summing up that most needs justifying; here I can largely draw on the very impressive work reported in recent years by the distinguished Swiss genetic psychologist, Professor Jean Piaget. This has provided a novel and arresting unified picture of the fundamental dynamic of individual intellectual development, supported by a great weight of fresh experimental evidence; and this picture seems to me to carry full conviction.

I can, of course, only bring out here the essential pattern; but it will be evident how much this has in common with the characteristic aims and methods of natural science. From the infant's first few weeks onward he begins on his continually expanding course of watching and following, observing and registering. From certainly 3–4 months onward he explores, manipulates, and experiments and goes on to compare, distinguish and sort out. He combines and connects; he learns increasingly by trial, error and assiduous practice to produce and control particular effects; he generalizes, falls into error, and learns from his errors how to correct and improve his generalizations; he looks for causes and gropes for explanations. And along all these ways he carries out week by week, month by month, a single cumulative process of finding out and piecing together, till he has built up for himself a usable rough working scheme, or 'cognitive map', of his surrounding world.

All this he does during his first 18–21 months, almost without help from language, up to a surprising level of accomplishment. It is all part of his continuous striving to establish himself in his world. For this he needs to know how to deal with what he encounters; to foresee and adjust, or respond, appropriately; to be able to use and exploit the diverse opportunities around him; and to secure the power of planning his own course and of choosing and realizing his own goals in his world. Growing and connected dependable knowledge is what he requires as the basis for all his action and all his own further growth; and on that is concentrated much of his main energy and resources, with impressive success. To get the measure of this, one has only to note the variety and range of foresights and purposive ways of action of which he disposes by 19–21 months.

As language becomes more and more available to the child, from the latter part of the second year onward, we know that the scope of his mental life is further vastly enriched. Speech opens up to him endless new possibilities; but one of them at least is its use as a powerful new tool in the service of all his finding-out, linking-up and organizing activities. Most characteristic perhaps is his rapid discovery of the great open-sesame instrument of *question-asking*. Some of our chief types of *finding-out* questions are picked up as early as the third year; others are mastered in the fourth; and by the fifth most children are freely able to use all our main gamut. They then continually want to know: what things are – what they are made of – where they come from – how they began – what makes them happen – what makes one thing different from another – what are the reasons for apparent exceptions and anomalies, and so on. And we find that even as early as their fourth or fifth year they are so clear about what they want or need that they do not necessarily accept *any* answer. They seek one which they can join up with what they already know and understand, and if what they are offered fails by this test, they will press for further information or help, or will even raise queries or objections of a disconcerting appositeness.

These are the facts about our typical 5-year-olds, as regards one of the major aspects of their intellectual life. Of course, there are others that loom even larger, more particularly make-believe play and fantasy; but the various interlinked 'finding-out' activities continue their dynamic course. In spite of all the working knowledge the child has already built up, our kaleidoscopic world frequently confronts him with new situations, encounters, facts and happenings which he has no means of understanding, does not know how to deal with, and may find either puzzling or just stimulating or challenging. Therefore, if given the chance, he will still want to ask questions and thus to secure further knowledge and understanding; and if the opportunity opens up for him, he will continue to be excited and thrilled if he can find out the answers for himself. He is still ready to enjoy exploring, manipulating, experimenting, comparing, trying to discover causes or to think up the right explanations, discussing and arguing and putting to the test. And these precisely are the interests and activities which it is suggested that the primary school should take up and foster; for these are the living roots from which growth towards developed science can spring.

The important point is that, given the wish and the planning, the primary school can use these activities as one main instrument of education. Instead of actually displacing them by the usual school routine of classroom teaching and formal lessons, it can set out to organize a large part of school-life *round them*. Children can then not only go on with the vital 'real' learning work they have been accomplishing all along, but also carry it out far more effectively and fruitfully. In their pre-school environment, the opportunities for active exploration and discovery, after the breathless first few years when everything around was new, tend to get fewer and more restricted. And questions addressed to parents who are often either busy or insufficiently equipped will most commonly receive merely verbal answers, sometimes erroneous, frequently perfunctory, in many cases put in terms which the child only half understands. The school, on the other hand, can continually offer fresh stimuli and openings for exploration, in the most various directions; it can provoke questions or expressly invite them; and it can use any that are suitable in order to launch groups of children on their own cooperative quests for the answers. They can be encouraged to consider and discuss, and to put out ideas or suggestions either by way of actual solutions or at least for next steps. They can be guided and steered, helped over difficulties, and offered hints in the right directions or suggestive leading questions. In all these ways each inquiry that has been set in motion can be carried forward through exciting progress to a successful solution, and become an immensely educative experience for all the children who have shared in it. For not only have they thus built up by their own efforts some fresh scheme of connected knowledge and understanding, but they have also experienced for themselves some of the typical ways and methods by which such building up can be achieved.

A varied series of these cooperative group enquiries carried on week by week, term by term and year by year, on a growing scale, in various main fields which thus become progressively better charted and organized, should take children a long way towards a basic understanding of the meaning of scientific inquiry and of scientific knowledge. What they will achieve will, of course, not yet be fully-fledged 'science', but it will serve as the most authentic and the most valuable approach road towards it. And all this is not mere theory, but has been tried out in practice in a number of quarters and found to work.

Of course, what could be done in the primary school would still only be introductory to the more deliberate 'scientific' work of the secondary school, but it would provide the right introduction. Children would be ripe for this work as a *meaningful* next stage. Those who did not feel specially drawn in that direction would at least be well prepared to take in the broad general scope of science as a major human achievement, together perhaps with some closer study of a specific field – physical or biological or human, according to their individual trend of interest. That field would then, in effect, be seen as *representative* of the specialized work of science, with particular stress always on methods and criteria at the same time as on results. On the other hand, those children who were keen to go on with some particular set of inquiries, or to get to know and understand much more about some larger scientific field of their own choice, could be carried fairly quickly into the fully systematic study of all that had already been 'found out' on that theme.

Even here, however, the aim would always be to ensure the utmost continuity with what the children had already done. The first endeavour would be to establish a sense of the *questions and problems* which the chosen special field presented to those who wanted to build up 'science' about it. An effort would be made to project the pupils into the living history of the science. Particular attention would also be paid to the way in which the basic initial 'finding out' approach has everywhere come to be enriched and refined by an ever-growing body of special aids. Thus the vital contributions of all our specific instruments and techniques, of our controlled technical languages, and of that great universal tool of human thought, mathematics, would get their due weight – but would yet be seen as remaining dependent on the fundamental orientation which the pupils had already so long been experiencing for themselves, that is, the attitude of setting out to learn about the world from the world itself; a process always of thinking as well as looking, but with the looking in final control, and the thinking ever subject to the test of further looking of the most searching kind. Thus as the pupils took into their minds the full present structure of their chosen science, they would at the same time keep it firmly linked with the processes of sustained factual inquiry, imaginative yet also critical thinking, and rigorous factual testing, of which it represented the outcome *so far*. And the final result should be to give them the sense of themselves joining in something living and growing – the further building up of a great structure of which the end is nowhere in sight and which remains always open to fresh transformations and revaluations in the light of new horizons yet to be reached.

Up to a point the case I have stated might be regarded as complete. It could be briefly summed up as based on these two premises: (i) at this time in our civilized history, we all need some understanding both of what science means and of how it comes into being; (ii) we all have the roots of this understanding within us, since throughout our first years we are busily building up our own first fabric of mainly dependable knowledge in just the ways by which each individual science has begun. By the age of 5 we have already advanced a long way, and are still wanting to thrust forward further, if only we are given the facilities and help which we need.

It follows that the primary school could provide the great opportunity of taking up these drives, giving them guidance and scope, and carrying them to the very threshold of our developed sciences. However, since for the second of the above premises I have particularly invoked the work of Professor Piaget, I am bound to note that there are parts of his work which seem to suggest somewhat narrow limits to what children can actually accomplish during the primary school period. His investigations of intellectual development during the first two years had brought out all the cumulative active learning and psychic building up which children carry through in that time in terms of *behavioural* achievement. But he also holds that thereafter, when they go on to *verbal thinking*, they are in a sense obliged to start their learning all over again; and that then must come a long period of slow and laborious growth before they can attain any kind of *ordered conceptual and logical thought*. Moreover, this in turn only evolves very gradually from its first beginnings to the level required for even elementary science.

Thus Piaget sets out a wide range of experiments to show how at the age of 4–5 the thought of average children is still in a state of wholesale logical confusion and incapacity; and how it is only towards 7–8 that they attain their first structured and stable concepts in such rudimentary fields as number, or spatial notions like length or distance, or some of the basic logical relations. Even when by 7–8 they do achieve these concepts, their range is found to be very limited, and at around 11 a majority is still not able to handle freely the more abstract logical relations needed for most kinds of sustained reasoning, whether scientific or of any other kind. It is not until some time between 11 and 14 that average children become capable of operating (or understanding) the logical processes needed for solving fairly simple scientific problems. It would seem to follow that no real scientific approach can even begin before about 7–8, and that it must stay very sketchy indeed till some time *after* 11; which would perhaps not fit in too badly with what many teachers of science already believe.

However, there are, I think, good reasons for holding that the foregoing represents only one side of a picture which in fact has two faces. I cannot discuss this in any detail here, but Piaget's own account of the basic forces of intellectual growth as they emerge during the first two years makes clear, in my view, that his later negative findings cannot constitute more than part of the story. Obviously all the cumulative learning, building up and growth which can be noted in the pre-verbal phase goes on in just the same way after the mastery of language, and indeed in increased measure. It is true that language also ushers in a new era of assiduous and absorbed verbal *fantasizing*, and at the same time engenders a whole new world of vague and confused verbal ideas which are apt at any moment to pass over into pure fantasy forms. Nevertheless, the child continues to expand his experiences and activities, his knowledge and powers, in the real world, and here too he derives immense new help from language – above all, through those organized question-forms to which I have already referred.

Thus verbal thinking tends to develop on two largely separate levels: one on which it remains closely linked with children's own active experience and learning processes, is fully controlled by these and advances turn by turn with them; and another where for lack of experience, knowledge or direct active interest, it lags far behind and long remains unorganized, vague and fluid. Piaget's experiments tend to test children's capacity for ordered concepts and logical thinking in situations in which their own drives and inquiring interests are *not* actively engaged: that is, where they do not start from questions to which their own course has brought them and for which they themselves want to find the answers, but are plunged into alien problems from without. Almost all of these are, moreover, concerned with the formal world of number, space, time, etc., and their abstract relationships, which are fundamentally *uninteresting* to most young children. Therefore, Piaget's findings generally register a level of performance well below the best which they can achieve, within the living context of their own learning, thinking and growth. Furthermore, those findings refer typically to children in current educational settings and must to some extent reflect any basic limitations inherent in these. Thus they cannot, above all, be used to rebut the possibility of quite other results if we drew the right moral from Piaget's own fundamental work and provided the utmost scope and help for truly constructive learning and thinking – even in those fields where he finds growth *under current conditions* so slow.

For all these reasons I suggest that his more negative conclusions regarding the primary school age-range need only be kept in mind as partial ceilings applying under present circumstances and in certain limited directions – ceilings that have yet to be retested after more helpful conditions have been fully tried out. Moreover, even on the most rigid interpretation, they would leave useful scope for *approach*-work of the type outlined here – from 7–8 years onward for the average run of children, and a good deal earlier for the brighter ones. However, there is little ground for thinking that the ceilings would apply *at all* to children's powers of active constructive learning in the situations contemplated: namely, those of their own pooled efforts to find their own answers, under skilled guidance, to many of their own questions about the concrete world around them. Here again I can refer to the very successful work already recorded.

In conclusion, I have been arguing essentially that we should use the primary school years for the deliberate and sustained fostering of those 'finding-out' activities (and everything that goes with them) which are the common core and first root of all our sciences. My thesis has been that we can turn them into progressive approaches *towards* science, which will greatly help both the majority of eventual non-scientists and the minority of future scientists. The first will gain some real power of appreciation and understanding of the work of science as a whole. The second will have the right foundation for the most fruitful study of any one specialized science: a sense of the distinctive methods and criteria which achieve science as such.

Moreover, we should eliminate what may well be the main cause of the present marked division between science and the rest of our current world. I have suggested that we ourselves largely create this by the normal working of our educational scheme. The latter, in the first place, switches children right away from their natural, spontaneous, active, inquiring and finding-out processes (which might carry them closer and closer to science) and replaces all these by something altogether different – in setting, in subject-matter, and, above all, in the way of learning called for, that is, learning by being taught. Then, a number of years later, we start teaching to a relatively small body of pupils one or two selected sciences (most often physics and chemistry) as separate and self-contained intellectual systems or worlds. For everybody else these sciences, or the few others that might be similarly picked upon, remain closed books. There develops the general tendency for physics and chemistry to become the main normal image of 'science', and for physicists and chemists themselves to share this view, with the most closely analogous other sciences as an outer fringe, and everything else relegated to the non-scientific world. This leads to a far too narrow and static notion of science, which helps in turn to regenerate the same educational circle.

In fact, physics and its kin simply happen to represent our most advanced and developed sciences, now segregated in a very elaborate world of their own, a world of laboratories, physical instruments, technical language and mathematical tools. But though we do have here the present highest level of scientific achievement, it simply constitutes the current summit of a slope on which a number of other sciences are struggling at various points, each as truly a science in virtue of its aims, methods and criteria as physics itself. It is these that have launched physics and its kin on their course; and they equally constitute the motive force of such human sciences as psychology, anthropology or economics, even if for various reasons of later start and more complex and fluid subject-matter, these sciences are still in a less developed phase as regards their results.

Once this much more comprehensive and dynamic view of science is adopted, we can easily see how it joins up with the educational approach put forward here, and how our existing division into two cultures, scientific and lay, disappears. Whether children eventually grow into physics or chemistry, or into biology or geology, or into psychology or archaeology, or into the law or letters, or into some art or craft or technical skill, or into any other of our thousand and one human occupations, they will have in common a vital, unifying groundwork of experience and constructive learning. They will share the same developed sense of how we have come by all our most dependable organized knowledge of our world, and the same ensuing power of entering in at least some degree into the visions and perspectives which that knowledge has to offer. Here, surely, lies the most valuable contribution of science to the education of all of us. But that contribution depends first of all on our making the right use of the interests, drives and capacity for personal active 'finding out' with which most children enter our primary schools.

11   Ausubel's Theory of Meaningful Learning and Its Implications for Primary Science

Gerry McClelland

A central reason for teaching anything to a child is that the child, by learning it, will gain understanding and control of some aspect of the world of experience. Through ideas of number and the four processes of arithmetic a truly enormous range of problems can be solved. Through ideas of right and wrong people learn to live together. Through science pattern and order may be imposed on apparently diverse and chaotic experiences. Through all of these and many more, but particularly through science, the idea that the world of experience is governed by rules, and that it is worth while to seek for such rules, can be developed. The more we have a theoretical grasp of how such learning takes place and how it fulfils these functions, the better the position we will be in to make decisions about what to teach, when, in what sequence, and how. Ausubel's theory of learning provides such a framework which, to date, has been neither widely understood nor disseminated, largely, I think, because it has been framed (Ausubel *et al.*, 1978) in very careful, but far from easily accessible language. By re-expressing some of the main aspects of the theory in less technical language I am bound to distort it and to lessen its subtlety and rigour.

Ausubel's Theory of Meaningful Learning

From the many changes of behaviour or capability which can be termed learning, Ausubel concentrates on a restricted range, that of learning meanings expressed in symbols, mainly words. This makes it particularly relevant to school learning. He distinguishes two independent aspects of the learning process as shown in Figure 1, the degree of meaningfulness and the way in which the material to be learnt is encountered.

Probably no learning experience is ever entirely rote nor entirely meaningful, but pure rote learning would form no link with anything already known, would not help further learning, and would necessarily be learnt 'by heart'. Learning is meaningful according to how well it fits into the network of what is already known, extends it, and improves the ability to learn still more. A child who can work out the exercise 12 × 23 to get 276, but cannot find the

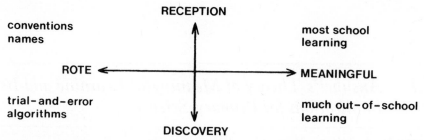

cost of 12 chocolate bars each costing 23 units or the area of a rectangle with sides of 12 and 23 units, and so on, has not learnt multiplication meaningfully. Meaningful learning is demonstrated by the appropriate use of the ideas in hitherto unseen situations.

Three Conditions for Meaningful Learning

Learning will not be meaningful unless three conditions are met.

1 What is to be learnt must make sense, or be consistent with experience. This is logical meaningfulness. (The material does not have to be true.)
2 The learner must have enough relevant knowledge for the material to be within grasp. This is psychological meaningfulness.
3 The learner must intend, or be disposed, to learn meaningfully, that is, to fit the new material into what is already known rather than to memorize it word-for-word.

While these conditions are seen as necessary, they are not sufficient. For example, inherently meaningful material will not automatically be learnt, given the other two conditions. There are problems of medium, sequence, timing, exemplification and expression to be solved.

Relevant knowledge and the way it is interconnected will vary from individual to individual. Learning is an individual, constructive activity leading to an end-product which is different for each person. It is easy, as a teacher, to think of the content of a lesson as being 'transmitted' but this is a misleading analogy. One product of this idea is to view errors or gaps in pupils' knowledge as being 'their fault' rather than as the results of failure to meet the second condition. Another is to focus attention on specific facts and details rather than on a broad grasp of ideas, both in teaching and in testing.

An intention to learn meaningful is based upon a perception by the learner that it is worthwhile to learn that way. If children are rewarded for 'parroting' back what they are given, this will promote rote learning. If the new material has no obvious use or value (beyond pleasing a teacher) there will be little intention to learn it in any form. Young children have fewer yardsticks by which to judge usefulness and value than older children and will show interest in almost anything; this should not be abused.

It bears mention that the three conditions do not specify whether material is presented or discovered. This is seen as a separate dimension, that is, didactic presentation and discovery methods can equally range across the spectrum of meaningfulness. Something essentially arbitrary, with little connection to any existing network of knowledge may be discovered by a child, while highly meaningful material can be learnt through being heard or read. Discovery is a double-edged weapon: it is perfectly possible to discover something which is false.

Concepts

Most areas of human understanding may be analyzed into hierarchies of concepts of ever greater degree of abstraction. An example from biology is Rover, dog, mammal, vertebrate, chordate. What is known by an individual is not open to such simple analysis. It is also organized hierarchically but in a much more confused and overlapping way so that different individuals have different structures covering the same general areas.

According to Ausubel, it is the concepts at the highest level of abstraction in an individual's organized knowledge which are the most stable and useful. That is, they are the most valuable for dealing with new situations and the most resistant to forgetting. Formation of high-level concepts, to draw together the many experiences we have, is the central feature of human ability. It is this rather than the ability to accumulate pieces of information which gives human thought its power, and it happens spontaneously. Children are natural theory-builders. High-level concepts are stable because they are used, and each successful use deepens and strengthens their base. Situations where they lead to inappropriate action give rise either to their modification or to avoidance behaviour. The higher the level of a concept, the greater the range of phenomena and situations to which it applies and the more likely it is to be used and stabilized. Part of the trade-off in this process is loss of exact recall of specific instances and information. Requiring precise memorization may well inhibit formation of higher-level and more beneficial ideas.

The task of the teacher is to help children to develop useful high-level concepts, that is, to organize learning experiences so as to promote rapid and efficient meaningful learning of the abstractions which link and underlie specific phenomena and experiences. If children study the life-cycle of a small animal or send table-tennis balls along the floor by blowing through straws, it should not be because we think they should be knowledgeable about these phenomena, but because they can exemplify more general ideas. Particular experiences are relatively unimportant and are freely interchangeable with others. They are not the content but the vehicle for learning it. If what we teach does not exemplify higher-level abstractions, children will invent their own, almost certainly incompatible with a modern view and often reminiscent of aspects of Aristotelian science. If what we teach is not perceived as useful by an individual, it will not be stabilized but forgotten.

Higher-level concepts cannot be pinned down by simple definitions or lists of attributes. Research on such trivial concepts as identifying 'blue triangles' from sets of coloured shapes can have little bearing on how children develop a concept of 'force' or 'adaptation'. High-level concepts are developed, not selected from alternatives. They can be more or less clear, cohesive, all-embracing and applicable to new situations. My concept of energy is probably more elaborated in these respects than yours, as I have spent a great deal of time thinking about it, but your concept of justice may be much more usable than mine. It is a matter of degree, not of absolutes. High-level concepts are more than a means for coping with existence; they also determine what we perceive out of the mass of information which constantly bombards our senses. Shelley's skylark blithely poured forth profuse streams of unpremeditated art: mine is on red alert defending its territory.

Learnability of New Material

The degree to which something new is potentially easy or difficult to learn depends on two factors: its internal complexity and its relationship to what is already known. These can be viewed as independent dimensions. Internal complexity is the quality which distinguishes the exercise 23×47 from 2368×4759. The direct effect of an increase in internal complexity is to increase the time required to process the information. For an individual there may be a ceiling to the degree of complexity which can be tolerated. In what follows it will be assumed that internal complexity is kept constant, and below such a ceiling. Six levels of relatedness to pre-existing knowledge can be distinguished, each of which leads to different learning characteristics. For the sake of brevity only two will be considered in any detail. The list is more or less in order of difficulty, given that reasonably large amounts of material are to be learnt:

1 deducible or derivable from what is already known;
2 extends, elaborates or recodes what is already known;
3 draws together low-level concepts into one higher-level abstraction;
4 although meaningful, cannot be directly related to what is already known;
5 arbitrary (or approached in this way);
6 meaningful but conflicting with or negating what is already known.

Although children bring to school a great deal of knowledge and experience, it is not usually highly elaborated nor organized, so much school learning is likely to fall into the fourth category. Some may fall into the sixth.

Strategy for Presenting New Material

Where new material does not link directly with what is already known it cannot be actively 'fitted in' and may be quickly forgotten unless some means is arranged to give it temporary stability. Ausubel describes a strategy designed for this purpose. The new material is presented as a short set of statements at a high level, followed by specific lower-level instances, used to develop their meaning. Initially the general statements have little meaning and the concepts they express are vague, limited and possibly confused. Experience with the widest possible range of situations to which they apply clarifies and refines them to the point where they can take over the task of explaining and incorporating further examples. At first the statements act as a clue that something worthwhile is to be learnt, and as a guide to what that learning will be like. There is a considerable analogy with how a new word is learnt. Met in isolation it can only be learnt by rote and is soon forgotten. Met in context its meaning develops, and the wider and more complete the range of contexts, the more rapid and complete the process.

Unlearning

New information which conflicts with or negates existing concepts is the most difficult to learn and the process may even be painful. If the concept under threat has been hitherto useful, and so is highly stable, the most likely course of action is to try to deny or discount the new information, or to avoid circumstances in which it must be acknowledged. The reception given to evolutionary theories by Christian fundamentalists exemplifies these processes. It is for this reason that I would strongly argue against either allowing children to form their own scientific concepts through experience or taking their concepts as a starting point for lessons (Albert, 1977; Driver, 1980; Erickson, 1979; Harlen, 1980; see also Chapter 5 in this book). Most physical science is based on theories which fly in the face of naive observation, and later attempts to displace perfectly successful but incorrect theories may well contribute to the well-known flight from physical sciences at school. Even practising scientists are not immune to this problem. It has been said that ideas in science change not because individuals change but because old people die. The ideas which a person discovers or invents are more strongly held than those which are learned from others so if they are wrong they will be at least a stumbling block to further learning. Better a tentative and vague grasp of a useful idea than a firm and clear grasp of an erroneous one. As Mark Twain put it, 'It ain't what you don't know that causes the trouble. It's what you know that ain't so.'

As a general rule I should argue that any concept or theory which has not been discovered nor invented by adults in other societies than our own is unlikely to be discovered or invented by young children in ours, however well-planned the experiences given them. If misconception and error is to be avoided, such concepts and theories must be presented in contexts where they can be used to make sense of experience. If misconceptions already exist, it is vital to know about them, and this may mean quite careful probing of children's talk. The use of standard phrases and terminology may well disguise differences in meaning. Misconceptions cannot be expected to be uprooted quickly. Children do not usually have so elaborate, stable and interconnected ideas as adults. Also they are reasonably accustomed to having got things wrong, so the task is not impossible, but it can be expected to require more repetitions of the new ideas with accompanying experiences than would learning the same material from zero. It is not enough to present the new ideas and hope that the old ones will wither away.

High-Level Ideas in Science

What does all this imply for teachers of primary science? To be worth teaching at any level, ideas should help to impose order on diversity, draw as wide a range as possible of phenomena into one scheme and increase our ability to understand and explain what we experience. To be feasible they must not require knowledge or skills beyond the capability of the learner – or the teacher. Two very pervasive, useful and accessible ideas in science are that living things are adapted to their life-style and environment and that energy is conserved. Another, which will not be considered in detail, is that every material is made up of atoms and molecules. This is not a definitive list for 'science' but it is adequate to create a basis for later learning in biology, physics and chemistry or for any other course which draws upon these disciplines.

Following the Ausubelian strategy already outlined, each idea must be expressed in 'powerful' statements, that is, statements which express the full range of the idea, and which can be presented to the learners over and over again. As most primary classes, however little science they experience, work with plants and animals, I shall give my approach to *Adaptation* in most detail, again with the caveat that my statements and approach are not definitive, although I consider them to be adequate.

Adaptation

Two statements can encapsulate this concept:

> Plants and animals have to solve three problems: (i) how to get food; (ii) how to avoid being eaten; and (iii) how to breed.

> Plants and animals have different shapes, sizes and ways of doing things which help them to solve these problems.

The three problems provide a ready-made structure for studying organisms. There are many ways to get food. Animals, for example, may eat plants or other animals by hunting, scavenging or parasitism. Animals which hunt are likely to have binocular vision. If they run down their prey they have long legs and narrow bodies. The more they use sheer speed, the more these features are accentuated. If they scavenge, they have at least one very acute sense and the ability to cover considerable distances without using much energy, like buzzards, or they associate themselves with hunters, like jackals and pilot fish or they live in a place where dead animals accumulate, like a seashore. If they eat plants and rely on flight, they are likely to have wide-angle vision and long legs, or wings. If they live in trees, they are likely to have grasping feet or claws. If they live on the ground, they are likely to have relatively rigid feet.

After having various examples of this type pointed out, new examples can be seen in the same light and inferences drawn about their way of life. Alternatively, given a habitat and source of food, the type of organism which would thrive there can be hypothesized and compared with what actually exists. An excellent game, 'The Animal That Never Was' (Michael, 1977), uses some of these ideas. Children decide on the life-style of an imaginary animal and put it together using standard parts. Others must then guess how it solves the three problems. (Unfortunately, two other games in the same pack require modification if they are not to introduce misconceptions about the speed and inevitability of evolutionary processes.)

There is similar richness and variety in solutions to the other problems. As each organism has to solve all three simultaneously there is always compromise and the issues may not be at all clear cut. Initial choice of examples should be for clarity and ease of interpretation, but it should not be supposed, by teacher or children, that it will always be easy to work things out. Very often answers will not be obvious and no one could be expected to know them in advance or to give them on the spot. It will be necessary to observe, investigate, and consult reference books.

The choice of adaptation as the starting point is the result of an attempt to combine direct accessibility of the ideas with explanatory power. This means that I have not included cells, classification, physiology, nor, at the other end of the scale, ecology or evolution. The approach I have outlined leads naturally to most of these over time. Organisms with similar strategies cry out to be classified together, and the need to reconcile different criteria should become apparent rapidly. Some mutual aspects of adaptation are quickly visible, giving rise to notions of food webs and mutual interactions in an environment. Ideas about evolution should also arise naturally out of ideas of adaptation and variability. Whereas the idea of adaptation can be easily and directly related to observation and experience, and so can stand alone, I do not feel that the same is true of the others. Before dealing with physiology I should like to develop concepts of energy, and, before cells, those of atoms and molecules.

One practical problem which is likely to arise is that many plants and animals are encountered in very artificial settings. Those kept in a classroom or school are highly protected and pampered. Domestic animals and plants are bred for features adapted to human intentions, and much of the work of a garden or farm is devoted to ensuring that they survive and thrive. Looking at them another way, they have solved the three problems by training man to look after them, and, on this criterion, grasses may be seen to be the dominant earthly species!

Energy

Partly because of the historical development of the concept and partly because of its strong associations with mechanical work, energy has been seen as the preserve of the physicist and so outside the grasp of anyone else. Yet perfectly valid and useful ideas about energy can be grasped by 7-year-olds (McClelland, 1970). Energy can be seen, quite generally, as the 'ability to make changes'. I have used the following statements:

Energy is the ability to make changes;
Every change needs energy to make it happen;
Energy is never lost or destroyed: it is changed from one form to another;

together with the following list of forms, always kept available for consultation:

Kinetic Energy
Moving things: running, spinning, rolling

Elastic Energy
Stretched, bent or twisted things

Potential Energy
Things which can fall or slide down

Chemical Energy
Things which can burn, explode, and so on, plants and animals

Electrical Energy
Things which are electrically charged

Magnetic Energy
Things which are magnetized

Thermal Energy
Things which are hotter than their surroundings

Light Energy

Sound Energy

The three statements and the list of forms of energy constitute a considerable learning task. To give them meaning, and to follow Ausubel's strategy, it is necessary to arrange for a wide range and variety of changes to be experienced as quickly as possible. Changes should be in both directions for any pair of forms of energy. Many short experiences are to be recommended. More time-consuming investigations should be delayed until the general ideas have been formed. Very many changes can be shown or experienced without the need for elaborate or expensive equipment. Study of the mechanisms used to transform energy can lead quite naturally to ideas of force, work, efficiency, fuels and so on. It is definitely not recommended that ideas of energy be approached piecemeal, and particularly not in the sequence of their historical development. Neither is it recommended that topics such as 'the energy crisis' or 'nuclear energy' be considered until the general concept of energy has been developed.

Atoms and Molecules

As these terms are now part of everyday language some treatment of them is advisable but, because atoms and molecules are invisibly small, even using a microscope, atomic and molecular properties can only be inferred from larger-scale phenomena. This must limit their accessibility to young children, so I should not recommend extended treatment at primary level. Possible statements include:

Every material is made up of tiny pieces called atoms;
The smallest piece of a material you can have is called a molecule;
A molecule is a special group of atoms;
Atoms and molecules are too small to be seen.

Just as Lego pieces can be put together to make a wide variety of things, or bricks and blocks can be built into entirely different shapes and appearances, so a limited number of different atoms can make up everything we see. One relevant activity would be crystal growing. Taking things further would depend on an individual teacher's confidence and knowledge.

Investigation and Experiment

At the beginning it was stated that science provides a very good, but not unique, vehicle for developing the ideas that the world of experience is bound by rules and that it is both possible and worthwhile to seek them out. For this to happen investigations and experiments carried out with and by children are essential. It is often argued that the methods and processes used are valuable in their own right. From an Ausubelian perspective this is not so. Like the ability to multiply numbers, the ability to hypothesize, measure, classify, observe or carry out a classical experiment is empty unless it can be chosen appropriately in context. Without a context there is no basis for observing or measuring one thing rather than another. As the development of such skills is highly desirable, it is important to arrange suitable contexts. The scheme suggested here will automatically provide suitable contexts, but all areas of the curriculum should be used to generate appropriate investigations involving such processes. They are not the preserve of the sciences, and it would be unwise to give the impression that they were. It would be even more unfortunate to give the impression that, in themselves, they constituted science.

Mathematics and Technology

Contexts for investigations which strongly overlap with science are found in mathematics and technology. Like scientific concepts, mathematical concepts are inventions which draw very different phenomena into their ambit. To be learnt meaningfully they need to be stated and widely exemplified. On the basis of Ausubel's theory it would not be predicted that children, given limited specific experiences with stereotyped equipment like blocks and rods would be able to develop abstract concepts, expressed in symbols, and capable of being applied to situations involving birds or bicycles. Instead it would be recommended that children carry out activities and investigations requiring counting, measurement and so on, in as widely differing circumstances as can be contrived, with the relationship of the activity to the mathematical ideas always made explicit. It should be pointed out that, if these activities involve plants, animals, magnets or batteries, this does not make them part of science. If their purpose is to develop mathematical ideas they are part of mathematics. A mathematics programme should provide many opportunities for investigations. If it does not, I believe that it will be unproductive for all but a few children and that it misconceives the nature of mathematical concepts at this level. Indeed, the idea of mathematics as separate from any direct physical link is highly sophisticated and very recent.

Technology is often described as the application of science to practical problems. I think this is highly misleading, particularly as it suggests that you cannot have technology until you have science. I see it as the application of whatever knowledge, skills or hunches are available, to the solution of practical problems. If there is nothing better to use, systematic trial-and-error is a perfectly respectable technique. Many investigations may be carried out by children to solve a technical problem before they have developed much knowledge of science. The nature of the problem determines which processes would be appropriate.

In practice, the boundaries between science, mathematics and technology are not clear, and a given investigation may include any or all. Provided that the high-level ideas to which they relate and which they are intended to develop are clear to the teacher, this does not matter. All are valuable. What would be wasteful would be exercises in investigation whose ultimate purpose was not clear, or which were carried out for no other reason than to practise investigation. Even more wasteful would be abstract statements of concepts, theories, laws or rules, in the absence of activities and experiences. It is the combination of the words with experience which leads to meaning.

Following an Ausubelian strategy does not predetermine what the important concepts may be at any stage in a child's schooling, how they are expressed, or how they are exemplified. Individual teachers have to reach decisions about all three aspects, but those who have limited understanding of the ideas themselves are not favourably placed to make sensible decisions at any level. I do not subscribe to the view that some public measure of scientific attainment, such as O-level chemistry, Grade C, is prerequisite to competence to teach, at primary level, the sort of science which is advocated here. Instead, a relatively short course, much more condensed than would be suitable for a child, and including the underlying rationale, should be adequate to allow any competent teacher to draw into use the many resources and materials already in existence.

My own experience, using both media, strongly suggests that a short burst of individualized instruction, for example, by the audio-tutorial method (Postlethwaite *et al.*, 1972) is more efficient at developing fundamental concepts than is conventional classroom instruction. I believe that this is so for two reasons. One is that a taped lesson of some fifteen minutes can gain a level of continuous and undistracted attention which is rare in a class-room, while providing a much higher density of exemplification of the powerful ideas in action. The other is that the personalities of learner and instructor do not intrude upon the exchange. For this reason my ideal system would combine groups of about five such lessons in any term with what-ever relevant experiences and investigations a teacher and class may wish to pursue.

Using normal classroom techniques alone it may be expected that the transition from an initially vague and uncertain grasp of the ideas to one which is clear enough to be used to give meaning to new experiences will be slow in many cases. These are not grounds for criticism of the strategy. Whatever skills and information would be gained by children from experiences, activities and investigations under other circumstances, would be gained under these, and further activities would always be available to clarify and reinforce them. Any move towards development of higher-level ideas is an added bonus. Because higher-level ideas are not acquired in an 'all or nothing' fashion it is entirely acceptable for activities which relate to them to be carried out by children of widely differing speeds of learning, with all gaining something and no one being irredeemably left behind.

References

ALBERT, E. (1977) 'Development of the concept of heat in children', *Science Education*, 62, 3, p. 389.

AUSUBEL, D.P., NOVAK J.D. and HANESIAN H. (1978) *Educational Psychology: A Congnitive View*, Holt, Rinehart and Winston.

DRIVER, R. (1981) 'Pupils' alternative frameworks in science', *European Journal of Science Education*, 3, 1, pp. 93–101.

ERICKSON, G.L. (1979) 'Children's conceptions of heat and temperature', *Science Education*, 63, 2, p. 221.

HARLEN, W. (1980) 'Selecting content in primary science', *Education 3–13*, 8, 2, pp. 19–23.

McCLELLAND, J.A.G. (1970) 'An Approach to the Development and Assessment of Instruction in Science at Second Grade Level: The Concept of Energy', unpublished PhD thesis, Cornell University.

MICHAEL, W. (1977) *Animals*, Hamilton College of Education.

POSTLETHWAITE, S.N., NOVAK J.D. and MURRAY H. (1972) *The Audio-Tutorial Approach to Learning through Independent Study and Integrated Experience*, 3rd ed., Burgess.

PART V

Approaches to Curriculum Development

Introduction

As a practical activity, developing any part of a school's curriculum is likely to be a difficult exercise requiring as much in the way of 'political' skill as technical expertise. As a theoretical activity, explaining how different areas of the curriculum have been developed over time is also difficult, again requiring technical expertise (though of a different kind) and 'political' insight. To provide a context for the developments discussed in this section, three approaches to curriculum development are identified, based loosely on the ideas of Havelock (1975). It needs to be recognized that the descriptions of the approaches provided here emphasize procedures and tend to obscure the political interplay among interested parties which occurs whenever the existing curriculum (and the balance of power and interest embodied in it) are disturbed.

From the Hadow Report of the early thirties to the beginning of the sixties the development of the primary curriculum (including science) took place in an *ad hoc* way. Individual teachers or schools introduced changes, more often modifications to existing practices, less often more fundamental ones. Such changes became known to others through contact with colleagues in neighbouring schools or through the agency of HMI or local inspectors who passed on reports of 'good practice'. Sometimes, such developments featured in courses for teachers; less often they featured in the educational literature. Changes such as the introduction of elements of physical science to complement nature study were introduced by enthusiasts and became known through informal and formal contacts. This interaction was not managed centrally; it was not conducted systematically, nor made public for the benefit of the teaching profession generally.

Though never totally replaced and still functioning as an important means of disseminating ideas and practices, this approach through social interaction was displaced by the national curriculum project era of the sixties and seventies. Curriculum projects such as those discussed in Chapters 12–16 were investigations into curriculum problems made over a limited period by teams expressly employed for the purpose who usually operated on a national basis. Projects were essentially 'temporary systems' existing alongside established educational institutions and attempting to catalyze them into some form of action. All the primary science projects aimed to influence teaching and learning methods and attitudes towards science; some such as the Oxford Primary Science Project were more concerned with curriculum content than others such as Nuffield Junior Science. Except for the Learning through Science Project and Nuffield Combined Science (originally designed solely with the 11–13 age-group in mind), the projects featured in this section concentrated on producing materials for teachers rather than for children. All sought to make a contribution to teacher development. Three main sub-strategies of the project approach can be distinguished among English projects: those based largely on academic expertise, on teacher expertise, and on teacher-project cooperation in areas where special expertise was non-existent or, at least, not readily identifiable (Taylor and Richards, 1979).

The first project style assumed that new approaches to science were not being attempted in schools except on a very small scale, and that therefore a central team needed to be gathered together to initiate and manage the development of work in primary science. The central team created new materials and set up a network of trial schools in various parts of the country to try them out. Practising teachers were involved but very largely as responders and adapters rather than initiators. None of the projects featured in this section fell neatly into this category judging from the accounts reproduced here, but both the Oxford Primary Science Project and Science 5–13 had strong elements of 'academic expertise'.

As Chapter 12 illustrates, the Oxford Primary Science Project was concerned with both research and development; it attempted to discover what scientific concepts primary children could form and to identify experiences which could help children form particular concepts. The project team's scientific expertise was used to examine the general ideas running through science (even to the extent of providing a one-paragraph description of the universe!), to identify a number of concepts around which primary science could be based and to communicate these through courses to teachers in 'pilot' and 'operational' areas. The teachers' role was not to question the basic approach but to suggest, on the basis of classroom experimentation, how children's understanding of these concepts could be extended. A final academic component was the evaluation programme, testing children's understanding through problems presented on film. The project thus sought to map out primary science in terms of concepts; the team was at pains to stress that 'concepts did not represent a scheme of topics to be worked through. Work arising out of particular concepts should only be done where it was relevant to the things the children wanted to do' (p. 138). Its approach was out of tune with the process-dominated ideas of the sixties; it disappeared almost without trace. Only one book (Redman *et al.*, 1969) was ever published.

Science 5–13 was another example of a national project based largely on academic expertise. The delineation of objectives, the relating of these to Piagetian stages of development and the sophisticated approach to evaluation were all important academic contributions to the curriculum development enterprise. The advocated planning approach, of working with objectives in mind, was an interesting attempt to provide a firm sense of direction for primary science, without depriving teachers of the choice of activities to pursue. As Parker-Jelly points out in Chapter 14, the 5–13 project offered guidance to teachers at reflective and pragmatic levels. Accepting the basic philosophy of its predecessor (Nuffield Junior Science), it sought to provide 'a child-based structure as a framework for child-centred activity' in primary science. In doing so it involved a large number of teachers in many parts of the country, but mainly in trying out draft material rather than in producing it. Its publications (all directed at teachers) have sold well, but, as Parker-Jelly's contribution suggests, questions remain as to the significance of its impact.

A second project style worked on the assumption that interesting approaches were being developed, and could be developed, by teachers themselves, but that support needed to be given and communication improved if such approaches were to be given wider currency. Project teams gathered information about 'good practice', codified it in terms of principles, illustrated it by examples and published it in a form in which it could be used by others. Judging from the account in this section of the book, Nuffield Junior Science could be interpreted as an example of a 'good practice' project. Wastnedge remarks: 'of all the projects, this must be the one which was most firmly based with teachers in classrooms. Helped and supported by the team in the field, it was teachers who did the research and pointed the way ahead; the team were there to interpret the teachers' findings and to feed more suggestions and questions into the system' (p. 142). Conferences, courses and meetings in teachers' centres (many newly established for the purpose) were all forms of social interaction deliberately used by the project to foster its ideas. The project helped clarify the nature and role of primary science and to establish the importance of the process approach in this area of the curriculum. It did not provide guidelines on subject-matter, believing that content would take care of itself if teachers chose a suitable range of starting points and planned topics together to avoid duplication. The project produced not a set of objectives nor a list of concepts but a number of broad principles as to how to proceed in primary science (see p. 143), discussed in detail in its first publication (*Teacher's Guide 1*) and illustrated by case studies in a second volume (*Teacher's Guide 2*). At the end of his contribution to this volume Wastnedge, its organizer, sums up the nature of its achievements. Some educationists, however, have criticized the project for failing to provide a firm enough rationale in terms of skills, concepts or content, and for underestimating the difficulties faced by teachers in revising their preconceptions and/or practices with regard to science.

A third project style involved practising teachers neither as major initiators of change nor as relatively passive recipients of others' ideas but as partners with project teams in investigating problems within particular subjects or in exploring and clarifying ill-defined areas of the curriculum. A primary science project which exemplified this 'partnership' approach was the Progress in Learning Science Project, referred to in Chapter 8, but not discussed specifically in this section of the book. In this project the small central team explored with groups of teachers ways of determining children's levels of development in relation to skills, concepts and attitudes, and ways of developing these further (Harlen, 1977a, 1977b).

For over ten years curriculum development in primary science was dominated by national projects all of which produced materials for teachers. Since the late seventies two important developments have occurred – one related generally to development strategies, the other specifically to primary science.

With some important exceptions such as the Micro-Electronics in Education Programme, there has been a shift away from project-based development towards school-based development involving problem-solving strategies. With this approach, individual schools themselves are responsible for the process of change through identifying areas of concern, through translating general concerns into definable problems and through devising solutions to these either through their own efforts alone or through calling on help from outsiders. The stress is on school-generated initiatives and school-wide commitment to reform, with materials from national projects seen as resources to be adapted, sometimes very extensively, to suit local circumstances. Though itself a national initiative, the Learning through Science Project (Chapter 15) has attempted to service problem-solving activities through involving groups of teachers in thinking out strategies to help schools devise policies for science, through involving other groups of teachers in the production of a handbook on resources (see Chapter 21) and through the production of tape-slide sequences designed to foster discussion at staff meetings or in teachers' centres. The direct development approach of early projects focussing mainly on individual teachers has been replaced here by a managerial/resource supply strategy focussing on schools as institutions.

The Learning through Science Project also illustrates another marked change which has occurred in the years following the publication of the HMI Primary Survey (Chapter 4). A major aspect of the project's work has been the production of materials for children. Material has been produced which 'helps put problems in the paths of children and gives help to the teacher on ways of encouraging and guiding the enquiries' (p. 163) – a reversal of the policies adopted by the Nuffield Junior Science and Science 5–13 Projects. The remaining chapter in this section also illustrates the same trend. Holford examines the principles underpinning the material produced by the Nuffield Combined Science authors for top primary and middle years children. These, he argues, have much the same features as are evident in the recent upsurge of material published for primary schools, especially for children aged 7 to 11; for these, too, the intention is to provide for teachers a resource which is flexible in their hands as they plan lessons, married to a card resource for children which is durable and efficient as a stimulus and support to learning. It is too early to evaluate the impact of workcards professionally produced as learning aids, but there is no doubt that their publication meets a need felt by many teachers who have lacked children's material they can use flexibly. However, some of the contributors to this book, such as Conran and Wastnedge, have already voiced their misgivings.

Twenty years of curriculum development have witnessed a series of attempts to remedy areas of weakness in primary science. Nuffield Junior Science sought to provide a general orientation to the enterprise; Science 5–13 provided a clear sense of direction; Progress though Learning Science gave attention to the evaluation of children's development in science; Learning through Science helped in the formulation of school policies and in the provision of resource support. The Oxford Primary Science Project does not fit easily into that overview of past developments. Its concept-based approach was still-born in the sixties, but could perhaps be built on and developed further in the eighties. Holford argues that 'the pendulum now seems to be swinging towards a conceptual view, following a decade of studies of how scientific ideas develop or fail to develop over time, and of the role of perception and language in children's learning' (p. 169; see also Chapter 5). Would greater attention given to concepts lead to a tighter view of the content of primary science or to a greater concern for the order in which materials and activities are introduced to primary-aged children?

References

HARLEN, W. *et al.* (1977a) *Raising Questions*, Match and Mismatch, Edinburgh Oliver and Boyd.

HARLEN, W. *et al.* (1977b) *Finding Answers*, Match and Mismatch, Edinburgh Oliver and Boyd.

HAVELOCK, R. (1975) 'The utilisation of educational research and development', in HARRIS, A. *et al.* (Eds), *Curriculum Innovation*, Croom Helm, pp. 312–27.

REDMAN, S. *et al.* (1969) *An Approach to Primary Science*, London Macmillan.

TAYLOR, P. and RICHARDS, C. (1979) *An Introduction to Curriculum Studies*, Windsor NFER.

12 Young Children and Science: The Oxford Primary Science Project*

Stewart Redman and others

There are still doubts in the minds of many teachers as to the proper place of science in the primary school. Part of the trouble stems from the memory they have of the science in their own school careers. This was a subject with a special mystique of its own and one they found difficult. It required special rooms and facilities and used a jargon which they never felt they fully understood (see Chapter 24.2).

Primary teachers are also aware that there are pressures from some secondary schools to inhibit their undertaking to teach science. Some secondary teachers will say that science is better left to the secondary stage; that it will merely be badly taught in the primary school and that the children will have to unlearn much of what they have been taught when they start their science courses in secondary school.

The stages of intellectual development described by Piaget, and confirmed broadly by others who have worked in this field, suggest that children cannot reason about abstract ideas until, on average, they have entered secondary schools. While it is important that we learn as much as possible about the learning processes of young children, in science and all other fields, it may be argued that any real understanding of science at the primary stage is unlikely because the child is unable to handle abstract ideas and to form the concepts involved. If science, on this view, is undertaken with young children, it will have to be so drastically over-simplified as to be valueless as a basis for later studies and the work done will have to be unlearned and a new foundation laid. Opposed to this is the view that children can recognize the common elements in situations in their own experience – a number is an abstraction recognized as a common element in, say, twelve apples, a dozen eggs, 12 o'clock and a foot ruler – and that the child at the primary stage may be able to make abstractions about the scientific experiences which he has, and to form scientific concepts in a simple, unsophisticated form. If it is possible to discover which scientific concepts children can form and to identify the experiences which are fruitful in helping children to form concepts, this may be a valuable pointer to the work in science which it is profitable for children

* From *Trends in Education*, 12 1968, pp. 17–25.

to do in primary school, and this work might come to be seen as an appropriate foundation for the science schemes to be followed later in secondary school. Susan Isaacs, in her book *Intellectual Growth in Young Children*, wrote that the thought processes of young children can be quite complicated when they are concerned with something that interests them deeply and that they do not always think in the same way, nor do they always conform to the modes of thought suggested by Piaget (see Chapter 10).

The Project

The first stage in the research was to find out what was already being done by teachers in the way of developing scientific concepts with primary school children. Teachers were asked in a questionnaire which scientific concepts they thought children might have formed as a result of their science lessons and the answers suggested that the term 'scientific concept' meant little to them. Apart from the difficulty introduced by this unfamiliar term, the returns gave little indication that the teachers were aware of what ideas or principles they were trying to bring to the understanding of their children, or that they were doing more than following the lines of development of a topic as seemed sensible to them or as it was suggested in a science book. The topics, too, appeared to be quite distinct and self-contained and it seemed that a child might do a piece of work on magnets, and later a project on electric circuits, without fully realizing that he had been looking at the two sides of the same coin. Science topics, particularly if they are followed as experimental schemes, have a danger of being divorced from the other work of the class and they may inhibit the interchange of ideas.

Perhaps we ought to look at what is meant by a concept. Lovell (1961) defines it as the ability of a person to discriminate or differentiate between the properties of the objects or events before him and to generalize his findings in respect of any common feature he may find. The use of language is clearly important in the process of concept-formation and the words the children first learn are thought by adults to categorize objects in the most useful way for everyday life. In some cases the child uses words denoting a large category first before he uses words to denote members of that class, whereas in others he uses words to denote particular objects first and later learns the words which embrace the whole class.

Aims of the Research

It was felt by the research team that the research project into the formation of scientific concepts should not be just an opportunity to devise a new scheme for primary school science, but it should be angled to produce something of value for primary schools. The team would look into the whole field of science and examine the large, all-embracing ideas which run through it. If it is agreed that children sometimes think in terms of larger categories first and then think in terms of particular examples inside the group, there is a real argument for identifying the important global concepts of science and attempting to find out how the children form these – or if they can form them at the primary school stage. Nevertheless, at the school level, it was recognized that the child's experience must be structured in order that his understanding is gradually refined and deepened. If these concepts could be identified, it was felt that they should be investigated in the situation of the primary teacher with his class. In order to cover a significant range and number of children and teachers, it was decided that the concepts should be identified first; an attempt should be made to communicate these ideas to primary school teachers, many of whom would have had little if any scientific training; and then the teachers asked how these ideas could be illuminated by the experiences which children have in their schools.

It was recognized that the teacher could form only a subjective opinion of the understanding of his children and of their formation of a particular concept. The combined findings of many teachers, supported by the work the children had done, would be valuable but still only subjective, and it was recognized that methods would have to be explored for evaluating quantitatively the formation of science concepts with a view to testing some of the children in the schools collaborating in the research. The first hurdle was the identification of the important concepts of science and the framing of a conceptual picture of science which would be broadly acceptable to a large number of scientists. The second hurdle was the communication of the scientific ideas in the face of the difference of teachers.

Identification of Concepts

Discussions were undertaken with scientists in universities, colleges of education, schools and industry and a variety of suggestions were received. Some scientists were not happy to attempt an answer to what seemed to them an unusual and indefinite question. They were naturally aware that the research was to be concerned with primary school children and their own ideas about the understanding of young children frequently affected their answers. It was intended that the scientists should give their ideas on the important concepts of science purely from the standpoint of themselves as physicists or chemists or biologists, but frequently their knowledge of their own children's development, for this was the only experience on which they could call, influenced their suggestions. The research team was conscious of a dilemma. Obviously it was essential to arrive at a conceptual picture of science which was broadly acceptable to scientists, but this needed also to be expressed in terms which could be understood by teachers.

Discussion of biological concepts particularly, turned up some different opinions. To the non-scientist the differences between living and non-living things are so obvious – discounting awkward groups like the viruses which he would be unlikely to consider – that the division between physical and biological sciences is a natural corollary. The research team felt that this division should be reflected in the conceptual picture of science. Some biologists, however, did not accept that there were distinctly biological concepts. One view was that everything distinctive of living organisms could be understood under the concepts of energy and structure.

Eventually, it became clear that some ideas were accepted as being fundamental. These were linked together in a brief paragraph called, for purposes of reference, '*A Description of the Universe*'. It was agreed that the ideas embodied in this should become the subject-matter of the research.

One element it was felt to be essential to include in any statement about science was that of chance and uncertainty. Children can very easily grow up to think of science as something certain and predictable, for the view of science as something which knows all the answers is a common one held by the person who does not profess to understand science. In everyday life so many things are accepted as uncertain, others as more or less probable, that it seems only sensible to bring children to a realization that the scientist is doing the best he can with an uncertain world; that the laws he discovers are not certain but are frequently statistical laws – in Professor Porter's phrase 'Laws of Disorder'.

From this thinking it became clear that basic scientific ideas fall into four groups under the headings 'energy', 'structure', 'chance' and 'life'. 'Life' was retained as a separate entity because it was thought it did have its own system of ideas which were distinct from those of the physical sciences. No claim was made for this as a definitive list of concepts and a standing invitation was given to scientists to write their own 'descriptions of the universe'.

A Description of the Universe

The universe is the product of the interaction of energy and matter. In circumstances not yet understood, the interaction of energy and matter produces life, which has characteristics not found in non-living matter. The non-living universe is the necessary result of very many chance occurrences and tends to 'run down' to an equilibrium. The universe of living things tends to differentiate into specialized forms in temporary equilibrium with each other and with the non-living universe. Matter has a discrete particle structure. The characteristics of a substance are determined by its particular structure. A substance may undergo physical change, including change of state, while remaining intrinsically the same substance. Substances are either elements or compounds. They can undergo chemical change to form different substances. Such changes involve a rearrangement of particles with accompanying energy changes. Energy occurs in interconvertible forms. The transmission of energy through space or through a suitable substance creates a field and may often conveniently be described in terms of wave motion.

The ideas in this description of the universe may be set out in four concept groups.

Energy	*Structure*
Work	Relationship
Field	Force and forces in equilibrium
Wave	Particle structure of matter and cell structure
Reflection	Chemical change: element/compound;
Refraction	atom/molecule
Absorption	Particles in motion and pressure
Interconvertibility	Change of state
Equilibrium	

Life	*Chance*
Metabolism	Uncertainty and probability
Diversity	Disorder and randomness
Interdependence	Pattern
Adaptation	
Inheritance	

Organization of the Research

It was felt to be essential to work through a large number of teachers with their classes, and to plan the programme of research in two main stages – a pilot stage and an operational stage. The concepts of energy, structure, chance and life were explored with different groups of teachers in successive terms. A small group of teachers attended a weekend course on energy. In this course, the science was presented to them at an adult level and the aim of the course was to give them an understanding of what is meant by energy. Some tentative suggestions were made as to work which might be attempted in school, but the attitude taken was that these teachers were the experts in primary teaching and it was they who must decide what was relevant to their classes. The remainder of the term was to be devoted to thinking their way around energy; they were asked to have energy in mind for their teaching in the spring term and during both the preparation and the teaching terms the research team would visit the schools and be available to help in any way possible. After the teaching term the teachers were asked to send in a report, preferably accompanied by children's work, and a preliminary attempt would be made at exploring techniques of objective assessment of concept-formation.

Courses on structure, chance and life, were mounted in succeeding terms with different groups of teachers in the Oxford Institute of Education region, and their terms of preparation, teaching and reporting followed successively. News of these courses and of the whole research project spread and as a result invitations were received from other institutes of education and LEAs to mount courses in their own areas. These invitations were accepted as they gave the team the opportunity to try different methods of presentation of the science and they offered the possibility of securing the cooperation of teachers in other parts of the country in the research project.

The Pilot Stage of the Project

The four courses mounted in the Oxford region were regarded as trial runs and the experience gained in discussion with the teachers who attended these courses was invaluable in suggesting ways of improving the presentation of science. In these courses, too, attempts were made at suggesting possible ways in which the scientific ideas might be related to the work going on normally in class. The reactions of the teachers attending these courses varied widely, some feeling that the concepts provided them with a useful framework for their guidance of their children's activity and others feeling that this was foreign to their method of teaching and could not be reconciled with it. The experiences of these teachers in school afterwards were invaluable in letting the team know which of the teaching suggestions were worth pursuing and which did not work and should be dropped.

If the experience of the teachers on this course was to be of any relevance to others schools, it was essential that they should not be a handpicked group keenly interested in science and already teaching science with their classes. On the other hand, it would be equally inappropriate to insist that the teachers had no interest in science. It was made clear that knowledge of science was to be regarded neither as an essential condition nor a handicap as far as the teachers were concerned. In this first stage then, a small group of teachers was invited to collaborate in the research, as far as possible representative of a body of primary teachers, and drawn from a variety of types of primary schools.

No prior knowledge of science was assumed by the research team, but it became apparent from discussions with teachers involved in the pilot stage, and other teachers over a period, that they were in fact assuming unwittingly a knowledge of science which the teachers did not possess. This illustrates the difficulty that individuals who have been trained in science and pursued scientific activities have in appreciating the standpoint of people whose training and careers have been orientated towards the humanities and away from the sciences.

Some Second Thoughts

The end of the academic year 1964–65 seems a suitable point at which to review the impressions which had been formed as a result of giving a number of courses to teachers, listening to their reactions and assessing some of the work which had been done in schools. By the summer of 1965, the pilot courses on energy, structure and chance had been given in Oxford, and the life course was in preparation. Repeats of courses had been given in other centres and the whole range of ideas had been explored for the first time at Hereford. Teachers' reports on energy and structure had been received and the work attempted and opinions formed by the teachers were known in some detail. The group of teachers attempting to introduce ideas of chance were visited in the summer term and their reactions were known from discussions during the course and from visits to schools afterwards.

It was essential to take a long, hard look at the concepts in the light of previous experience. One of the first clear pointers to be given by the teachers was their preference for the large concept, energy structure, chance and life; although chance was unpopular with some this was by no means universal, but numerous teachers felt that it did not arise as naturally as the others. However confused one may become in tackling the philosophical questions: What do we *mean* by energy? What do we *mean* by life? there was little doubt that they meant something definite to the teachers and they were accepted by children as the key to the multitude of things going on around them. About some of the sub-concepts the teachers were much less certain and, as a result, misconceptions were more common.

Armed with tentative conclusions from the pilot stage of the research, the time had come at the beginning of the academic year 1965–66 to review the energy, structure, chance and life courses, to make amendments on the basis of feedback from teachers and to present the science in terms of an integrated framework of concepts.

During the second year of the project further courses were given to groups of teachers who had already become involved in the research and these, for the sake of completeness, follow more closely the lines of the pilot courses, though cross-references were constantly made.

In planning the presentation of the science on the operational phase, it was not intended to devise one integrated course and to repeat it in exactly the same form several times. It was hoped to ring the changes on a basic structure and to see if any significant difference emerged from the different methods of presentation.

Analysis of Results

It was suggested that each teacher should fill in an index card for each approach to a concept and accompany it with an account of the work at greater length and examples of children's work. Records in card form would be most valuable for storage and retrieval if the number of teachers should reach considerable proportions, as seemed likely from the interest shown in many quarters. Nevertheless, many teachers found it irksome and difficult to complete the cards and preferred simply to write out their accounts, often at considerable length.

When an analysis was made of the variety of activities that teachers were engaged in at the operational (final year) stage of the project, it immediately became obvious that some concepts – for instance, equilibrium and disorder – are difficult to put over to any primary age group; that some topics are moderately successful – refraction, absorption; and that the discussion approach, highly favoured by teachers, was a dimension of the other forms of activity.

Conclusion

The research was seen as a positive attempt to help the primary teacher, rather than an academic exercise. The results of this work convinced the team that it is not enough for the teacher to decide what to teach and then to do it. It is necessary to make him aware that what appears to be transparently clear and obvious may strike the child as mysterious if not alarming. Awareness of the child's limitations in thinking and conceptualizing is essential in the teaching of science and it is necessary to find out when a child is reaching the stage of readiness for a particular range of concepts and not assume, as we have done for so long in science, that it is best to play safe and leave it all to a later stage, perhaps in the secondary school. To do that is to avoid running any risk of anticipating a stage of the child's development, but at the cost of wasting the wide possibilities of the child's primary school career, with all its excitement, enthusiasm and the genuine joy of inquiry and discovery.

But to make suggestions of possible approaches to science in the primary school is only half a job; without a conscious attempt to assess the success or failure of such approaches in terms of the understanding of the children all efforts are valueless. The evaluation of the work in schools was discussed with teachers at all stages and various levels of assessment were envisaged. At the first level, each teacher was able to say how fruitful or otherwise a particular topic or line of inquiry had been; and he is the best judge.

Even without any precise measure of the understanding of the concepts by the children, the number of teachers who recognized particular concepts in their children's activities was of some significance. All through the research it was stressed that the concepts did not represent a scheme of topics to be worked through. Work arising out of particular concepts should only be done where it was relevant to the things the children wanted to do. When a concept such as equilibrium figures in only a tiny proportion of reports of work, it was taken to be an idea of limited usefulness at that stage. There could be various reasons for this, a notable one being that the teacher had not himself made sense of the idea and therefore could not apply it in everyday situations. Where failure occurred consistently, it seemed sensible to assume that this was a concept which did not hold much for the children of this age range on the basis of their experience at home and school.

An evaluation of the operational stage of the project was carried out by the Research Unit of the University of Bristol Institute of Education. Over a period of a year the performances of four groups of children were compared; two of these were experimental groups from the Oxford and Doncaster areas, one was a control group being taught no science and the other was a control group whose science was guided by the Nuffield Junior Science Project. Group objective tests took the form of problems presented by means of an 8mm film-sequence and responses were recorded in an answer booklet. About 1500 children between the ages of 7 and 11 were tested, the items being devised to test the objectives of the Oxford Project. It was found that for the concepts of energy, structure and chance, the Oxford group was superior and the Doncaster group was superior for the energy and chance concepts. These very general conclusions do not, however, apply equally to all sub-groups: there were important differences according to age and sex.

One might conclude that the Oxford Project was successful in achieving some of its objectives.

Reference

LOVELL, K. (1961) *The Growth of Mathematical Concepts in Children*, University of London Press.

13   Nuffield Junior Science: The End of a Beginning?

Ron Wastnedge

Background

As they reminisce nostalgically, older people, especially older teachers, will often tell you that nature study is as old as primary education itself and that, before the war, the nature table, nature walks and 'object lessons' about animals and plants were an accepted part of the elementary school curriculum. It is a very attractive idea but I suspect that distance in time probably lends enchantment to the view, and most of us who were pupils in the elementary schools of the twenties and thirties would be hard-pressed to summon up firm memories of actual visits to woods or streams, of direct observation of living material, or of specific pieces of teaching based on nature tables.

After 1945, however, events in primary education took an interesting turn. The object lesson had gone, but the nature table was still common, and here and there individual teachers began to take a broader view of nature, recognizing that it had a physical, as well as a biological, component. Physical science became one of the things to 'do' in primary schools and by the late 1950s a fair number of teachers were deeply and excitedly involved in this latest development. Usually teachers based their science teaching on what they remembered of their old grammer school courses; they selected those topics which seemed to match what they judged to be the stage of development of the children, and they used 'make do and mend' equipment rather than the sophisticated and prohibitively expensive apparatus of the secondary school laboratory. Publishers provided support in the form of sets of work cards and books of suggested experiments. So did the BBC with excellent programmes on radio and television – Harry Armstrong, where are you? We have need of you again! (See Chapter 2.)

At its best, science was seen as a way of providing experience appropriate to the developmental level of the children. At its worst, it was, and was often referred to as, 'cookery book science', where children and teachers followed sets of instructions, often even being told the answers they should get if they followed the instructions precisely.

Parallel with this interest in science there were other important developments. For instance, in Bristol, Marianne Parry and her co-workers were examining the education being provided in nursery and infant schools and were pointing out the need for change. It was a movement which was to have a profound effect on early childhood education, and not only in Britain, as witness the excellent Open Corridor Project of Lillian Weber in Harlem and the Bronx, which still struggles on in spite of financial difficulties and the entrenched attitudes of many of the educational establishment. Essentially, nursery and infant teachers were being asked to ignore what junior schools were trying to dictate to them – have the children reading and setting down tens and units in columns by the time they are 7. Instead, it was suggested they should look carefully at the children themselves, find out what was known about how children learn, and then provide what they saw as the most appropriate educational experience they could devise. It would then be incumbent on teachers in the later phases of education to carry out similar exercises and build on the foundation the nursery and infant schools had laid. All this, of course, was powerful stuff and it gained support and encouragement from the fascinating information which came through about the work of Piaget in Geneva. Indeed, one of the most rewarding experiences of the early sixties was to attend teachers' courses and hear the enthusiastic and often remarkably well-informed discussions about the relevance of Piaget's work to contemporary British primary education.

So the climate was ready for the various curriculum development projects which burst on the scene in the mid-sixties. The wealthiest of the British primary projects was Nuffield Junior Science, funded to the extend of £75,000, to run from January 1964 to December 1966. But it should not be forgotten that there were other smaller but no less important projects operating at the same time. For instance, the British Association for the Advancement of Science sponsored a project at the Froebel Foundation. The Director was Nathan Isaacs and he and his team reported and commented on the findings of thirty teachers whose classes had carried out scientific activities arising from children's interests and questions. The final analysis, together with important sections on such key issues as the role of the teacher, children's questions, and record keeping, was published by the Foundation in 1966 under the title *Children Learning through Scientific Interests*. At the same time, Stewart Redman, with a small grant from the then Ministry of Education, and a team of two, based in the Oxford University Institute of Education, was looking at the problem from a different viewpoint. He published his statement in 1969 (Redman, Brereton and Boyers, *An Approach to Primary Science*, Macmillan). This was of special interest because, whereas the Nuffield and Froebel projects began from children and how they learn, Redman started by considering the universe and the main themes which seemed to him to run through all scientific studies – energy, structure, chance and life. His final statement was designed to help teachers by giving them information about subject-matter and suggesting possible teaching approaches which might be adopted in schools (See Chapter 12).

In parallel with these British ventures there were comparable groups at work in the United States, the one with which the Nuffield Junior Science Project had the closest ties being the Elementary Science Study (ESS), based in Cambridge (Mass.). It was one of the development programmes established by the Educational Development Center, an organization established to develop 'new ideas and methods for improving the content and process of education'. ESS had been founded in 1960 and was funded at first by the Alfred P. Sloan Foundation and the Victoria Foundation, but later by the Natural Science Foundation. Professor David Hawkins directed the team which assembled teaching materials for trial in schools, ran workshops for teachers and finally published an interesting selection of support materials which included teachers' booklets, kits for classroom use, film loops and films. It is interesting to recall that in one of our discussions David Hawkins and I compared the ways in which we had chosen our teams. He had gone for scientists – physicists, engineers, mathematicians – usually with a university background. I had chosen primary school teachers. We agreed that, with hindsight, we would each have started on the middle ground with a mixture of the two. I still think that would have been right. Certainly, as his project developed, David became increasingly, and very perceptively, fascinated by the response of young children to his materials and to his teaching, and by what he could see of the learning techniques and strategies they employed.

That was the backcloth against which Nuffield Junior Science developed. The ground was fertile and enthusiasm was high.

The Project

As a team we knew that in three years, which included the awkwardness of starting on 1 January rather than in September, we had to produce materials which would help teachers to include and exploit science in their teaching programmes. As things turned out, the major contribution of the project was made at a more fundamental level and concerned the nature and role – if any – of science in primary education. Until that had been done the appropriate teaching materials could not be devised, although we did not realize it at the time. Exactly how all this would be done was determined by the team with the support of a Consultative Committee chaired by Dr Jack Kerr (later Professor Kerr) of Leicester University. We knew that we needed to know much more about children's responses to scientific problems and we were also very conscious of the exciting trends in primary education. We were extremely aware that we had to keep people informed, and one of my first actions was to write to every teacher training institution in the country telling them of our existence and offering to visit and speak with groups of tutors and teachers. Most of them responded with an invitation. A memorable aspect of the meetings was the positive response of teachers, advisers and lecturers in some of the institutes, notably Bristol, Nottingham and London, where they left us in no doubt about their feelings. They told us that if we intended to produce work cards and/or kits (ESSO had recently produced a science kit for preparatory schools) they did not wish to be included in the project's trials since, to quote Bristol '... we left those behind long ago'.

With these pressures in mind and with no great pool of experience in curriculum development on which to model our activities, we began our work. We needed, above all, to know much more about how children would respond to scientific problems. We needed to know about their ability to experiment, to observe, to generalize or find patterns, and to predict, and we had to determine whether science could fit easily and naturally into the most advanced primary education of the day.

We started work in a few schools in a few 'pre-pilot' trial areas, in Kent, Nottingham, Kesteven, Leicester, the North-East, Liverpool and Wiltshire. Experience there enabled us to write the trial teachers' guides which would be used in the twelve trial authorities. Initially, we asked teachers to report their observations of children at work with science. Indeed, of all the projects, this must be the one which was most firmly based with teachers in classrooms. Helped and supported by the team in the field, it was teachers who did the research and pointed the way ahead; the team was there to interpret the teachers' findings and to feed more suggestions and questions into the system. Meanwhile the ground was being prepared for the trials, with an initial conference for representatives from the twelve trial areas, followed by a series of residential courses for teachers, advisers and administrators. The general administration for this programme was undertaken by the newly-formed Schools Council, strongly supported and helped by several HMIs who were officially attached to the various projects, notably Edith Biggs, Gwynneth Jones, Norman Booth and Len Ennever, who later was to direct the 5–13 project.

As the preparations went ahead, it became clear that the pilot areas would benefit from having properly equipped centres where teachers could exchange views, where courses could be based, materials stored and so on, so we made it a requirement that each trial area should establish a teachers' centre. This was a remarkable development which was to have far-reaching effects. The idea was not new; indeed, some areas such as Birmingham and Carlisle already had them. But it gave a fine opportunity for many people in local authorities to set up the centres of quality they had long wanted. By the time the second of the in-service courses was held in Leicester in June 1964 the thinking of the team about the nature of primary science courses had moved on considerably. From presenting teachers with specific problems to solve we moved through a phase of giving them problems arising out of children's questions and ultimately to asking them to observe the environment and define their own problems. This way they had actually to work at their own intellectual level in the way we hoped they would work with children. They were operating at the educational level of the best British primary schools.

This started fierce debates and there was a good deal of resistance from those who held that we should be laying down rules, or at least guidelines, as to what subject-matter should be taught. It also worried those people who were committed to work cards or books, since it is impossible to construct a work card which allows children to ask the initial question to start an investigation. The debate was fierce and filled with emotion, with all sides stoutly defending their positions.

The work went on. The team had developed considerable expertise in running courses and we were soon able to circulate a list to all areas of the names of teachers, advisers, college tutors and others who had reached a high level of competence in the in-service field, and might be invited to organize and assist with local courses. Looking back, it was a remarkable assembly of enthusiasm, talent and expertise. In addition, the information supplied by teachers allowed us to compile a collection of techniques and ploys for overcoming problems of classroom organization, shortage of storage and working space (most classes had over forty pupils, some more than fifty), and about successful and productive starting-points for study. All these, together with the general 'philosophy' of the project which had by now been worked out, were written into the teachers' guides and circulated to the trial areas. It seemed to us to be in accord with the best primary school practice and with existing theories of learning and of child development.

In essence, the project was saying:

(i) An important aspect of primary education is that of helping children learn how to learn.

(ii) In learning, they will employ a number of different strategies, one of which we call science.

(iii) Children do not see the world in terms of adult-conceived disciplines, rather as a totality. But they will ask questions about it, whose solutions will require the application of those specific disciplinary skills, one of which we call science.

(iv) At this early stage of development children learn and understand as a result of concrete experience, and there can be no substitute for this, although learning from books, film and other secondary sources may, indeed should, follow.

(v) Following first-hand experience, children will usually want to communicate their findings in various ways – words, paintings, collage, models or mathematical symbols. However, these expressions of a child's ideas are often more than communication; they are also a child's way of examining his own ideas in a concrete form so as to understand them more fully.

(vi) Choice of subject matter (it seemed to us at the time) will be taken care of through a carefully-planned range of starting-points for study. Appropriate selection will ensure not only a proper balance between the biological and physical sciences but also that every scientific idea of importance (and within the competence of a primary school child) will be met at some time by every child in the primary school. The great emphasis, however, is on the so-called 'processes' – observing, pattern-seeking, hypothesizing and planning experiments (See Chapter 1).

(vii) Children's questions are of paramount importance because
(a) they provide maximum motivation and
(b) the only person who can pitch a question at the exact level of difficulty for anyone is that person himself.

That was the project's philosophy. We knew that it worked in classrooms – very early so far as children were concerned, although teachers needed more help than we appreciated or recognized at the time. The emphasis was on 'processes' and 'environment'. The 'content' would be taken care of by choosing a suitable range of starting-points and by a school staff planning topics so as to avoid duplication and ensure a suitable balance. That was what we actually told the teachers who asked for a scheme of work.

In 1965, thirty or more second phase areas became involved in more trials. In order to convince teachers that it could be done with 'ordinary' children in down-town schools we made a film, *Into Tomorrow*, to be followed by *The Explorers*, which showed the science going on in all age groups in one school. A third film, *Children Observed*, was about children either at play or confronted with unfamiliar materials or situations, and with no teacher intervention. The idea was to show children investigating naturally. One copy was handed to Molly Brearley, Principal of the Froebel Institute, who added a commentary, emphasizing child development. Another had a commentary by Professor Lunzer who looked at it through the eyes of the psychologist. The point many people missed was that it was not a film about teaching, simply about children.

By then, the project was nearing its end, but it was clear that the work had really only just begun. We had established what kind of science was appropriate in primary schools, that it could be achieved with the brightest and the slowest children, including those in ESN schools, in 'streamed' as well as mixed ability groups, and with boys as well as girls. We had shown that, given support, all teachers could achieve it. But now it was important to produce support materials for teachers. I hoped that the Foundation would agree to an extension, my idea being to relinquish the job of Organizer but to stay on as a Consultative Committee member. However, the Foundation did not feel able to continue its support – by then it had spent more than a million pounds on curriculum development – so I went to the Schools Council and presented my case, together with several sheets of questions about primary education, which had emerged from the work of the project. Happily, they decided to fund a new continuation project which eventually became Science 5–13 whose job was to produce support materials. It also launched into the field of evaluation, an area we had avoided largely because we had neither the time nor the resources available, although I had discussed the problem with Dr Margaret Donaldson in Edinburgh.

There was now a painful gap of nine months between the two projects, during which time I tried to maintain links with the second phase areas on two days each week from my home. But it was not very successful and there was some sourness in some second phase areas which had laid out considerable sums of money and felt, understandably, that they were having a raw deal.

Achievements in Retrospect

So what was achieved in 1964–6? Above all, the project had acted as a focus for those who were interested in primary science education, and it provided a forum for discussion and debate on fundamental problems. Out of that debate came a generally accepted idea about the nature of primary school science and its role and place in primary education. That this had been established was made clear in the basic assumptions of Science 5–13 and by the ideas expressed in all of the fourteen conferences arranged by the Inspectorate in 1979. Whilst there were still disagreements about important issues such as the extent to which 'content' mattered or the amount of direction the teacher should employ, nevertheless the Science 5–13 project inherited and accepted most of the basic ideas of the Nuffield Project. They still placed the emphasis on 'processes'; they continued to emphasize the use of the environment, the need for concrete experience and the desirability of starting from children's own questions (see Chapter 14). The Nuffield Project also helped to set a pattern for in-service education. In particular, it recognized that most teachers, because of the way they had been taught, or because they dropped the subject at an early stage, or both, lacked understanding of many scientific ideas, were often unskilled in practical work and had no experience at all of using processes such as experimental design. Yet these were the very things we were asking them to encourage and develop in young children. The pattern, of course, where teachers are asked to work at adult level but in the manner in which the children will work, is still the norm (see Chapter 24). Beyond all doubt, the project established that children really can work scientifically – indeed it seems to be a natural form of learning for them. They rapidly become acute observers, and they have a great facility for designing experiments, many of which are rigorous and elegant. This was true of all children aged between 5 and 13 in all normal schools and in ESN schools, for girls as well as boys. The evidence was overwhelming. The difficulty did not lie with children.

It was teachers who had problems, and yet we established that, with support, all teachers, from the newest probationer to those approaching retirement (for example, a 64-year-old lady in Kent), could undertake the work successfully. What we did not recognize sufficiently was the time-scale involved if success with teachers is to be assured. Indeed, only now are people recognizing that it needs continuing support, often for two or more years, to overcome the fear and insecurity of teachers and to release the undoubted reservoir of potential which seems to exist untapped within the teaching force.

Teacher's centres became essential components of all local education services and by the early seventies there were 600 or more in England and Wales. Their importance lay in the fact that discussion of common problems helped in their solution and that professional exchange was an important contributor to teacher development. I also believe that once the central project had served its purpose of acting as a focus the natural development was towards regional and local activities. The centres encouraged and facilitated such a development. A remarkable change which came about, and which is rarely considered, was the opening up of classrooms to other teachers. When one team member in 1964 took teachers from Leicester to visit teachers in their classrooms in Nottingham it was considered a daring (and perhaps unprofessional?) experiment. By the late 1960s such visits were becoming not only commonplace but also a highly desirable part of ATO/DES courses. I believe that the sharing of ideas, the admission by teachers that there were problems, difficulties and failures and the willingness to discuss those problems openly, marked a major step forward in the professional development of teachers. By its very nature, a national project encourages that type of development.

However, what was not so clear at the time was the limited effectiveness of the printed word in implementing curriculum change. Like all other projects at the time, we believed that if we collected information and advice from teachers in schools and wrote it down clearly other teachers would read it and act upon it. How wrong we were. For a variety of reasons, most teachers do not read the teachers' guides and, if they do, they tend only to read the headlines and not the small print. The result is misunderstanding – for instance, the project's insistence on children's own investigations of concrete materials was often interpreted as 'fill the room with materials and turn them loose so that they can teach themselves'. But even if teachers read it all carefully it seems that translating what has been read into action is an unsurmountable obstacle unless continuing practical help is available. Yet we continue to produce printed words in formidable quantities. It seems that curriculum developers never learn! Probably we should apply to teachers the philosophy expressed by John Dewey, and which the project adopted as its basic approach to teaching children: 'Children are people. They grow into tomorrow only as they live today.'

References

Publications from the Nuffield Junior Science Project

Source books:
    (1967) *Teacher's Guide 1*, Collins.
    (1967) *Teacher's Guide 2*, Collins.
    (1967) *Animals and Plants*, Collins.
    (1967) *Apparatus*, Collins.

Background booklets:
    (1967) *Autumn into Winter*, Collins.
    (1967) *Science and History*, Collins.
    (1967) *Mammals in the Classroom*, Collins.

Associated publication:
    BAINBRIDGE, J.W., STOCKDALE, R. and WASTNEDGE, E.R. (1970) *Junior Science Source Book*, Collins.

14   Science 5–13: Reflections on Its Significance

Sheila Parker-Jelly

Editorial Introduction. *The Science 5–13 Project was set up in 1967 for five years and later extended to permit further work on dissemination. It was jointly sponsored by the Schools Council, the Nuffield Foundation and the Scottish Education Department. It was established to consolidate and extend the work on primary science teaching initiated by the Nuffield Junior Science Project (see Chapter 13). Its aim was to assist teachers in helping children, through discovery methods, to gain experience and understanding of their environment and to develop their powers of thinking effectively about it. This was done through the identification and development of topics or areas related to a framework of objectives appropriate to children's stages of educational development. In all, about 150 objectives were delineated, and each was related to (a) one of three stages of development in children (Stage 1: transition from Piaget's stage of intuitive thinking to his stage of concrete operations; Stage 2: the concrete operational stage; Stage 3: transition between concrete operations and thinking with the aid of abstractions), and to (b) one of eight general aims for science teaching (observing, exploring and ordering observations; developing basic concepts and logical thinking; posing questions and devising experiments or investigations to answer them; acquiring knowledge and learning skills; communicating; interpreting findings critically; and appreciating patterns and relationships).*

The project team produced a series of units for teachers on subject areas such as Time, Metal *and* Minibeasts, *and on themes such as* Change, Like *and* Unlike. *Each unit consisted of one or more illustrated books and gave advice, starting-points and background information. The publication,* Early Experiences, *was designed especially for those teaching younger primary pupils. The basic project thinking was set out in an introductory book,* With Objectives in Mind.

Early trials involved groups of teachers in twelve LEA areas in England, which had been designated in connection with the Nuffield Junior Science Project; the number of pilot areas was later increased. (Arrangements for Scotland were made on a slightly different pattern.) Schools and teachers' centres in non-pilot areas were free to take part in trials but it was only in pilot areas that the evaluation process designed by the project staff was conducted. The process of evaluation, reported by Harlen in Science 5–13: A Formative Evaluation *(Macmillan Education, 1975), was used to further the project's long-term aim of helping teachers to identify their own objectives and think creatively about their work, as well as helping teachers to recognize their pupils' stages of educational development.*

Any reflection on the significance of the Science 5–13 Project must address two important questions: significance for whom? and significance in what context? These questions are to an extent interrelated but for convenience each will be given a distinct focus and then re-examined in a final consideration of ways in which with hindsight the project might have achieved a greater significance.

Significance for Whom?

If asked this question during the project's lifetime it would have been a simple task to identify those for whom the project *should* have significance. The list would include teachers, people concerned with the support of teachers in their working situation, pre- and in-service teacher educators, HMI and, perhaps less obviously, children and their parents, publishers and others currently engaged in similar curriculum development work. Such a list is still pertinent more than a decade later but to it must be added another category of people for whom the project has acquired significance, namely those interested in general issues of curriculum development and in what is sometimes called curriculum theory. Quite clearly Science 5–13, as other projects, has a varied receiving clientele: less obvious is its particular significance for differing people within that clientele.

The remit of the project was summarized succinctly by Len Ennever, the Project Director, as being 'to help teachers help children learn science' and here, immediately and obviously, teachers are identified as the project's main target. Readers interested in a detailed chronology of how the team set about helping teachers and so making the project significant to them will find events fully documented by Harlen;[1] discussion here centres on a retrospective examination of the nature of this significance which will be developed by considering the interaction between teachers and the project during its lifetime and also certain post-project events.

From the outset the 5–13 team held the view that practising teachers should be actively involved in developing the project and, as Harlen records, very many teachers helped to shape the nature of trial materials, the way the trials were carried out and the revisions necessary to produce final publications. Undoubtedly for teachers involved in such tasks the project had considerable significance at the time, but significance of what kind? and for how long was it retained? These are difficult questions to answer with certainly, as is the question of the extent to which the project has significance for other teachers not involved in its developmental phase. Nevertheless, they are important questions and worthy of at least speculative comment.

When considering teacher involvement with Science 5–13, it is important to note that the project was trying to help teachers by offering guidance on two fronts. At what might be called the pragmatic level it was producing materials directly concerned with the practicalities of teaching primary science.

Thus, acknowledging problems of classroom implementation, a strong emphasis was placed on obvious teacher-perceived needs such as ways of making a start, ideas for children's activities, guidance about the resources required and, to a lesser extent, help with background knowledge of science in order to generate increased confidence. But such pragmatic concerns were embedded in an organizing structure derived from the main thrust of the project which was to offer teachers guidance at a reflective level in order that they might, by 'working with objectives in mind', gain deeper understanding of what was seen to be desirable for children of differing stages of development to achieve through their work in science and, through such understanding, gain confidence to cope better with the practicalities of teaching and at the same time improve the quality of their planning implementation and evaluative activities. In a sense, a reflective concern for objectives was the project's message: pragmatic concern its medium.

Whilst it is pertinent to separate the pragmatic from the reflective in understanding the project's intent, it must be stressed that such a separation did not characterize the project's interaction with teachers in its developmental phase nor was it intended in the way in which other teachers would perceive its published materials. For this reason any examination of the project's significance for teachers must be based on the nature of their response to its intentions concerning pragmatic-reflective relationships. To advance the analysis it is useful to identify three sets of responding teachers, distinguishable by the nature of their contract with the project's ideas.

Two sets of teachers helped the project during its developmental phase. One set had frequent sustained contact with team members in the task of producing first draft material that would be tried out by a second set of teachers in trial schools. These 'first-set responders' were small in number but became great in their enthusiasm for the idea of working with objectives in mind, even though the concept was new to them and in many cases initially quite difficult to grasp. The value of an objectives framework for the practicalities of teaching science became firmly established in their thinking and it acquired significance not only in relation to their own classroom practice but also in the recommendations they made for helping other teachers to work with objectives in mind. Indeed, the strong commitment of the first set of teachers to the objectives thrust is reflected in the decision to publish in full a statement of objectives for children learning science, originally intended solely as an internal working document, and in the prominence given to objectives as an organizing focus for the early trial units which conveyed the project's pragmatic-reflective intent to teachers in trial schools. Over 500 teachers took part in trial work monitored by the project. These 'second-set responders' derived their understanding of Science 5–13 from direct or transmitted involvement with team members at a short pre-trial residential course, from the materials on trial, from infrequent contact with project personnel who visited them in their schools during the trials and from contact with the project's LEA representatives and locally initiated activities organized to foster the work of the project. The response of trial teachers was more varied than that shown by the first-set responders. Evaluation of early units showed that, contrary to the expectations of the first set of teachers, many trial teachers found the treatment of objectives somewhat confusing and in some cases it was clear that its organization formed an unintended barrier to guidance offered on the pragmatic front. Accordingly, later trial units were revised substantially in order to communicate to teachers a more obvious concern for the pragmatic whilst adopting what might be described as an objectives-by-stealth approach to the reflective. The change of strategy affected the way many second-set teachers interpreted the project's intent and made judgements about its significance. As Harlen records, it became possible to identify trial teacher response along a satisfied-dissatisfied dimension and it is interesting to tease from this dimension relationships between the pragmatic and a reflective concern for objectives.

The writer's interpretation of teacher response to the project in its developmental phase is that supportive project and LEA structures were vital for successful implementation. Where teachers had strong support many increased considerably their confidence and practical competence in teaching science; favourable response to the objectives content was, however, largely dependent on the extent to which teachers employed, or were willing to develop, child-centred methods and the extent to which they had sustained contact with people able to communicate the practical advantages of working with objectives in mind.

Turning now to the third set of teachers, namely those who relate to the project after its funded life, it is sensible to examine the significance of Science 5–13 in both quantitative and qualitative terms. How many 'third-set responders' have been affected by the work of the project and to what extent is there a match between project intent and current teacher activity? Unfortunately, no comprehensive and definitive evidence exists for answering these questions although they may be approached by considering certain indicators. For example, the Schools Council Impact and Take Up Project[2] found that in visits to 740 randomly selected schools nearly 70 per cent of teachers who could be expected to do so never used the Science 5–13 Project and the postal returns from 1146 schools gave a similar figure of around 65 per cent. This is not encouraging evidence of the project's significance for teachers at large but it is supported by smaller local surveys such as that of Bradley[3] and my own survey of all primary schools in one LEA.[4] Yet the sales figures for Science 5–13 currently stand at well over a million copies, of which 60 per cent relate to the home market; in publishing terms the project is highly successful. Interestingly, the sales figures peak in 1977–78 and so invite speculation on current interpretations of the Impact and Take-Up data acquired before the peak; was the impact of Science 5–13 investigated too soon, given the acknowledged slow progress of any innovation through the school system, did the enquiry itself stimulate a new sales impetus and to what extent is there a relationship between Science 5–13 sales and HMI activity relating to the 1978 survey of primary education in England (see Chapter 4)?[5] Issues of this kind point the complexity of obtaining hard evidence regarding the project's current significance for teachers, and three crucial questions remain unanswered and are likely to remain so: How many teachers currently know about Science 5–13? How many of these make use of its products? Of these, how many use the project in ways intended by the team?

Whilst there is a dearth of hard evidence about the project's significance for primary teachers at large, there is considerable evidence to show that it has significance for other people. In quantitative terms project influence has spread from the initial development team to encompass a variety of interested people whose work is likely to affect teacher response. It is rare, for example, to find an initial training course for primary teachers that does not make use of Science 5–13 materials. 'Method' courses include the publications in their bibliographies and most make practical use of the units in student workshop activity. Additionally, and as a result of the academic interest of people such as Sockett,[6] Stenhouse,[7] Lawton,[8] Blenkin and Kelly[9] and Open University contributors,[10] many students encounter the project in theory courses concerned with general issues of curriculum development. A similar pattern emerges in relation to in-service courses available to practising teachers (see Chapter 24). Clearly Science 5–13 has acquired significance in the content of many courses organized by people concerned with pre- and in-service teacher education – a significance likely to rub off in their less structured teacher contacts. At the same time the influence of the project can be detected in a variety of publication that include policy statements from the Association for Science Education,[11] APU science reports,[12] accounts of non-science-specific curriculum development of the kind recorded by Tempest,[13] Blyth,[14] and Ashton,[15] and in science-focussed curriculum development publications such as Harlen's *Match and Mismatch*[16] and Richards' Learning through Science Project (see Chapter 15).[17] At a more circumscribed level project influence can be seen in a further range of material such as the Starting Science Materials[18] and the Sciencewise Series[19] produced to help teachers with the practical task of implementing science. Quantitatively the project's significance for others in a position to influence teachers has increased considerably since its funded life; qualitatively the situation is obscure.

In qualitative terms the significance of the project for others likely to affect the work of teachers requires an understanding of how different people mediate Science 5–13 intentions in attempts to improve the quality of teacher action. Some, believing that the best help for teachers is to give them increased confidence and competence in the practicalities of teaching science, use the project for its pragmatic guidance and ignore, or considerably underplay, the objectives thrust. An example of this form of mediation would be LEA activity concerned with providing resource kits for teaching Science 5–13 or structured work cards for children based on the practical suggestions of the units. Whilst such action can improve classroom activity in the sense that children may as a consequence extend their science work, the mediating role is one that denies to a large extent the reflective thrust of the project because much of the thinking about the appropriate selection and development of children's activities has been done by others for the teachers concerned. This is not to denigrate mediation of this kind but to point out that it has an incomplete match with the total Science 5–13 intent and in these terms the project's qualitative influence is restricted, however much it has contributed to the improvement of teaching at a pragmatic level. Similarly, mediation of the kind that focusses on the objectives thrust without relating it to the reality of improving children's experience represents a reduced response to project intent, however successful it may be in helping teachers in their grasp of quite complex curriculum issues. Undoubtedly, various forms of mediation currently exist between the pragmatically-focussed and objectives-focussed extremes and the overall significance of Science 5–13 must be judged against the context in which such mediation occurs.

Significance in What Contex?

Science 5–13, like any other project, has an associated time dimension of preceding events which shaped its thinking, transactional activities that occurred during its lifetime and post-project happenings consequent on its work; placement in time is important in the retrospective appraisal of the project in any context and particularly so within the context of the general development of primary school science and, relatedly, in the context of general issues of curriculum development.

When the project was established in 1967 its terms of reference[20] were shaped significantly by the preceding work of the Nuffield Junior Science Project (see Chapter 13).[21] The main direction of the new project was seen as 'extending the lines of development initiated by the current Nuffield project whilst paying particular attention to the needs of older junior pupils and pupils in the early years of the secondary schools.' Its principal aim was to be 'the identification and development, at appropriate levels, of topics or areas of science related to a framework of concepts appropriate to the age of the pupils', and its development was to focus on the need 'to assist teachers to help children, through discovery methods, to gain experience and understanding of the environment, and to develop their powers of thinking effectively about it.' The team was given complete freedom to work out appropriate means for implementing the proposals and the significance of its subsequent activity must be judged against the contextual climate of the times.

In the late sixties science received very little attention in the curriculum of primary schools despite earlier efforts of the Ministry of Education,[22] the British Association,[23] the National Froebel Foundation,[24] the ASE[25] the Oxford Primary Science Project (see Chapter 12)[26] and the Nuffield Junior Science Project (see Chapter 13). The overall picture was extremely depressing but did contain within it some excellent examples of science work (see Chapter 2). The problem faced by the small team in the early days of Science 5–13 was that of deciding how best to tackle its terms of reference given the general situation in schools. Initial work towards this end involved reflections on Harlen's evaluation of the Oxford Junior Project,[27] study of the Crossland evaluation of Nuffield Junior Science,[28] a close scrutiny of relevant curriculum development in the United States[29] and general discussion of appropriate action that was based on the particular past experience of individual team members. What emerged was a commitment to the philosophy of the Nuffield project and a conviction that its further implementation would be best fostered by offering teachers some underlying child–related structure to their work. Science 5–13 was to acquire significance in the development of primary science as the first major project to offer teachers a child-based structure as a framework for child-centred activity.

The child-related structure of the project did not emerge overnight. At first efforts were directed towards the framework of concepts deemed desirable in the terms of reference, and recollection of this period in the project's life is one of intense mental activity associated with attempts to produce a hierarchical/network map of the concepts involved in various science topics appropriate to children in the 5–13 age range. At the same time, and following the evaluator's earlier experience with the Oxford Junior Project, team members were attempting to thrash out exactly what it was they were trying to achieve and this line of thinking, which was consistent with the curriculum design theory of the time, turned the project's structural focus towards objectives and resulted in a statement of objectives for children learning science that was matched to a Piagetian view of child development (see Chapter 10). The framework for the project became one based on objectives organized to accommodate the work of Piaget; in this respect Science 5–13 became significant as the first primary project to adopt the approach in its guidance for teachers.

Reactions to the decision to promote an objective framework have been examined in the previous section, but the significance of Science 5–13 in the general development of primary school science warrants further comment concerning the two major science projects that stem from its work. Science 5–13 extended the Nuffield Project by introducing what might be described as analytical pedagogical theory in its guidance for teachers. It required of them a high level of conceptualization about the process of helping children learn science whilst at the same time requiring them to take from its practical guidance that which they judged to be relevant. In short, its target teacher model was a highly sophisticated one and experience has shown that the expectations were too high for teachers in general. Some did find the conceptualization appropriate and valuable: many did not. Many were helped by the project's practical suggestions but a considerable number found them deficient in direct help with organizational problems. From such experience the subsequent projects emerged. Match and Mismatch developed largely from the favourable response of trial teachers to evaluative checklist activities associated with 'working with objectives in mind' and so extends the conceptual pedagogy of the project (see Chapters 1 and 8); Learning through Science developed largely as an attempt to remedy the project's limitations in helping with particular problems of organizing science in a primary school and so extends Science 5–13 on a pragmatically-focussed front (see Chapter 15).

Undoubtedly, Science 5–13 has made a major contribution to the development of primary school science and it will be interesting to see the direction of new work in the field; most probably it will have a great concern for concepts than that shown by 5–13 and the two projects it has generated.

Turning now to the significance of Science 5–13 in the context of general issues of curriculum development, it is appropriate to reflect on both issues of curriculum design and strategies for curriculum change. The project's design model is a variant of the classical planning-by-objectives approach of theorists such as Tyler[30] and Taba,[31] departing from it in certain significant ways. For example, the team did not embark on a systematic formulation of objectives as a necessary first step in planning, rather it groped its way towards an objectives framework in a diffuse manner, having a view of objectives as useful guidelines rather than prescriptions for action. For this reason, Science

5–13 objectives are stated at a level of generality not acceptable to the 'purist' school. This was deliberate team policy because specific objectives would make the project too mechanistic to be acceptable to teachers and, critically, because more specific treatment would deny the firmly held conviction that teachers should be responsible for decisions about the detailed practice of their classrooms. The generality of the objectives presented certain problems of meaning and associated difficulties concerning the extent to which they could generate effective evaluative procedures, but since the objectives were stated in behavioural terms the project acquired significance for many in helping them move from considering science solely in terms of what children might do to thinking about what it was desirable they should achieve and how such achievement might be recognized. Early units attempted to convey this message by the classical approach of selecting appropriate objectives for each developmental stage and then linking them directly to learning experiences likely to help children achieve the objectives. However, following trial use, subsequent units abandoned this classic sequential approach and Science 5–13 became significant in adopting a more flexible model which recognized differing planning styles in the relationship between objectives and activities. [32]

A further significant design feature of the project is the nature and role of evaluation in its work. Science 5–13 was the first primary project to have an evaluator as a team member and, as a consequence, a rigorous formative evaluation programme. Details of the programme are set out in Harlen's evaluative report, but the significant activities would seem to be the extent to which they involved practising teachers in understanding and enjoying the use of quite complex procedures and the experience gained which turned thinking from a classic psychometric mode of focussing evaluation on the children's achievement of objectives to a more open and varied transactional activity involving extensive participant observation.

In terms of strategies for change the project's activities are best described as a variant of the RDD change model. [33] Thus a central team produced materials that were trialed, revised and made available for diffusion through the system. However, unlike most projects of its time, it made considerable use of teacher expertise to augment central team thinking and its trial materials were made freely available to others not involved in development work. This latter and apparently trivial variant of the model became significant in the diffusion of project ideas. Nevertheless, despite the rudimentary diffusion network of LEA representatives, events have shown that the spread of Science 5–13 was disappointingly slow and patchy. This is understandable since, operating in the climate of the time, the project did not build into its work a planned dissemination programme of the kind recognized as necessary by the Schools Council in 1972, [34] although it did approach the dissemination problem by developing a unit, *Understanding Science 5/13*, designed to help with uptake barriers. Unfortunately, the unit remains unpublished and one can only speculate about its likely affect as a dissemination aid. What is clear when reflecting on the project's significance in the context of strategies for curriculum change is that the project gave insufficient attention to the large-scale planned spread and uptake of its work, although it did stimulate significant instances of curriculum development at local level which in some cases promoted change across the primary curriculum.

Could the Project Have Achieved Greater Significance?

The old adage that it is easy to be wise after the event cannot be applied too strictly in reflections on ways by which Science 5–13 might have achieved greater significance. For, whereas it is reasonably easy to identify causal factors that account for the limited uptake of its full intent, it is very difficult, even with current understanding, to know how such barriers might have been overcome. What follows represents the with-hindsight speculation of one team member concerning features of the project which account for its restricted significance, namely its view of teachers, the form in which it offered them a structure for their science work and the rudimentary nature of its dissemination strategies; the speculation is recorded in the form of questions intended to promote reader response.

Was the project's view of teachers appropriate given the wide variation of teacher attitudes and aptitudes?
Was it a mistake to produce material that had to be all things for all men?
Might it have been better in a project centred on individual differences in children to acknowledge more explicitly individual difference in teachers?
Would it have been useful to promote a staged model of teacher development (of the kind introduced in the unpublished unit *Understanding Science 5/13*) in which attention to objectives developed from considerable experience with pragmatic concerns?
Might the project have made more impact on schools if it had not rejected work cards for children as running counter to its philosophy?

Was the project's framework of objectives the most appropriate one for tackling the problem of 'structure' in science?
To what extent was the project promoting an objectives thrust before the time was ripe?
Given that objectives *per se* were acceptable to some, was the invitation to work with objectives in mind totally unrealistic given the 150 or so identified by the project?
Might it have been better to restrict the number of objectives or would this have promoted an over-simplified view of the complexity of the task?
Would a simpler and more restricted categorization of intent for children (say, into knowledge, skills and attitudes) have achieved greater success?
Might the focus on children's achievement in science have had greater meaning for teachers if the project had paid more attention to 'development norms' in particular situations?

Was the project's dissemination strategy the best it could have achieved?
Was the project's LEA network of representatives used to full capacity?
Might it have been profitable to involve the representatives in a more conceptual treatment of dissemination problems?
Would it have been useful to identify more clearly what constituted an appropriate supportive network for teachers undertaking science 5–13 work and so match local provision against an optimum?
Is there an optimum?

To what extent must local circumstances influence the way a project is utilized?

Could the project in its lifetime have undertaken the dissemination procedures recommended by the Impact and Uptake Project?

Is there a lesson to be learnt from the overseas use of the project where several states have provided each school with Science 5–13 publications and expectations about their implementation?

Does the real implementation problem reside in the paradox that teacher freedom to decide what to do in the classroom carries with it freedom to decide not to give science the serious consideration.that is given to language and maths work?

Answers to these and similar questions must remain speculative. Perhaps the most fitting final comment on the significance of Science 5–13 is that it did what all science should do, namely it adopted a working hypothesis (for improving primary school science) to test within the current scene; that it is found lacking in some aspects of its work is undeniable but equally the extent of the project's success has more than justified the large sum of money invested.

Notes

1 MARTEN, W. (1975) *Science 5–13: A Formative Evaluation*: Schools Council Research Studies. Macmillan Education.

2 STEADMAN, S.D. *et al.* (1978) *An Enquiry into the Impact and Take-up of Schools Council Funded Activities*. Schools Council Publications.

3 BRADLEY, H. (1976) *A Survey of Science Teaching in Primary Schools*. Univ. of Nottingham School of Education.

4 PARKER, S. (1978) *A Survey of Science in Avon Primary Schools* (unpublished).

5 DES (1978) *Primary Education in England*, HMSO.

6 SOCKETT, H. (1976) *Designing the Curriculum* Open Books.

7 STENHOUSE, L. (1975) *An Introduction to Curriculum Research & Development* Heinemann.

8 LAWTON, D. *et al.* (1978) *Theory and Practice of Curriculum Studies*. Routledge & Kegan Paul.

9 BLENKIN, G. and KELLY, A. (1981) *The Primary Curriculum* Harper & Row.

10 See for example HARLEN W. (1978) 'Science 5–13 Project' in GOLBY M. *et al Curriculum Design*.

11 For example ASE (1974) *Science and Primary Education* Paper No 1.

12 For example APU *Science Projects Report* 1977–78.

13 TEMPEST, N.R. (1974) *Teaching Clever Children 7–11* Routledge & Kegan Paul.

14 BLYTH, A. (1973) 'History, geography & social studies 8–13: A second generation Project' in TAYLOR, P.H. & WALTON, J. *The Curriculum: Research Inovation and Change*. Ward Lork Educational.

15 ASHTON, P. *et al.* (1975) *Aims into Practice in the Primary School*. Univ. of London Press.

16 See Match & Mismatch Publications. Oliver & Boyd 1977.

17 See *Chelsea College Project* (1978) *Teaching Primary Science* MacDonald Educational.

18 SCHOOLS COUNCIL (1980) *Learning Though Science* MacDonald Ed.

19 DERBYSHIRE SCIENCE PROJECT (1976) *Starting Science* Macmillan Educational.

20 PARKER, S. and WARD, A. (1978) *Sciencewise* (Teacher Books) Nelson.

21 NUFFIELD FOUNDATION (1967) *Junior Science Project* Collins.
22 MINISTRY OF EDUCATION (1961) *Science in the Primary School* Pamphlet 42. HMSO.
23 BRITISH ASSOCIATION (1962) *The Place of Science in Primary Education* BAAS.
24 FRÒEBEL FOUNDATION (1966) *Children Learning Through Scientific Interests* NFF.
25 ASSOCIATION FOR SCIENCE EDUCATION (1966) *Children Learning Through Science* ASE.
26 See REDMAN, S. *et al.* (1969) *An Approach to Primary Science* Macmillan.
27 HARLEN, W. (1967) *An Evaluation of the Development of Scientific Concepts in Children*

30 TYLER, R.W. (1949) *Basic Principles of Curriculum & Instruction.* University of Chicago Press.
31 TABA, H. (1962) *Curriculum Development: Theory and Practice.* Harcourt, Brace & World.
32 See for example *Science 5/13. With Objectives in Mind* MacDonald Educational 1972.
33 HAVELOCK, R.S. (1971) The Utilization of Educational Research & Development. *Br. J. Ed. Tech* 2 (2).
34 Schools Council Working Party on Dissemination 1972–73.

15   Children Learning through Science: A Report★

Roy Richards

Initiatives

During the past twenty years a great deal has been done to help teachers promote science in primary schools. The materials from curriculum development projects and the wealth of commercial publications available, of which the best are very good indeed, constitute a rich and valuable resource for teachers. It is, therefore, an irritation to hear critics claim that such materials have not been successful. Many teachers have proved them so through their vital, exciting and worthwhile practice. There is no question that science can be done by primary school teachers, the problem is getting all to do it! Compared with work in language and mathematics, science is much more meagrely treated. It is often thought of as an optional extra. Why? One answer is contained in an observation made in the Primary Survey (DES, 1978), 'the general impression given by heads' statements was that only a small minority recognized the important contribution which science could make to children's intellectual development' (Chapter 4). This is at the crux of the matter. Those teachers who do science well know how essential it is to a young child's development. They see their children improving in observational skills, asking questions, thinking out ways to find answers, discussing and arguing and putting to the test, perceiving patterns and relationships and communicating often excitedly and vitally with others. They see their children developing in curiosity, prepared to listen and argue and yet maintain an open-mindedness, prepared to cooperate, show responsibility and persevere when things are difficult. They would not want any less for their children. Not only do they help give their charges a greater insight into the world around them and 'tools' for investigating that world, but, importantly for this nation, they send on to the secondary school children with attitudes formed and forming that may stay with them throughout their lives.

A School Policy

How can we persuade more teachers to be like these? This is a major task facing the Schools Council Learning Through Science Project. The project

★This is a later version of an article first published in *Education 3–13*, 8, 2, 1980 pp. 4–7.

team made a beginning by involving a large number of teachers (fifty regional groups) in thinking out a strategy whereby teachers might formulate a policy that was pertinent to their own children, their own school and their own school environment.

What should such a policy contain? In the first instance, almost all the groups reported that any guidelines should make clear what was meant by science with children of primary school age. It was a cry from practitioners whose understanding of young children made it abundantly clear to them that the image of science as an activity carried out by white-coated laboratory workers was not applicable to their children. As equally inapplicable was the idea that science was a great conglomeration of facts that their children had to absorb like gluttonous Billy Bunters. Yet what was 'science' if not the stereotyped image that many people hold? Wynne Harlen (1978) captures their views when she argues that 'our central concern in primary science should be to develop the abilities to observe, raise questions, propose enquiries to answer questions, experiment or investigate, find patterns in observations, reason systematically and logically, communicate findings and apply learning.' There was thus general agreement that a school policy should begin by making a clear statement of the aims and objectives or reasons – call them what you will – of why a school staff wants to pursue science with its children.

The next step is to consider how these aims are to be achieved. What *experiences* can be put before children? Where can teachers get help? This, of course, is where the very large amount of literature available can be put to good use. It is a relatively straightforward matter for individuals or, perhaps better still, small groups of teachers to scrutinize source books and take up the topics they suggest or use them as a source reference for an original theme decided upon within the school.

Interestingly, a number of the groups of teachers that reported back to the Learning Through Science Project thought that there were major underlying themes that should be tackled during a child's primary school years, though these could not be organized into a tight four-or-seven-year syllabus. Put very simply and briefly, teachers seemed concerned that children should know *about living things*, about the cycle of plant and animal life and should be concerned not only with looking after living things but with making comparisons, measurements and carrying out simple testing procedures where these were appropriate and proper. Certainly everyone seemed convinced that children should know *something about themselves*, about the ways parts of their bodies work, and testing here was thought to lead to many opportunities for discussion and questioning. Again, there was universal agreement that children should investigate *their immediate environment*. Weather studies and other seasonal changes were thought to be of great intrinsic interest to children and important in involving them in collecting data and looking for patterns and relationships. Energy and energy studies took their place not only because world attention has focussed on such issues, but because they embody basic scientific experiences that lead to an understanding of profound scientific concepts. Understanding of the nature and properties of materials (beginning in the infant school with active exploration of sand and water, paint and clay) was felt to be vital, too. Working through topics or setting out basic themes to run through the years of a child's primary education were seen as two feasible ways of proceeding. Other teachers – especially teachers of infant children – often favoured taking their science from everyday situations, such as creative play in home bays, cooking or construction work. Yet other teachers reported that an excellent way to consider what experiences to put before children was to make maximum use of the school and the school grounds.

The besetting problem facing many teachers is not the substance of what is to be done, but how on earth can one teacher organize it with thirty or more children? In primary education the class is usually largely or completely taught by one teacher and this can give a flexibility often denied to those operating in the secondary sphere. Teachers can and do use a variety of teaching styles and patterns of organization. Any school-based guidance on organization must recognize this fact. Experienced teachers vary their preparation to suit different patterns of organization. Teachers inexperienced in presenting scientific activities might well be advised when starting off to limit the number and the range of their initial investigations. (The rest of the class can carry on with routine activities that are more easily managed.) With experience, the number and range of activities simultaneously made available to children can increase. Certainly, there is much to be said for staff discussion on methods of organization and for teachers to spend some time observing and discussing the ways their colleagues proceed, especially where these differ from their own.

Another important aspect of any policy should be a proper consideration of how to *evaluate* children's progress and how to keep records of such progress (see Chapter 8). The main question about the form of record kept seems to be whether it should list activities or development. Keeping records of activities is useful as an *aide-memoire* to prevent unnecessary repetition during a child's school career. It is, however, not sufficient on its own, for it gives no indication whether a child is improving in observational skills, getting better at devising tests and identifying variables, attaining basic concepts and so on. The subject is not a simple one and points to keeping different records for various purposes.

Science with its emphasis on 'things' demands careful teacher preparation, but the dividends that come are compound. There is nothing that acts as a surer catalyst to children at the concrete operational stage of thought than confrontation with an object or objects. It is the 'I, thou and it' of science – teacher, child and 'thing' must interact.

Talking of 'things' raises the question of *resources*. Careful organization and planning are needed for purchasing, collecting, storing and maintaining specimens, equipment and materials. Materials and apparatus will be needed for:

- arousing and maintaining children's curiosity;
- collection of specimens and data;
- housing animals;
- the development of enquiry skills;
- the scientific aspects of topic work;
- aiding communication.

Again, the project team has involved a number of teacher groups throughout the country in framing a text (Richards *et al.*, 1982). The result is a handbook that gives information on what to collect, buy and make, and how to store and organize resources. It contains practical suggestions and detailed examples of what can be achieved, including case studies of work done in schools. There is also a list of suppliers, and an extensive bibliography. Used in tandem with a school science policy it should help school staff to lay firm foundations for their science curriculum (see also Chapter 21).

Thus the way forward, the project team suggests, is for a school staff to sit down and argue out its own policy for science and get it implemented. In all this, the role of the headteacher is crucial. He or she is the main provider of support, encouragement and guidance in the development of scientific education. Our other published text lays down a strategy whereby any primary or middle school can determine its own policy for science (Richards *et al.*, 1980). Our hope is that this national initiative will be complemented by action at local level and that all schools who have not so far done so will seriously consider forming a school science policy. It is also hoped that LEA inspectors and advisers will use the text on their in-service courses.

Pupil Material

The main aspect of the project's work has been the production of pupil materials. The challenges in writing such material have been many! It would have been relatively easy to write prescriptions of things to be done, but this would scarcely have been conducive to getting children to show initiative, to think out good and fair ways to test things, to challenge ideas and interpretations with the purpose of reaching deeper understanding. In other words, it would probably have negated the whole idea of getting children to 'develop an enquiring mind and a scientific approach to problems' as spelled out by the Science 5–13 Project. It would even have been dubious whether such a prescription would teach facts about science, since tasks carried out by rote often lack the basic understanding that intellectual involvement brings. We accepted that children needed to develop certain abilities, attitudes and concepts, but many questions went through our minds as we began to write the first pupil material: What core of experience do we include? What concepts is it to embody? How can such experience help children develop abilities and attitudes? What is a reasonable amount of material to offer children at any one time? Should there be an order of presentation? How can we stretch the able and the less able child?

A start was made by delineating certain areas of experience commonly featured in schools teaching primary science. The recommendations made by our regional groups of teachers on the major underlying themes they thought valuable for primary science were borne strongly in mind as this was done. To the list thus formed were added two areas of experience that the project team felt were of great interest and importance to young children, and yet were sadly neglected in the curriculum – studies of the sky and space, and a study of rocks and minerals. The resultant list of units is:

Ourselves	Sky and space
Colour	All around
Materials	Out of doors

Moving I	Electricity
Moving II	Which and what?
Earth	Investigations

Each unit has been presented as a series of twenty-four cards, each card being four-sided and A5 in size.

The material helps put problems in the paths of children and gives help to the teacher on ways of encouraging and guiding the enquiries. In essence, each card presents a mini-topic for children to pursue which is so written as to be very flexible in use. Any one page tries to keep to one basic idea, but the aim of each four-page card is to try and present a unit of work which allows children flexibility in the way they tackle the task in hand. Often it leaves scope for children to bring in new ideas. Our intention has been to present each card in such a way that the work could be attempted at many levels and leave scope for children at varying stages of development to take things as far as they could. In practice this has worked. Children of all abilities seem both able and willing to take up the starting-points. In no cases have there been any real difficulties with the experiences suggested; this is not surprising since we have seen many of them work in schools in the past. The cards have not been presented in any set order, nor has there been any intention that a child or group of children should necessarily complete everything set out on an individual card. Work on a particular card can be done by an individual, a group or by the whole class. The teachers' notes explain the aims of particular cards, discuss where children may find difficulty, tell how the tasks in hand may be taken further and give additional information.

The material is for children who have reached Stage 2 of the developmental sequence set out by the Science 5–13 Project and are moving towards Stage 3, that is, those who learn best through working with things concretely through to those who are, albeit tentatively, beginning to think about things abstractly.

It is important to point out that, as with all the project's work, these units have been first produced as trial versions, tried out in schools nationally and then rewritten in the light of teacher comment and observation by the project team. Often rewriting has had to be extensive and we are enormously indebted to the very many teachers, headteachers, advisers and inspectors who have given much time and effort to helping us make the material as astringent as possible. The resultant body of material is not only comprehensive but also sufficiently detailed to allow teachers to pursue studies in depth with their children if any particular theme or topic engenders such treatment.

'Slow Learners'

Another aspect of the project's work concerns the problems of slow learning children. The Warnock Committee (DES, 1978) proposed that all children with special educational needs, apart from the gifted, should be described as 'children with learning difficulties'. Their difficulties range from serious physical, mental and behavioural disabilities to those caused by mild temporary problems which may need remedial help or special attention from a class teacher. The majority of children with learning difficulties are in ordinary classes and every teacher in primary and middle schools is likely to teach such children. We have borne this in mind as we have framed a series of teacher guides to help with the teaching of science to these children. The guides are complementary to the pupil material produced by the project team and references are made to those project cards for children which could easily be modified by teachers for their children with learning difficulties. The teacher guides attempt to bring out the processes of science and are based on topics which arise from children's interests or everyday surroundings, and integrate well with the rest of the curriculum. Short practical investigations are suggested which often repeat the same experience in a number of ways to reinforce children's understanding. Simple and quick recording methods are suggested and some discussion points are put forward to help the teacher bring out patterns and relationships. Some of the guides are concerned with a child finding out things about himself; 'Me and my shadow' is an example of a title in this series. The other guides are on a range of topics: 'Batteries, Bulbs and Magnets and 'Weather' are two examples. These guides in no way constitute a course or syllabus and are merely set out as examples of a method of approach to science with children who have learning difficulties.

Slide/Tape Sequences

Finally, the project is also concerned with the production of slide/tape sequences for in-service use by teachers and advisers. These have been developed in conjunction with the Association for Science Education. The titles of some of the versions give a flavour of these: 'Starting points for infants', 'Starting points for juniors', 'Science from the building site'. They are intended for use in school, in teachers' centres or, indeed, anywhere where teachers meet together.

Summary

The Learning through Science Project team has aimed to develop its work on three broad fronts. It has been particularly concerned that primary and middle schools form their own school policies for science. It has given help and guidance on this matter and strongly feels that the best policy is one framed by a group of teachers for their own school and for the particular needs of the children within that school.

The question of resources is also of great importance. The need for adequate, properly stored, well maintained and well used equipment and materials is obvious, and the team has produced a text to help.

Given a well formed school policy and proper resources, a good start can be made by any school. However, the quality of science experience in schools will still be very dependent on the kind of thinking that children are encouraged to do for themselves. The role of the teacher is of paramount importance. Not only must teachers encourage children to observe and question, but they must lead them on to propose ways to find answers to their questions. This necessitates planning experiments, sorting variables, using controls, repeating tests, looking for patterns in observation and examining work critically. The emphasis of our pupil material and teacher guides is on developing these processes of science, and time and time again they take children into problem-solving situations. What is now needed is a concerted effort by all those concerned with the education of children to help teachers realize the importance of such scientific processes and to persuade them to pursue such processes in their classrooms. There is a wealth of material to use.

References

DES (1978) *Primary Education in England: A Survey by HM Inspectors of Schools*, London, HMSO.
DES (1978) *Special Educational Needs* (The Warnock Report), London HMSO.
HARLEN, W., (1978) 'Does content matter in primary science?', in *School Science Review*, 59, (also reprinted as Chapter 7 in this book).
RICHARDS, R. *et al.* (1980) *Learning through Science: Formulating a School Policy, with an Index to Science 5–13*, MacDonald Educational.
RICHARDS, R. *et al.* (1982) *Science Resources for Primary and Middle Schools*, MacDonald Educational.

Learning Through Science Materials

Pupil material

Colour	All Around	Earth
Ourselves	Out of Doors	Electricity
Materials	On the Move	Which and What?
Sky and Space	Moving Around	Time, Growth and Change

Teacher Guides

Learning Through Science. Formulating a School Policy with an Index to Science 5/13

Science Resources for Primary and Middle Schools

Science for Children with Learning Difficulties

Filmstrip/Tape Sequences

Primary Science – Ways Forward

16 Nuffield Combined Science: Themes for the Eighties*

Derek Holford

Following the recent appearance of updated versions of Nuffield O-level texts, it was natural to suppose that revision of the 11–13 Combined Science Project would soon follow. Instead new material has been added, the *Nuffield Combined Science Themes for the Middle Years* (Bingham, 1977–80). The decision not to revise was doubtless influenced by the knowledge that the project's books had from the early seventies achieved greater market penetration than any others in science from Nuffield or Schools Council (Booth, 1975), but it also reflects confidence in their continuing suitability for courses in middle and secondary schools.

Why Themes for the Middle Years?

The roots of the *Themes* lie in the early seventies. From 1971 Bingham and Elwell (1973), coorganizers of the Combined Science Project, surveyed science provision in the new middle schools. They found that some had already begun to introduce material from the Nuffield Combined Science scheme for their younger pupils in preference to alternatives such as Science 5–13. Though not designed for this target audience, its 'real' science with 'real' apparatus had attracted them more. The *Themes* which Bingham and his colleagues ultimately wrote are, therefore, intended to fit situations not envisaged in the original texts – where the 9- and 10-year-olds are taught in a science area or classroom rather than a laboratory or where teachers, with help and advice from science-trained colleagues, wish to teach the subject. However good the intentions, it seems likely that previous sets of materials for middle school pupils such as those from Science 5–13 over-estimated the level of expertise that many teachers have for science and grossly over-estimated the time they can give to lesson preparation. The *Themes* attempt to provide the level of support in the classroom that these teachers may need in order to be sufficiently confident to begin. Some may view this as the thin end of the

* This is an edited revised version of an article first published in *Education 3–13*, 9, 1, 1980, pp. 38–42.

wedge, arguing that however worthy the intentions, to encourage the inexperienced puts children at pedagogic risk. Middle school teachers are likely to disagree, pointing first to the informative teachers' notes and second to the quality of science the *Themes* contain. They make use of simple everyday materials for genuine investigative activity and offer sufficient flexibility for science activities to develop from work in other subject areas. This approach, one of enrichment of the whole curriculum which the pupil experiences in school, rather than its compartmentalization with science taught as a discrete subject, fits the preference of many teachers. Nevertheless, vigilance *is* required for two reasons. Where teachers are seen to cope with science while lacking mains services, standard apparatus and technical assistance, their claim for laboratory provision to open up other options is likely to be undermined. And unless the teacher systematically builds onto lessons their acquisition, this is an approach which does not readily foster the development of *scientific* skills.

Morley (1979) noted a great deal of modification where teachers felt the scheme was too difficult, and Charles (1976) pointed out that 'pupils at the extreme ends of the ability range become increasingly frustrated in the second year', noting, for example, that much of the material on energy was beyond the least able. It is the latter who have benefitted least from Nuffield. The *Themes* attempt to put this right. Features they share with other new schemes are symptomatic of an increased sensitivity to these pupils' limited capacities. Work cards direct and support their experiments, whilst leaving scope for personal resourcefulness by those who have first mastered the essentials. Vocabulary demand and textual density are reduced, although further simplification should perhaps have been attempted in a scheme where reading is advocated as a central activity. It is teachers in middle schools, especially of the 9- and 10-year-olds, who are likely to be the main beneficiaries of the *Themes*. However, it is the expense of each *Theme* through providing work cards of improved durability that is more contentious. Teachers would probably prefer rough and ready material they can readily adapt for their particular contexts.

The *Themes* are also intended to broaden the range of alternatives for teaching mixed ability groups and for independent learning. Competition there is much fiercer. ILEA's Science Project (Marshall, 1978) is just one that offers instructional material to support different rates of learning through a core plus extension format. Both schemes have recognized that *flexibility* matters by producing curricular units which can be arranged in any preferred order. One perspective on the *Themes* is that they provide, in effect, 'polyfilla' to fill gaps in teachers' existing Combined Science courses. They can buy individual units and then select the activities and cards from those that attract them.

Into the Eighties: Have We Got It Right?

Addition of material to the existing stock is the Combined Science Project's insurance policy for the early eighties based on prediction of current trends. By choosing simple activities which enrich understanding of some of the same concepts as the parent texts, concepts such as 'temperature' and 'time', the new

Themes are on safe ground – such safe ground, in fact, that the now proliferating schemes for the primary years, schemes such as 'Look' (Gilbert and Matthews, 1981) and 'Scientific Horizons' (Hudson and Slack, 1981), cover much the same core of basic concepts, at a yet simpler level. They too use durable work cards for pupils, link their material with that of other school subjects under broad thematic headings, and presume their teacher audience to be rather inexperienced in science. Where they tend to differ from the *Themes*, interestingly, is in offering a tighter rationale for the mapping of content and skills, and in having rather more technological exploration, most evident in 'Science Skills' from Scotland (Mills, 1981).

The *Themes* also fit the likely outcome of the process–content debate. Is process supreme in science, suggesting the need for plenty of practice in specific skills such as observation and inference? Or should content rule, implying the need for experiences which lead to the progressive enrichment of concepts? Certainly the process approach had a strong influence worldwide on course design through the sixties and seventies. The pendulum now seems to be swinging towards a conceptual view, following a decade of studies of how scientific ideas develop or fail to develop over time and of the role of perception and language in children's learning. From this perspective, scientific processes may be just one outcome of holding certain concepts in mind. If someone has a rich understanding of the concept 'variable', it seems likely that he will succeed in the corresponding process of designing a fair experiment. Processes remain a powerful *aide-memoire* in the planning of courses, but as an aid towards concept enrichment rather than ends in themselves. Questions such as, 'Can pupils be asked to observe with more than one sense? . . . compare and contrast? . . . make a prediction?' do, however, enable planning activities to be upgraded in order to focus more sharply on engaging pupils' minds.

How then might we seek to improve present practice with older middle years pupils? A start towards more sophisticated design of courses is to map the interrelationship of content and process in a matrix. It might be better, however, to spilt broad thematic headings into the discrete concepts subsumed and to broaden 'process' to include a range of intellectual as well as practical skills before examining how these various skills could better contribute to development of the concepts. Similarly, by using these same concept and skills headings for recording and assessment procedures, evaluation of curriculum can be more closely related to planners' intentions. Some schools have indeed created schedules for record-keeping which try to map more effectively their pupils' attainment, expressing these in terms of levels of mastery of skills and attitudes. Fewer have included concepts but this may be the more productive direction to follow. Harlen (1977) provides examples. As important as the creative task of devising schedules has been spin-off from discussion of criteria. Some teachers, for example, have started to set more imaginative tasks to break the 'neatness, presentation and accuracy' syndrome that can infect science work.

The Combined Science Project's guidance on assessment was very limited. Schools have since devised proficiency tests and examinations assisted by banks of published questions but the idea of testing for different levels of concept mastery is in its infancy. First it implies that the teacher chooses the correct tool for the job. On most occasions the teacher's intention is not to select *per se* but to diagnose learning difficulties or to gain feedback on the effectiveness of learning. Criterion- rather than norm-referenced testing is then appropriate with many short tests employed rather than a few large ones and items carefully designed to reveal proficiency levels. Shayer (1980) has now illustrated a 1980 mechanism for the diagnostic testing of concepts, following his earlier research on pupils' difficulties in understanding them (Shayer, 1978).

The Nuffield approach is fundamentally one of guided discovery, implying at least some degree of open-endedness and pupil-generated enquiry. Some teachers have recognized that certain topics do afford good opportunities for them to encourage skills such as the design of experiments and hypothesis-testing to be pursued, but for many, lack of examples and time have been effective barriers to their inclusion. The pedagogic approach has been substantially tailored to fit individual preferences rather than *vice versa*. Now, with technical help and finance to maintain equipment in short supply, the trend may well be away from pupil practical work, imaginative or not, to more passive ways of learning. The challenge is to find ways of getting a better quality of learning from the practical work that remains without *just* looking to a process approach to achieve this and to find more ways of engaging pupils in active learning when they are not doing experiments.

The Bullock Report focussed attention on the importance of language in learning. Many teachers' response was to concentrate on finding ways of increasing readability of texts and on the more sensitive introduction of technical terms, whereas Sutton (1980) suggests that these are just two ways of facilitating a more desirable end, the *active search for meaning* in texts. From this perspective, much that children do in science has rather passive, routinized elements concerned more with developing procedural competence than engaging them consistently in a search for meaning in their experiences. A further 'message' from Bullock, supported now by more extensive research into the place of spoken language in children's learning, is that what we should really be attempting in science teaching is to give pupils more opportunity to 'talk themselves into learning', for example, by getting them to compare and contrast two situations orally or to sort out ideas before putting them to a small group of peers. Experiments with a greater variety of short task-centred reading, talking, listening and writing activities are now becoming more of a reality as exemplar material appears (Fisher, 1979; Sutton, 1981).

The acid test of success in the eighties will be whether by these or other means the time that children actually engage in meaningful learning is increased – meaningful in two respects, first that it interconnects well with their previous experience, second that when internalized the learning is rich in action potentiality. We need better ways of translating knowledge in mind into action knowledge and among other things this suggests an enhanced role for metaphor and analogy so that pupils have a richer store of meanings to bring to bear.

The Combined Science texts are at their most persuasive when presenting the 'structural scaffolding' of science, its concepts and its principles (in which concepts are related to one other). Three ideas underpin the choice of practical activity. The teacher is encouraged to value children's existing perceptions, their theories based on limited insights; to extend the attributes of each discrete concept introduced towards incremental growth of understanding; and to introduce instrumentation by first creating a functional need for it through activities in which pupils recognize the limits of their unaided senses. All this fits current thinking on the ways in which children may learn best. The specific activities do, however, require careful orchestration by the teacher, especially skill in discussion leadership to pull together what can sometimes appear to be disparate strands of experience. Some teachers seem to be naturally gifted in this respect, others find it more difficult to achieve a sense of success but may be helped by emerging ideas.

For a decade teachers of science have said that what they most wanted was the chance to consolidate their courses further rather than face yet more innovation. Given continuing economic stringency and falling school rolls, that opportunity is now with us. If consolidation is not to become stagnation, more varied ways for engaging pupils in learning should be tried out. Extending the range of activities in the ways suggested is but a partial and hesitant response but it requires a less radical shift in teaching style than discovery learning presumes possible and guided discovery has managed to achieve. Better theories of learning and deeper insight into its association with language are likely to yield more subtle, penetrative methods for promoting and monitoring learning in science, for example, by yielding improved diagnostic tools to reveal the interrelationships between concepts in pupils' cognitive structures. Experiment with these approaches, allied to a rationale for curriculum focussed more on the enrichment and mastery of concepts, currently seems to offer the best way forward.

References

BINGHAM, C. (Ed.) (1977–80) *Nuffield Combined Science Themes for the Middle Years* Longman.

BINGHAM, C. and ELWELL, M. (Eds) (1973) 'Nuffield Foundation Combined Science in Middle Schools Continuation Project', in *Education in Science*, 51.

BOOTH, N. (1975) 'The impact of science teaching projects on secondary education', in *Trends in Education*, 1.

CHARLES, D. (1976) 'Nuffield Combined Science – an evaluation' in *School Science Review*, 5B.

FISHER, R. *et al.* (1979) *Setting Alternative Written Work in Science Lessons*, Occasional Paper, Leicester University School of Education.

GILBERT, C. and MATTHEWS, P. (1981) *Look!* Addison-Wesley.

GILBERT, C. and MATTHEWS, P. (1982) *A First Look!*, Addison-Wesley.

HARLEN, W. *et al.* (1977) *Raising Questions*, Match and Mismatch, Oliver and Boyd.

HUDSON, J. and SLACK, D., (1981) *Science Horizons – The West Sussex Science 5–14 Scheme*, Globe Education.

MARSHALL, D. (Ed.) (1978) *Insight into Science*, Addison-Wesley.

MILLS, G. (1981) *Science Skills*, Collins Educational.

MORLEY, P. (1979) *An Examination of Secondary Teachers' Views on Nuffield Foundation Combined Science*, unpublished MEd dissertation, University of Leicester.

SHAYER, M. (1978) 'Nuffield Combined Science – do the pupils understand it? in *School Science Review*, 60.

Derek Holford

SHAYER, M. *et al.* (1980) *Science Reasoning Tasks,* Concepts in Secondary Mathematics and Science Project, NFER.
SUTTON, C. (1980) 'Science, language and meaning', in *School Science Review,* 62.
SUTTON, C. (1981) *Communicating in the Classroom,* Hodder and Stoughton.

PART VI

Practice

Introduction

Very few accounts have been written by teachers discussing why and how their practice of primary science has evolved. This is not primarily because of the lack of impact of national initiatives in schools. Primary science may not have had the wide impact its advocates would wish, but it has been firmly established in a considerable number of schools and classes through the efforts of teachers such as Jean Conran, Peter Evans, Bill Thornley and Molly Wetton. Why then this absence of accounts from the 'chalk-face'? In part at least, the problem lies in the complexity and elusiveness of practice. Practice is a complex amalgam of many elements, some of them idiosyncratic; it is difficult to pin down as it constantly evolves. It is particularly difficult to communicate about one's own activities; so much is tacitly understood and not readily communicable to others, especially if they have no knowledge of one's situation. There are further problems: of time, of modesty and of a lack of self-confidence in the use of the written language to discuss educational issues. These difficulties are acknowledged. Even so, it is important that 'ideas should encounter the discipline of practice ... that practice should be principled by ideas' (Stenhouse, 1975, p. 3) and that accounts should be published by those involved first-hand in relating ideas and practice in school contexts.

In addition to a general article by Margaret Collis on the practical issues involved in the organization of resources to support practice in primary science, this section contains accounts by four practitioners whose writing reflects the interplay between the general ideas examined elsewhere in this book and the unique circumstances of their individual schools. The accounts are of practice in both urban and rural schools and involve children of infant, junior and middle school age. Bill Thornley's contribution focusses on one piece of work with one class, Peter Evans' on one unorthodox approach, and Molly Wetton's and Arthur Ashton's on the work of their schools as a whole. All the accounts reflect the enthusiasm and knowledge of their authors, but an enthusiasm and knowledge tempered by realism: the realism that some failures are inevitable where new approaches are being tried. Perspectives such as theirs need to be shared and complemented by other accounts, if teachers of primary science are to be, not lonely practitioners of some ill-defined, uncommunicable craft, but professionals with an expertise to refine.

Reference

STENHOUSE, L. (1975) *An Introduction to Curriculum Research and Development*, London, Heinemann.

17 Science in Practice: Infants on Merseyside

Bill Thornley

Editorial Introduction. *There are very few published accounts of work with infants. Here, Bill Thornley describes in some detail a piece of work carried out with, and by, top infant children at St Cleophas C.E. School, a new small open-plan primary school close to the South Docks on the River Mersey. At St Cleopas science plays a very important part in the infant curriculum, not as a separate subject but as a way of working which involves children in observing, thinking, questioning and investigating. Such scientific activities provide a basis for extending children's language beyond the local dialect in which the children are already fluent. In addition to developing language, science is used to help extend children's understanding of the local environment, to provide them with concrete experiences essential for understanding and to give practical problems for the children to solve. To develop the work throughout the school the head has had to overcome problems caused by turnover of staff, by teachers' lack of background knowledge and by their consequent lack of confidence. Regular staff meetings, inter-school visiting, encouragement to attend local in-service courses and the involvement of the head in taking groups of children for investigations or in working alongside the teacher with the whole class have helped to develop the work. The account which follows is a clear, straightforward description of science with infants; the style in which it is written belies the depth of experience and understanding of children's learning required to provide and sustain such activities for young children. The account is deliberately unfinished; the work at St Cleopas continues. . . .*

Beginnings

It was an unsettled, showery day when I called in to see the teacher of the top infant class. Whilst I was there I had a chat with the children about the weather. One of the questions I asked was, 'Where do you think water comes from?' The children gave the usual type of answers, for example, the tap, the clouds, from a big lake in Wales. One boy surprised us by saying that it came from behind a big black wall. At first we were puzzled, until we realized that he meant the local reservoir which indeed in surrounded by a large black wall. A general discussion followed and the class teacher and I agreed that it would be well worthwhile to follow up with a topic on water. She asked me to help her with this project.

The first thing we did was to take the children for a walk round the district when the rain had stopped. We looked at the wet roads, the puddles, the gutters and downspouts from which water was still flowing into the drains. I pointed out the many different kinds of roofs which served to keep out the rain. There were several types to be seen even from our own playground, for example, slates, tiles, roofing felt, and some roofs were in such a bad state that they had been painted with bituminous paint to make them weatherproof. We looked up at the sky and different patterns of dark rain clouds scudding across.

When we arrived back at school we looked at the clothes we were wearing on a rainy day. We counted the numbers of cagoules, anoraks, parkas, raincoats, overcoats, snorkels, etc. and made a histogram. This led to an investigation as to which materials were best for keeping out the rain. Several types of material were collected by the children and the teacher. Sample squares of each material were placed over beakers and a tablespoonful of water was poured onto the material. The children noted what happened: the water ran through some materials very quickly, through some only slowly, while others were completely waterproof. We also tested the drying properties of the various sample materials. The children weighed half-metre squares of materials when dry and weighed them when wet and compared the difference. The materials were hung on a line to dry and the children made a chart placing the materials in the order of the time they took to dry.

At this stage I asked the manager of a large departmental store if he could let us have any old dummies that were of no further use to him. The three dummies he provided were dressed in clothes suitable for rainy weather, cold weather and summer wear. We labelled different parts of the dummies and clothing to help with reading and spelling.

The next investigation was to test the heat-retaining properties of the materials. The children made model people using washing-up liquid bottles for the the bodies and adding heads. The various sample materials were draped around them: one was left without any material as a control example. The class teacher then poured hot water into each bottle. At intervals the children felt them to see which were staying warmest longest. A chart was made by sticking the sample materials in the order of which kept in the heat longest. Whilst these investigations were going on, four children collected the rain water from the rain-gauge each day and poured it into a clear plastic tube container. Day by day they compared the amount of water until at the end of the week these tubes placed in line formed an excellent histogram. Throughout the term different groups of children took turns in collecting the rain water.

One recurring questions was, 'Where has the water gone?' when it disappeared. We found a large puddle in the playground and outlined it with chalk. At intervals during the day we returned to the puddle and outlined as it grew smaller until it dried completely. The children all thought that the water was soaking into the ground. To show that this wasn't necessarily the case, we placed a large plastic sheet on the ground in which a puddle was formed. From their previous experience with materials, the children knew that plastic was waterproof. They realized that there must be another way in which the water was disappearing. We walked round the school and noticed that the pavements were drying up, but the children still did not realize what was happening to the water. When we returned to school we placed several containers holding water in various places, some cold and some warm. We marked the water level with red tape and over a period of time the children observed the water level was getting lower and lower. Some children noticed that the same thing was happening in the fish tank. The water was disappearing more quickly in the warm place than the cold place. After much discussion we watched the steam rising from a container of water that had been heated. The word 'evaporated' was introduced; other words they had come in contact with were: 'weather', 'rain', 'cloud', 'puddles', 'waterproof', 'plastic', 'weigh'.

The Colour of Water

During the discussions about water the children were asked, 'What colour is water?' They were divided on this issue: some said that water is blue – no doubt due to the fact that they use blue colour to paint sea scenes; others thought that water was white. Kelly held up a clear plastic beaker of water. The children could see that it was definitely not blue or green, but many still said it was white. Clare held up a beaker of milk alongside the beaker of water. When they could see what a white liquid looked like they realized that water was not really white. Beakers of water were coloured with different paints, red, yellow, blue, etc. The children further realized that water on its own has no colour and a new word was introduced – 'colourless'. Pieces of coloured card were held behind the clear plastic beakers of water. The water seemed to change colour but the children gradually realized that the colours were not in the water but could be seen through the water. Other things were held behind the beakers and the children could see them through the water. This introduced yet another new word – 'transparent'. Other transparent materials were shown to the children, for example, clear glass, cellophane, perspex, and coloured transparent materials were used to show that transparent does not mean colourless.

Sinking and Floating

While the class was busy with other work, a group at a time was given the opportunity to do some investigations with sinking and floating. The children placed various objects in a water tank (Figure 1) and were asked to predict what would happen: most children thought that light things would float and heavy things would sink. They were very interested in the objects that floated below the surface. They were very pleased to learn a new word – 'submerged' – which they used many times later.

Hollow balls, tennis balls, table-tennis balls, various blocks of wood, spoons, scissors, toy wheels, ball pens, rubbers, etc. were used. The results were recorded on already prepared lists under the titles 'These Floated', 'These Sank', 'These Submerged'. The children made drawings of the various objects

Left: *Figure 1.*   Right: *Figure 2*

to place on a group picture; new words that were used were: 'sink', 'float', 'heavy', 'light', 'cork', 'wood', 'metal', 'submerged'.

Later each group was given clear plastic beakers, marbles, washers, bottle tops and sand. The beakers were placed in the water and loaded. The children were surprised to see that even when the beaker was full of bottle tops it still floated well above the water. They thought that this was because the beaker and contents was still light enough to float. The beaker that was loaded with washers sank when fifty-nine washers were put in. The beaker loaded with sand sank when it was three-quarters full. The children were fascinated to see that when the beaker was filled with water it floated with the top of the beaker level with the water in the tank. This was discussed for some time. In the end the children agreed with Debbie's idea that it must be because the weight of the water inside the beaker was the same as the water it was floating in. (The beaker itself was so light that its weight did not make much difference.) The children made a chart illustrating what they had done. The beakers were then loaded in such a way that they would all float just below the surface of the water. They realized that they could not do this with the bottle tops because they were so light. (This will lead to density at a much later stage.) The children then compared metal foil trays of different sizes. They loaded each tray with washers to sinking point, and compared the size of the tray and the number of washers needed to sink it.

As another scientific activity, large pieces of polystyrene were pushed under the water and the children felt the upthrust (Figure 2). They really enjoyed this experience. Next they pushed hollow rubber balls, table-tennis balls, below the water. They were delighted when the upthrust made some of the balls jump right out of the water. New words were learnt: 'surface', 'above', 'below', 'sand', 'upthrust', 'ball'.

Some children were given two sponges of equal size. They observed that they were very light and full of holes, and said they floated so well because they were light. They pushed them under the water and watched the bubbles rising. Michelle said they were air bubbles and the air must have been in the holes. Janet said, 'They'll still float even though they are full of water. This must be because they are still light.' She also noticed that the part of the sponge below the surface looked darker. Now that air had been mentioned we discussed the fact that empty beakers and cans were not really empty as we had thought because they contained air. We made a Bubbly Can – a can sealed with a lid. A small hole was made at one end and a larger hole at the other. When the can was pushed under water the children were delighted to see all the air bubbles coming out of the can. When it finally sank to the bottom a rubber tube was pushed into the large hole. Carl blew gently down the tube and the children had a lot of fun watching the can rise to the surface. Everyone wanted to have a turn at this. New words learnt included: 'air', 'empty', 'full', 'sponge', 'bubbles', 'rubber', 'tube'.

To add interest to our project we took the class to the Maritime Museum in the old dock close to the Pierhead. On show were two of the types of buoys which are used to make the shipping lanes. One had a light for starboard and the other a light for port. We intend to make model buoys with flashing green and red lights. We saw many different kinds of boats in the Boat Hall and many model ships in the Exhibition Hall. Among the boats floating in the dock one in particular was of special interest: the 'Lively Lady' in which Alec Rose sailed round the world. The children were told the story of this voyage and a group made a large picture of the 'Liverpool Bay', a model container ship. The class wrote a poem about the visit. Everyone took part by making suggestions. Here is the result:

> Down by the river,
> I can see the boats,
> I like to see them toss,
> I like to see them float,
> I see the triangle blowing
> The clapping, clacking sails,
> The speed boats move like rockets,
> The rowing boats crawl like snails,
> Can you see the ferries
> And the Isle of Man's big boat –
> They are sailing on the Mersey
> Oooh it's windy – fasten your coat.

Ice and Snow

A change in the weather helped us to continue with our study on water. It was the first frosty day of the winter; a white layer of frost covered the school grounds and it was time to warn children not to make slides where they would be dangerous. This gave us the opportunity to talk about ice and snow. All the children knew that ice was frozen water. The words 'liquid' and 'solid' were introduced. We filled plastic bags with water and asked the cook to put them in the freezer so that we could make our own icebergs. The children put their 'icebergs' in the water tank and noticed that they floated, but also that a large part of the ice was submerged. We discussed the question – 'Why did the ice float?' They realized that the ice shapes must be lighter than water from their previous experience of things that floated. The small pond we have in the school was frozen over and was examined by the children. Tracey filled a glass three-quarters full with water and marked the height with red tape. Cook put it in the freezer for us. When we examined it the next day the top of the ice was above the red marker. We talked about what had happened and a new word was introduced – 'expansion'. They were told the story of the sinking of the 'Titanic' and one group made a collage to illustrate the story. By now many water pipes in the children's homes were frozen and there were several bursts. We discussed the reason for this. Following this the children were shown a centigrade thermometer and how to use it. The weather still seemed to be coordinated with our project. Just as we were completing our investigations with ice, to the children's delight, we had the heaviest fall of snow that we had experienced for many years. This enabled us to extend our work on water and the weather. What is 'snow?' How is it formed? This was the subject of our next discussion. The children took thermometers out into the school grounds and took the temperature of the snow. This proved to be exactly 0°C. Some of the children watched Mr Baines, the school caretaker, throwing a brown substance on to the snow and they gathered round him. Lyndsay asked if it was to melt the snow. Mr Baines explained that it was rock salt and that he was trying to clear the snow from the footpath. He gave them a container full of rock salt and told them that they could use it themselves. We marked a square metre on the paving stones and another on soil; the children sprinkled the salt all over the squares. When the snow started to melt the temperature went down 10° below freezing point. During the day the children observed what was happening to the squares. After a few hours the metre squares were completely cleared of snow. The temperature of the little slush that remained was still 10° lower than freezing point. Later in school several children mixed snow and salt in containers to see who could make the coldest mixture. The final temperature went down to approximately 19° below freezing point. The children filled 1-litre and 2-litre containers with snow and when it melted they noted that the space taken up by the water was only one-quarter of the space taken up by the snow.

The weather remained very cold so we repeated a previous ice investigation. We filled larger containers and left them outside to freeze and the expansion was far more spectacular than when we placed a smaller container in the school freezer.

When the thaw came, many of the houses in the district were without water because of burst pipes. The school had to close one day due to a burst main pipe in the road. As a result of their investigations the children realized, more than most parents, why the pipes had burst. To complete our work on ice and snow, to the delight of the children, we made orange ice-lollies and with the main work done by the teacher we made ice cream. This was a popular part of the project. During the time the snow covered the area....

18   Balloons, Solar Energy and Dyes: An Approach to Primary Science★

Arthur Ashton

Editorial Introduction. *As a complement to Roy Richards' contribution (Chapter 15), Arthur Ashton illustrates how a primary school in Kent has developed a policy for science which has informed its practice. He is firm in his advocacy of science as an essential part of a balanced curriculum but is realistic enough to realize that not every topic or experience offered children will be successful: 'It is important to put ideas into practice; failures are inevitable but fear through so-called ignorance of science is no excuse for failing to start.'*

Background

A number of excellent accounts of the development of primary science in England have been written. This chapter is not concerned with the national scene but tries to give a glimpse into how one school has developed and implemented a policy for primary science. The use of the indefinite article in the title is deliberate. Our primary is not elementary science, simplified secondary science or a series of unrelated experiments. We prefer to talk of scientific investigations rather than just science, as for many people, including teachers, 'science' suggests a formal discipline suited to older pupils. We accept that primary work should be wide-ranging with purposeful investigations, frequently of an interdisciplinary nature, crossing subject boundaries. We believe that such investigations provide opportunities for primary children to carry out the exploration of their environment in stimulated and astringent ways without too much concern for content and without thought of formal assessment.

As a staff we accept a number of other points which form a background to the description which follows.

(i)   There is no longer any need for debate over the place of science in the primary curriculum. It forms an essential part of a balanced curriculum.

★From *Education 3–13*, 8, 2, 1980, pp. 7–11.

(ii) The implementation of an approach to science is not dependent upon the innate ability or academic achievement of the children.

(iii) Content is not as important as process; obsession with content can be a danger.

(iv) It is important to put ideas into practice; failures are inevitable but fear through so-called ignorance of science is no excuse for failing to start.

(v) Science in the primary school does not require a particular organization or method. The encouragement of an attitude of critical appraisal rather than unthinking submission is what matters. This is an important point because investigative studies seem to have been associated with an integrated, informal classroom organization, and, though this may be desirable, it is not essential.

Policy

Our policy can best be summed up by part of a curriculum document which is a consensus of staff views plus guides to practice:

General Aims

To help children utilize the environment – both physical and natural, so as to learn from it and to evolve techniques of experimentation, develop their mental and physical skills and to obtain certain basic scientific concepts that will enable them to apply a scientific approach to problem solving in as many aspects of the curriculum as possible.

Detailed Objectives

Observing, classifying, collecting data and recording it in a sensible, structured way.

By quantitative as well as qualitative experiment and interpretation of results, to accept conclusions contrary to expectations, and to appreciate the value of negative findings.

To learn practical techniques of observation in the field and classroom, and to apply those techniques to the examination of results obtained from experimentation.

To use statistical diagrams, to summarize information and to reinforce mathematical appreciation of measurement and associated concepts.

Sources

Schools' Council, *Science 5/13 years; Teaching Primary Science*, MacDonald Educational.

Selection of books used: *Geary Science-craft*, Macmillan; Cox and Jenks, *Topics in Biology*, Blackie; Kincaid and Cole, *Science in a Topic*, Hulton; Bishops, *Outdoor Biology* John Murray; *Nuffield Junior Science*, Collins.

How did we come to formulate this policy for science? This process began in general staff meetings but we soon realized that these needed to be complemented by other activities. Informal talks were held with smaller numbers of teachers, usually those concerned with the same year groups. These meetings, held at weekly intervals, enabled us to exchange opinions and ideas and to learn more about personal day-to-day problems. Apart from the many suggested activities that were put forward, the need for adequate resources soon became evident – books, materials, apparatus and information about techniques for using more specialized equipment such as microscopes or overhead projectors. Working parties were formed to prepare assignments and work sheets and to contruct simple apparatus: self-help became the accepted practice. After a group meeting details of requirements would be posted in the staffroom, necessary raw materials would be made available and volunteer teachers from any year group would work at specified days and times. This team effort proved very successful – it meant that personal skills could be concentrated in the most appropriate areas and at the same time could be quietly disseminated by example. Scientific studies began with two or three enthusiasts developing work with their own classes. When these teachers were asked to assist with the county's in-service training programme, others who had helped the pioneers in making equipment found themselves sufficiently confident to encourage their own children to carry out investigations. This development was stimulated by information and ideas drawn from the Science 5–13 source books and discussions about them (see Chapter 14).

Now our meetings are a dynamic part of school life. Whereas original discussions were pre-arranged, now individual members of staff or small groups make their own plans for projects or for developing work that has arisen from children's starting-points. Senior teachers and others with special interests frequently become involved, with discussions taking place in the lunch hour, at the end of the day or during other odd moments. This greater measure of cooperation among staff and increased knowledge of one another's interests have resulted in the children seeking guidance from teachers other than their own. Frequently younger children can be seen working in rooms with older children or *vice versa*: either skilled help is being gained from another teacher or pupils are themselves acting as 'consultants' in the investigation being undertaken. A further benefit is that in offering these explanations and guidance older children are consolidating their knowledge and increasing their own understanding. The recognition by staff of the importance of scientific experience as an integral part of a balanced curriculum is one of the most important stages in the implementation of a programme. The development of personal knowledge and the provision of appropriate opportunities for the children will follow once conviction is there. A number of our teachers have now acquired expertise in specialized areas: plant propagation, butterfly rearing, identification of local flora and fauna – each thereby contributing to the technical resources available and acting as a spur to others.

Practice

General practice requires a termly class topic in which areas of science to be studied are identified and from this stem group and individual investigations. As experience is gained, further opportunities are taken as they arise – 'finds', for instance, with younger children where long-term studies are difficult to sustain. Another requirement is the collection of information to form a statistical bank which can be displayed and analyzed. This serves many purposes. Recently, for instance, those studying bird population in the playground wanted to find out whether or not there was a correlation between size of flocks, temperature and cloud cover – the availability of data assisted them considerably.

Here is a current list of observations for our data bank:

Evaporation rates
Soil temperature at .5 and 1 metre – air/soil temperature
Cloud cover
Air temperature in open ground and within vegetation
Changes in minibeast populations beneath a stone
Weather – wet or dry conditions at a particular time
A simple two-column comparison for younger children
Bird counts

Angle of sun – length of shadow
Length of day and night
Comparison of temperature inside and outside the school buildings
Bird varieties
Study of materials immersed in water
Moulds – foods left uncovered
Growth rates
Materials under stress
Wind direction/strength
Visibility
Dehydration rate

Many other incidental activities contribute to the evolution of our 'primary science': the slow organic growth shows in the language used, matters discussed, displays sent out.

Unfortunately, even with a flexible but well defined programme, early vigour sometimes flags and there is a constant need for positive support, good communication and selective praise. One way of catering for such needs is to encourage classes (and their teachers) to demonstrate publicly what has been done. For example, one lovely, clear, cold day in winter it was decided to have a balloon launch. Three classes had made them based on the design prepared by a teacher and as prevailing weather conditions were good it was an ideal opportunity. All classes were assembled in the playground: their excitement was evident, not in misbehaviour, but in attention, interest and controlled eagerness. One after another coloured balloons went aloft into the cool morning air each bearing the class name. One failed; it burst into flames but adequate precautions had been taken – an excellent opportunity to stress the importance of safety whenever practical activities are taking place.

Again, at the time of the Great Egg Race on BBC 2, a number of classes devised their own elastic band-powered machines. In the process they learned a great deal about energy transference and many perhaps gained experiences leading later to concepts of potential and kinetic energy. Certainly this practical demonstration given in the hall to a variety of children aroused great interest and curiosity – Could I make one? How does it work? Can I make mine go further? Why are some more effective than others?

It is not possible to go into detail on each of the investigations undertaken even in the last year but a few further examples at both ends of the junior range might be helpful. We must not forget that children today are familiar with a new vocabulary, solar energy, for instance – three solar panels have been constructed here. Many technological problems were encountered and overcome – appropriateness of adhesive, for example, being a difficult one when the glass tubing was fitted to the panel. This interest in solar heating encouraged another class to develop a parabolic solar furnace: the parabola was drawn onto a piece of ply, holes drilled and dowel rods placed through to act as a former for the reflective panel, made initially from silver paper but later from plastic. The angle at which the furnace was most effective depended upon the time of year and position of the sun, which meant that the furnace had to rotate horizontally as well as vertically. These and other problems were met and solved by groups of fourth year children under the guidance of skilled teaching. A further development was a really large model including a modified heat exchanger so that the furnace could be used for waterheating purposes.

With a class of younger children, the work began on a class basis with the examination of colours in materials which led to the subject of dyes. This resulted in the preparation of natural dyes from a variety of fruits and vegetables. A question of staining arose after an expedition in search of berries and the decision was taken to investigate which ones would wash out easily. Strips of suitable cloth were cut and subsequently stained with a variety of common liquids. Each member of the class then washed a number of strips after they had decided on simple variables and controls as follows:

Variables	*Controls*
Washing powders	Quantity of powder
Temperature of water	Length of time material rubbed

When strips were dried one child said that her stains had become fainter than a neighbour's, and the immediate comment was, 'She is a better washer!' 'She always rubs harder!' The teacher took the opportunity to raise the question, 'What is a fair test?' A suggestion which followed was that one person should do it all but it was decided that it was expecting too much. The following day a mother turned up with a battery-operated washing machine – she had heard about the problem and thought it might provide a solution!

Throughout the investigative work stress is placed on the quality of observation, the timing of inferences, the importance of fair tests – there must be progression and evaluation, for only in this way can we extend pupil capability and performance.

Environmental studies have their place throughout the school year and appropriate skills required can be taught prior to visits in some instances; for example, a transect on a home-made pond preparing the children for a field visit. Another group, having constructed small water wheels in the classroom built a large one rotating on a broomstick axle. They used it successfully in a narrow, fast-flowing stream and the next step was to harness the energy for useful purposes: they rigged up a block and tackle and hoisted a member of the class, much to their delight and his surprise. A local church provided a starting-point for a class but their investigations were concentrated on weathering and plant colonization of walls and gravestones. The results of their findings were presented in written reports, diagrams, vertical section plots, detailed drawings and models.

Many of the difficulties encountered in implementing the work are evident here but future development requires special mention – an awareness of what may be achieved rather than just what has been done. The potential of our own site has been explored more thoroughly and a scale model produced showing suitable stations for study. Other areas in the neighbourhood have been identified and contacts made to establish party access: a disused quarry, for instance, will provide a totally different environment for investigation. More work which might be called technology is appearing as children become more competent and experienced with a wider range of materials and tools. Last, but not least, links with secondary colleagues have been made, visits exchanged and additional support and specialist knowledge provided.

Outcome

Much remains to be done but we believe that primary children can carry out investigations which are intellectually challenging, provide rich experiences and foster the concept formation on which later science disciplines depend. Primary science does even more than this: it helps the decision-making process because evidence has to be considered carefully before judgements are made. It makes a significant contribution to language development and helps provide the knowledge needed for a responsible attitude towards the environment. As a final comment, it keeps alive that sense of wonder which, if not cherished, is lost perhaps for good. Who can quantify the harm that may do?

19 Science: Pure or Applied?★

Peter Evans

Editorial Introduction. *Peter Evans puts forward an insightful, irreverent but persuasive argument for the inclusion of 'technology' rather than 'pure' science in the primary curriculum. He observes: 'Of nuts and bolts and metal and wires used to conduct electricity, of practical reasoning, of the use of purposeful, controlled imagination – as distinct from the pixilated stuff of creative writing – and of the application of science and mathematics in the design of working gadgets, there is rarely a sign.' This may well be true, but isn't there still a place for tadpoles, levers, magnets and even the thrum-eyed primrose?*

Examples

In this ten-class rural primary school, d.o.b. 1846 and showing its age architecturally if not philosophically, that part of the curriculum labelled 'technology' is implemented for the purpose of 'enabling children to design and construct original devices which perform some practical function'. As a guide to the tracing of the educative wrinkles to be found in most of the children's technological experiences, the history of the 'Puff-meter' is offered in some detail, preceded by the reminder that children, who are apt to be childish, often take a serious and absorbing interest in matters which properly matured adults would regard as being downright daft.

George, a 10-year-old town bandsman, was the only child in the class who was able to raise a decibel from his French horn. Evidencing the school's failure to develop in her an enquiring mind and a scientific approach, one little dogmatizer said that George had the strongest puff in the place. Employing the 'impromptu' technique for initiating technological enterprise, the teacher undemocratically subdued the usual pondful of irrelevant quack-quack. Briskly he headed both expressions of relevant transactional language towards the crucial point when the problem was unambiguously identified and verbalized; what was wanted was a device that would measure puff-power.

★ From *Education 3–13*, 8, 1, 1980, pp. 16–23.

Peter Evans

Figure 1. Puff-meter Mark 2

Reliant as it is upon a flair for the instant recognition and exploitation of one of those rare classroom incidents which offer the teacher, as a font of interest, a faint and fleeting chance to compete with the incomprehensibly technological crew of the Star Ship 'Flying Enterprise', the 'impromptu' technique is liable to long periods of bankruptcy. Prods of a predetermined kind are more reliable. Some projects, or themes, or centres of boredom, or whatever is the latest tag, are more likely intrinsically to excite technological responses than others. Studies such as 'The Human Body', 'Measuring' 'The Elements' offer more scope for gadgetry than would a project on, say, 'Our Pets', although the 'Guinea-Pig Measurer', judged to be too tough on the compressed and disorientated pet, is filed under our 'Abandoned Projects'. Another productive ploy is to demonstrate unfamiliar items of equipment, such as the electromagnet and the electronically operated mechanical counter, and then, with nods, winks, prods and hints varying from the oblique to the direct, to try to coax out ideas for putting these things to some practical use (see Figures 3 and 4). Books are an obvious source of inspiration but, because it is essential to the aims of technology that the child is to some extent the designer, prescribed plans, as in Science 5–13 Units for Teachers, must be significantly improved by original modifications. One permanently standing technological challenge, which can be applied to every man-made thing, including the products of primary school technology is – improve on this!

At the initial stage of the search for a workable design for a Puff-meter, balloons were inflated and rudely deflated, sheets of card were blown along taut wires, and a table-tennis ball was puffed up an inclined map tube, all very joyously. None of these exploratory tests of a range of possibilities offered a solution, and therein lies a lesson.

The Puff-meter, in so far as the child was unaware of a similar design, is an invention, and its originality is confirmed by visitors having to ask, *'What* is that?' The reply, 'It's a puff-meter, mark 2, an instrument for measuring puff-power', followed by a vigorous demonstration, does tend to provoke a wary and quizzical look which suggests that the enquiring superordinate feels he has diagnosed a teacher under extreme stress who had better be humoured. This is what is meant by innovatory risk! It has to be explained to children, with reference to case histories, that no inventor ever shouted 'Eureka' at the first attempt, and this means that when originality is a requirement for success, initial failures are inevitable. The failure factor in technology, which very often causes the abandonment of a project, acts as an essential counter to the prevalent notion, inculcated in children by over-exposure to many of the traditional art and craft activities, that making things is a cushy undemanding way of passing a few pleasantly messy hours. So it is when no precision is required, when tolerances of 5cm plus or minus in all dimensions are acceptable, and when the assessment of the standard of quality is expressed solely in the eye-dominated comment, 'Ah, but it's so effective', said rhapsodically. In contrast, technological products are subject to a clear-cut test that the designers themselves cannot duck: does it work? Knowing the scene, and the characters who are acting the parts, the experienced teacher is able to distinguish between genuine expressions of the true explorative spirit of technology, and plain messing about. In any case, even those children with known form as messers about are no less gainfully employed than if they were to spend hours sticking layer upon layer of thin paper over a plasticine base to make a puppet head.

Puff-meter Mark 1 (not illustrated) can best be described as a one-armed anemometer constructed in the vertical plane. Mark 2 (see Figure 1) is a more robust and mechanically refined development. The indicator (left) is placed at zero on the graduated scale. Puff is directed into the cup (right) and puff-power is measured by taking a reading off the scale.

One problem which the children had to solve on this and other constructions was that, upon reaching its maximum point of traverse across the scale, the indicator fell back to zero before an accurate reading could be taken. Here, doing a bit of teaching at its crudest old-fashioned pre-Piaget level – someone who knows informing someone who needs to know – the teacher demonstrated the function of a pawl and ratchet, and left the child the further problem of fitting this mechanism. How exactly do these properly engineered parts match and function, where should they be fitted, how are they fitted, were posers with which the child was totally unfamiliar. Certainly he had never before had to apply his fine motor skills to the manipulation of anything as small as a grub-screw. This illustrates how teacher intervention of the sensitively judged kind, which falls short of telling the child exactly what to do, while preventing the avoidable abortion of a likely-looking project, is sometimes essential. A further problem, that of the application of just the right degree of tension on the pawl, was found not by teacher intervention but by the process of trial and error.

Surveys were conducted, statistics were recorded and analyzed, and conclusions drawn. George did not have the strongest puff, the record being set by seventeen-stone 'Sir'. Why? 'He's bigger than us.' Is puff-power related to weight or chest expansion? 'Find out.' Might it be possible to design a device for measuring chest expansion? It was. Rainbowed naturally in the full range of felt-tipped colours the display looked almost as effective as would, say, 'Our Norman Castle' walled in egg cartons. Everything is 'our' something in the primary school.

It is important to note that the Puff-meter scores are invalidated by variables in the test conditions which no child has as yet noticed. Spotting the defects in the design, and the incorporation of curative modifications, remains an opportunity for the child who is very bright in terms of practical ingenuity to identify himself or herself and be given further tasks to attempt which impose no ceiling upon high fliers. The blushes of musicians, visual artists and swimmers do not remain unseen, but the primary school curriculum rarely offers opportunities for young technological, scientific, engineering and mathematical talent to remain other than mute, inglorious and uncultivated.

Figure 2: Magnet Tester

Other Constructions

Another device constructed by the children is the magnet tester (see Figure 2). Here, the pawl is turned out of contact with the ratchet so that the paper-clip trembles, just touching the magnet. As the axle is slowly cranked, the clip is drawn downwards and the pawl, now tensioned against the ratchet, makes a series of audible 'clicks' which are counted. The number of clicks counted before the clip falls away is the measure of the strength of the magnet being tested. In fact the clip does not move an equal distance per Click', and this again is a problem to be recognized and solved by any child bright enough to do so. An electrically operated mechanical counter has been placed in suggestive juxtaposition to this device in the hope that some child will perceive a possible modification.

Barry has invented an automatic trundle-wheel (see Figure 3). Here, a strip of aluminium foil is fixed on the wheel and once per revolution it makes contact with two terminals which are fixed to the strip of pegboard. This

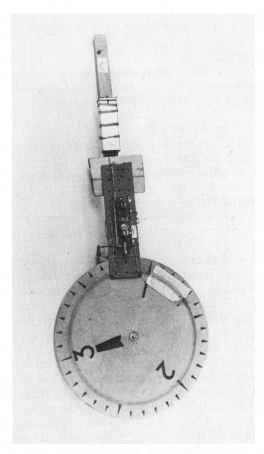

Figure 3: Automatic Trundle-wheel

completes the circuit (battery behind handle) so that the electrically operated mechanical counter (top of handle) registers '1' per revolution. Barry is a remarkable boy in that he is average; give him any kind of standardized test and his quotient will be 100. His interview was recorded on tape, and what follows is a verbatim transcript:

'Tell me all about this unusual trundle-wheel you have made, Barry.'

'Well, it's made out of an ordinary trundle-wheel really. I just connected – er well – stuck a piece of aluminium foil to the wheel, down from the top and about two inches long, and every time it took one revolution it would clock up "one" and so on, because it is connected to two terminals and an electricity current was sent up through the wires, up through the switch to the counted.'

'What causes it to clock up "one" Barry?'

'The current, a sort of shock thing.'

'And that current isn't flowing all the time, is it?'

'No, I've got a switch on there and when the wheel – how do I explain this – when the aluminium foil isn't connected up to the terminals it does not clock up'.

'It clocks up "one" for "one" what?'

'Metre – well it's a yard trundle-wheel but I've got a conversion scale for it.'

'For what purpose, Barry?'

'To convert 'n into the newest measurement.'

'What's its advantage over an ordinary trundle-wheel?'

'Well, you don't have to count the clicks up. It does it automatically for you, every time the wheel goes round one revolution.'

'Do you get any problems with it?'

'A few. It skids a few times. If you push it too fast it doesn't clock up "one". You have to push it really steady.'

'How do you keep the terminals pressing against the wheel?'

'With an elastic band. It goes around the wood and it pulls the terminals towards the trundle-wheel.'

'What about this skidding. Have you any answers to that one?'

'I could cut a tread on it, cut out little divots, or put tracks on, or stick nails in there.'

Barry's total verbal output, when he determines the subject, the place, the time and the listeners, is more a case for suppression than development. Here, he was obliged to talk to the point in circumstances dictated by a situation not under his control, and this is when 'average' primary school pupils tend to become mute. To shut a class up, ask one member to speak to a specific point! Pages could be used to show the links between technology and language development, but here it is sufficient to invite a glance at 'Bullock', pages 53, 54, 94, 95, 145, 188, 189. Barry's work sheet includes a written description, technical drawing, conversion chart and an 'Instruction Sheet' in the form of a flow diagram. Following 'Switch on', Barry's next instruction offers some sound philosophical advice, 'Face your destiny.'

Two versions of a jiffy-meter have been constructed. In mark 1, a broomstick released to fall freely down a map-tube is trapped with the palm of the hand. The greater the length of rod which emerges from the tube, the longer the reaction time. Scores are read off a scale marked on the rod at 2 cm intervals, and the time taken for the rod to fall through one interval on the scale is 'one jiffy'.

Mark 2 is the most complicated piece of technology yet made in the school. A thin metal strip is pulled by the string (left) to the top of the plastic channel (centre) where it is held by pressure from the lever mechanism (top right). When the lever is pressed, the red danger light (lower left) functions and, simultaneously, the strip falls. On seeing the light, the brake switch (bottom right) is pressed, the electro-magnet operates, and the falling strip is halted. Reaction time is read off the ruler fixed at the lower end of the central channel. Swindlers who attempt to operate the brake before the light appears are exposed by a wiring circuit which renders the magnet inoperative until the bulb comes on.

Mandy, using retort stands, G-clamps and vices to test and develop the long series of mock-ups which preceded the final construction, took a school

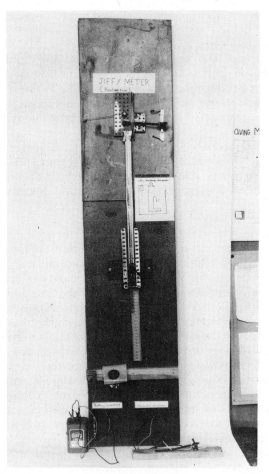

Figure 4: Jiffy meter Mark 2

year at the rate of one afternoon a week to complete this job. (Please Sir, did you say 'mock-up' or 'mess-up?) Again, where is the young genius who will point out that the 'jiffy' is not a constant measure of time, and prove it?! Those, then, are just four examples taken from the records of about 100 devices which actually work.

Appraisal

It is not known, in terms of properly validated research, what the educative influences of technology are upon the children. But, in the way that for the experienced it is not necessary to analyze a pint of beer and to find its specific gravity in order quite accurately to pronounce it off, flat or tasty, observant teachers do not always need the NFER, the APU or Neville Bennett to tell them when they are doing a sound bit of educating in terms of primary education generally, and science in particular. Adopting this connoisseur-type method of judgement, technology is believed to promote children's education in terms of:

(i) *Subjects:* applied science (consciously and intuitively); applied teaching of skills in isolation, whether in language or mathematics, does not produce the best results' (DES, 1978);

(ii) *Skills:* fine motor skills in the use of engineering media;

(iii) *Attitudes:* protracted application to largely self-activated, self-directed work;

(iv) *Intellectual processes:* meeting the intellectual demands of technology: define the need – accept the challenge – consider – possible solutions – test alternatives – select – design – construct – operate – test – appraise – modify – use – record; exercising practical inventiveness, ingenuity, creativity.

'Creativity' has become a cheapened word in education, its true value depreciated by over-use and mis-use. Its thoughtless application to just about anything produced by children, however commonplace, has the effect of hiding from teachers one big and important deficiency in formal education at all levels; the lack of opportunities for original thought and deed. At school level, it is doubtful whether teachers, any more than most authority figures, genuinely wish to encourage original thinkers. Such freaks, by definition, threaten the comfort of the *status quo* and are more likely to be labelled 'bolshie' or 'awkward' or 'bloody minded' than to be appreciated and encouraged. Universities, too, perpetuate a system that recognizes and rewards the ability to follow a prescribed course with leads towards a predetermined destination, but similar recognition is not open to independent explorers who drop far more and bigger beads of intellectual sweat during their longer lonely slogs which map new routes towards more fertile territory. In brief, the educational aim to encourage original thinking could well be phoney!

In our school, a genuine respect for the word means that, within technology, the accolade 'creative' is considered to be justified only when it is observably a fact that the device, wholly or in part, evidences.

invention: when, as far as is known to the child, the device is a prototype (for example, Figures 1, 2 and 4);

modification: when a familier device incorporates original modifications (for example, Figure 3);

improvization: when the device demonstrates ingenuity in the use of available materials as substitutes for unavailable standard items of equipment; for example, the use of graphite lines and water–filled tubes to act as resistors when a milliameter, in the absence of a voltmeter, was used to test circuits.

A most important feature of technology is that the emphasis is almost exclusively upon the physical sciences, and not, as is usually the case in primary schools, upon nature study. What, no tadpoles? No, and as an indication of the general philosophy, no maypoles either!

One boy's spontaneous appraisal: "This yer technology be a lot better 'n education" needs cautious interpretation. Did he mean this as a compliment for the innovation or as a condemnation of the rest of the curriculum? Interestingly, an undergraduate preparing a dissertation on 'Punishments and Rewards' found in the school that the favourite reward by far was 'being allowed to do technology'. (Incidentally, the most dreaded punishment was found to be a letter to parents inviting them to the head's office to discuss the child's behaviour – a bit of research which unusually has been found to be of immense practical use.)

The Current Position

It is now perhaps reasonably clear what is meant by the statement 'technology means the design and construction of original devices which perform a practical function'. German children do so, Japanese children do so, and possibly a few of the more cunning foreign DESs encourage their young to do so, but this is not the case in Great Britain. The current position in this country has been fairly put by Hugh Wassell, Engineering Director of GEC Marconi Electronics:

> Note that it is nearly always a she in the primary school and so it is not surprising that the use of educational media of an engineering nature is very rate indeed and we are doing practically nothing to introduce children of this level into the ideas of engineering applied to the man made things they will need to know so much about when they grow up even if they do not become engineers. Nor are we helping the first sparks of engineering flair to be kindled in children who might become first class engineers in later life', (Wassell, 1978).

The truth of this is visible in the display areas of nearly all primary schools where much of what the children make is seen to resemble those 'Presents from Tregluit' for sale in seaside gifte shoppes which cater expensively for the full range of bad taste. Shelves and walls of *objets d'art* of questionable decorative and aesthetic value are constructed almost excusively from soft materials, largely in accordance with step-by-step instructions passed on by teachers from books by authors whose names, paradoxically, have become synonymous with 'self-expression' and 'creativity'. Either the similarity of art and craft output from one school to that of so many others is in itself a denial of the claims made that this kind of work is self-expressive and creative, or, in the biggest psychological coincidence of all time, the inner self expressed by each individual child is genuinely almost identical to that of millions of others. Nevertheless, the authors of instruction manuals for creative activities do provide one not inconspicuous service; they answer the teacher's plea 'what the hell can I do in craft this week?' Of nuts and bolts and metal and wires used to conduct electricity, of practical reasoning, of the use of purposeful controlled imagination – as distinct from the pixilated stuff of creative writing – and of the application of science and mathematics in the design of working gadgets, there is rarely a sign.

Mr Wassell is, however, inaccurate, and unjust to men in blaming women teachers for this imbalance. It is little different in those schools – a majority – headed by a man, or in classes taught by men, and therefore full credit must be given to men teachers generally for making a very strong contribution to the almost totally feminine environment which primary schools offer to boys and girls alike. Girls do the traditionally girlish things, and boys do the traditionally girlish things. If anything, since the Act more boys take home their pyrexed goulashes than girls their wrought iron coat hooks.

Technology is one answer to Mr Wassell's complaint about the sparse use of engineering media. Since technology involves a form of craft, its wider adoption might go some way towards meeting HMI criticism that 'craft is making a smaller contribution to the work than is desirable', by adding to the range of possible activities one which demands new skills of both a physical and intellectual nature.

Technology and Science Education

The next and most important issue concerns technology in relation to science education. HMI state bluntly. 'Despite efforts by the Nuffield Foundation and the Schools Council, work in science is weak ... (DES, 1978). The product of the Schools Council's effort is, of course, Science 5–13, and therefore the safe implication to be drawn is that what HMI regret, in practical terms, is that Science 5–13 is very much neglected in schools.

It follows that as the powers respond to HMI exposure of this black hole in the curriculum, their INSET procedures will aim, more or less exclusively, to resuscitate Science 5–13. Certainly there are signs that this is the policy. Probably the most publicized, if very little known, recent publication which purports to promote science education in primary schools is *Learning through Science; Towards a Policy for Science in Primary and Middle Schools* (Richards *et al.*, 1978). Practitioners, the recipients of much fatuous advice, are so rarely able to reply in print that this opportunity must not be missed. Authors, by the act of publication, invite open criticism against which the imprint of the Schools Council should offer no protection. Trite restatements of the perfectly obvious, like 'all teachers are teachers of English ...' and 'in larger primary and middle schools it is necessary for the headteacher to take more positive steps to ensure the involvement of all teachers' are irritating in their condescension. The suggestion that a policy for science should be drawn up by whole staffs working together could only be made by those whose daily practices do not bring them face to face with the realities of the human forces involved. But the biggest criticism of the document is that it contradicts the very spirit of science by stating nothing new. Stripped of its plastic upholstery it advocates nothing more enterprising than a tortuous and impracticable way of implementing Science 5–13. Three photographs which appear in an article on 'Learning through Science' in Schools Council Newsletter No. 3, Summer 1979, are worth a glance in confirmation of their boring predictability. Certainly nobody would take a second look.

Course content also confirms that the bandwaggon is beginning to creak over the inset route towards Science 5–13, along which, during the first trip, most schools hopped off (see Chapter 24.2).

At this most tricky point in the discussion it is necessary to differentiate clearly between the major objectives of Science 5–13 and those of technology. A diagramatic representation of the aims of Science 5–13 occurs twice in *With Objectives in Mind* (Ennever and Harlen, 1972). At the hub is the general aim, 'developing an enquiring mind and a scientific approach to problems'. The implications of this for children are stated in eight less broad aims. None of these aims makes any mention of encouraging children to put science directly to some useful purpose. Technology, in contrast, aims to enable children to design and construct devices which perform a practical function. There is, then, a considerable difference between the prime aims of the two approaches to science education.

The activities proposed in the Teachers' Units reflect the Nuffield Junior Science team's definition of primary school science as being 'essentially a practical investigation of the environment' (see Chapter 13). Technology causes children to investigate the environment, but it also aims to introduce children to the concept of *changing the environment* by adding to it something useful which did not exist before. Within the process of designing and constructing the automatic trundle-wheel, Barry investigated the environment in so far as he found out much about electricity, but the truly significant aspect of his science education is that, at a simple level appropriate to his age, he constructed a device which performs a helpful function. He was able to perceive that science is a subject which offers scope for original thinking and doing.

Technology helps 'to develop the enquiring mind and a scientific approach to problems', but in addition it has the effect of developing the practically ingenious, inventive, creative type of thinking which finds its visible expression in resultant hardware.

In short, Science 5–13 is pure science, and technology is applied science. Traditionally, and currently, it is a very firmly fixed notion, taken as read, that science in primary education means pure science and nothing but pure science. That this is so is confirmed by the APU: 'The monitoring at 11, being concerned with processes, will reflect the view of science at the primary level as a way of thinking, the development of skills and attitudes of enquiry and the formation of basic concepts which help in understanding the environment' (APU, 1978 and Chapter 9). This is a factual statement of current thinking, but it might be taken by teachers generally to imply guidelines for what officialdom considers to be the ideal science curriculum for the future. If this happens, the APU, perhaps inadvertently, will have added a strong reinforcing rod to the concrete which supports a restricted concept of science education.

Science: Applied or Pure?

Pure science it was, is, and might be forevermore unless this new issue is discussed: within a school policy for science education which should take precedence – pure science or applied science? Relevancy is one little consideration. As children, most teachers must have watched the magic of magnets drawing patterns of iron filings with their invisible forces, counted the beats of pendulums, calculated the mechanical advantage gained by levers and peered at the private little places of the thrum-eyed primrose. Leaving aside obvious incidental benefits such as millions of enquiring minds who approach problems scientifically, of what direct use is this pure science except to a very few potential boffins? Teachers apart, the number of practising pure scientists must be very small, but the nature of science teaching remains influenced by the plainly unsupportable assumption that all children will become pure scientists. In a society in which there is no such thing as a free lump of plasticine, all citizens need some awareness of the economic importance of design and engineering. The overwhelming majority, as purchasers, users, repairers, DIY problem-solvers and garage-bench improvisers, need some preparative 'hands-on' experience of science in action, as do those who will become engineers. For all but potential laboratory scientists, pure science in the primary school is as irrelevant as the teaching of number bases other than ten.

What of the national need? Until recently this question would have been anathema to teachers who saw, or pretended to see, the whole business of education as being solely in the interests of the individual child, as if the ensuing rounded personality could roll through life undeflected by exterior influences like MLR, IMF, OPEC, EEC. But HMI have stated that curriculum priorities should be decided in accordance with national needs, and this makes it safe to make connections between education and reality even at interviews. That the national need for a society whose aspirations depend upon the successful application of the industrial arts is for applied science, was bluntly put by Lord Kearton, when he said that engineering must take precedence over science for a few decades; without practical application science could be no more 'than a form of self-indulgence'.

Science 5–13 is, of course, in a very superior class of its own as an approach to pure science education. The alternatives, those work cards on the usual heat, light, water, electricity, have as their only comparative attraction, simplicity of operation in the classroom. Science 5–13 has its place in this policy for this school. But for the reasons threaded throughout this chapter, it has been decided that the activities proposed in the teachers' units are potentially far less educative and relevant, in terms of primary education in general and science education in particular, than the experiences which technology offers. This is particularly the case in relation to bright children.

Therefore, as far as resources permit, technology is given precedence over Science 5–13, and intra-school INSET has, as its major objective, the strong confirmation in practice of this order of priority.

A Concluding Example

Recently, at long last, the DES has begun to advocate technological activities in primary schools: 'More emphasis than at present should be placed on work in three dimensions and some of this might be of a simple technological kind aimed at designing and making things that work' (DES, 1981). But there remains the danger that technological activities – applied science – will be regarded primarily as media for the teaching of pure science. One incident illustrates the strength of that kind of traditional thinking. A visitor said of the Magnet Tester (Figure 2), 'What an interesting way of teaching about magnetism!' To us, this was like saying to the Wright Brothers, 'Well now, Wilbur and Orville, you sure have gotten yourselves a mighty fine experiment in aerodynamics there!' True, the Magnet Tester teaches something about magnetism. Since the child at first used flat strips for the upright supports and later found that L-shaped girders provided a more rigid structure, experiments on deflection offered opportunities for investigations of the pure science kind. But the shining significance of the Magnet Tester, which our visitor should have recognized, is that it is an invention – the produce of a 10-year-old's creativity, originality, ingenuity and intellect applied towards practical ends which are rarely recognized as being either desirable or feasible in primary schools.

References

APU (1978) *Science Progress Report* 1977–78, London, HMSO.

DES (1978) *Primary Education in England: A Survey by HM Inspectors of Schools*, London, HMSO; see also Chapter 4 in this book.

DES/WELSH OFFICE (1981) *The School Curriculum*, HMSO.

ENNEVER, L. and HARLEN, W. (1972) *With Objectives in Mind*, MacDonald Education.

RICHARDS, R. *et al.* (1978) *Towards a Policy for Science in Primary and Middle Schools*, Schools Council Publications; see also Chapter 15 in this book.

WASSELL, H. (1978) *Engineering*, Design Education Supplement, June.

20 Science in a School of Social Priority*

Molly Wetton

Editorial Introduction. *This account by the late Molly Wetton provides an affirmative response to the question posed by Kerr and Engel in Chapter 5 of this book. Her views of children's investigations and scientific ideas are in line with those of Ann Squires (Chapter 6). It is clear that science can be taught very productively even (?) in a school of social priority.*

Science with 8–12s

All education at the middle school stage is exciting and challenging, with science possibly the most rewarding discipline of all. The least academic of the new intake arrives with a background of experiences to which he can relate and all the pupils have an understanding of some simple concepts. As an added bonus, there is freedom at the top of the middle school to develop the interests and talents of the most able for we have no formal set of examinations to impose a ceiling on learning.

Science education at this stage does not mean the acquisition of a body of facts but a wider and increased knowledge of concepts. This can best be accomplished through direct and shared experiences. Whatever the differences in childen's background, age and ability, for a few years they share a common interest in their school, and this environment can provide a basis for rich and stimulating teaching situations at all levels. In addition to understanding concepts, preparation must be made to help each child to benefit from the next level of education. Children need considerable practice in observation, measurement and recording. They need to be able to read from their records and eventually to form a hypothesis. In order to make satisfactory records, examination of the properties of objects must be undertaken, together with work involving area, volume, weight, density, force, time and speed. Classifying material objects of the world is another essential part of our work in the middle school. The same teaching situation can provide work for different levels – simple sorting by the youngest age groups and complicated Venn diagrams for the more advanced pupils. Middle school children must also understand something of relationship, dependence, interaction and

* From *Education 3–13*, 8, 1, 1980, pp. 13–15.

systems. The school and its surroundings can provide material for all this work. The detailed study of a tree will show a highly organized structure, a short length of hedgerow a complex natural community and a study of the weather will introduce the concept of systems.

Science on the Timetable

Science teaching at Heathcote Memorial Middle School has to cater for a very wide ability range for we are designated as a school of social priority. There are some very able and talented pupils and also a large group of reluctant scholars. Science, as a separate discipline, is timetabled for the third and fourth years only. All children in these two years have one hour per week and are taught by a teacher with enthusiasm for the subject, in an equipped laboratory. Because these groups are half classes, each child, as the need arises, can have experience in the more sophisticated techniques used in scientific exploration, such as filtration, evaporation, distillation, chromatography etc. Displays of apparatus and work can be set up, labelled and left for others to view and gain benefit. From this room lenses, microscopes, springs, magnets, thermometers, etc. can be borrowed, books referred to or advice sought. The science room and its facilities are in constant use for it is part of the area used in all the team teaching projects.

With so much to do, it is quite unrealistic to confine science teaching to this one period a week. It is integrated throughout the school into much of the other work. Whatever the theme of each year's team teaching project, all have a section concerned with a scientific aspect. Classes explore topics of their own choice with the help of a few simple pieces of equipment. Anything which changes or moves captures the interest of children at this stage and the problem is not getting them started but selecting and organizing their contributions into order and progression. During maths lessons they measure, record and read from their charts and graphs. Weather patterns are plotted from the meteorological screen. Written English results from objects and situations seen in science lessons. Valuable work often results from liaison between craft and science lessons. The wood carving group discern the relative softness and hardness of the material they are using and then with a binocular microscope can clearly see the spaces which gives the hard wood its distinct property. Leaves are printed in art lessons and then examined for differences in science lessons and sorted into sets. Colours and patterns of the natural world enrich the art work and in examining and recording these children begin to understand how structures are built up. Plaster casts from different parts of a tree trunk show how time changes one part of the tree's structure and can also show such wonders as a tree's ability to heal over wounds.

Learning Science Work Through Project Work

All our science projects start with a situation familiar to the children and involve materials from around our own school. The titles, themes and starting-points vary but all projects are alike in that they are planned, objectives listed and a record made of experience covered. Each child keeps a written record of work as it develops and this, together, with drawings, diagrams, graphs and photos, is made into a book. At the end of each project, work is displayed and children have the opportunity to read one another's books. Experiments and displays set up are available for all to look at. Slides and tape recordings from one project are used to enrich other work. The camera can record all the changes which occur on one tree during the seasonal cycle. It can remind us, as we study a chrysalis in winter, of the starting colour and patterns on the peacock butterfly which we saw on the stinging nettles in summer laying eggs, one of which eventually became our chrysalis.

Complex and diverse work can develop from a simple starting-point. An interesting study resulted from an examination of bare patches around the school grounds brought about by trampling. Measurement and recordings illustrated the relationship between term time and decrease in plant growth on specific areas. As a preliminary, food chains were worked out and these stressed the importance of soil to life itself. A display of sands from different beaches and from different parts of the same beach helped the children to see how the basis of all soil is broken down rock. The disaster caused by their own feet compacting the soil was easily understood by children who were given opportunities to see for themselves, with a microscope, relationships between size of particles and air spaces in soils of different types.

A variety of local soils such as sand, clay, chalk is always available and children test these for permeability and find the pH value. Dry soils are handled and wet clay formed into shapes and baked in the kiln, giving us further material to test and examine after the changes brought about by heat. With attention focussed on soil, we have examined leaf litter, made wormeries, soil monoliths and learned something of the importance of acids and alkalines.

Science and School Environment

A combination of contributions from forward-looking teachers from the past and resourceful staff now means that material for much of the science work is readily available. Heathcote Memorial School was built in 1860 by the church and was certainly never intended to be used as a resource. To shut away from scholars all aspects of the world around them appears to be the chief objective of the architect. Windows set high in the rafters would have let in little light and were never meant to be looked through. Inside walls of uneven brick could never have supported a display, and from the log book we learn that fumes from the coke stove were lethal to all forms of life less hardy than teacher and pupils. The problems of light and heat have now been overcome and countless alterations and extensions have provided narrow corridors, numerous walls, shelves and recesses, all of which are put to good use displaying pictures, charts, apparatus and material from the natural world. Exposed tie beams of the trusses supporting the high arched roof make a splendid place to hang pendulums of varying lengths, pullies and springs. Water coursing down valleys made by joins in various roof pitches ensures a constant supply of mosses growing on old damp porous bricks and we can always find an example of decomposers at work on the woodwork. Finding out the properties of the different materials in the buildings, iron, lead, stone, brick, wood, asbestos, glass fibre, etc., and looking for differences between the roof felt covering the new part and the well burnt durable clay tiles of the original school, lead to many science investigations. As a basis for work on structure, we often look at the various types of bonding showing clearly on the outside brickwork and the joins, corners and angles made by the walls provide us with every type of niche – wet, dry, sunny, shady, sheltered and exposed.

Protecting and augmenting natural material around the school is a most important part of planning middle school science. Our trees and shrubs now provide examples of hard wood and soft wood with leaves of many different shapes, sizes, patterns and textures. They supply us with a great variety of blossoms at all times of the year and show the differences in colour and structure between flowers pollinated by insects and those pollinated by the wind. Berries, nuts, cones, winged seeds, etc. can all be seen a few steps from the classroom and the arbutus tree which displays fruit and flower together every autumn keeps us supplied with aphides all through the year. Herbs supplement the shrubs in illustrating how some plants manage to reach the light. We have plants which twist, scramble, climb or use tendrils or hooks, etc. to support themselves up posts, the chain-link fence or various stronger other plants. The ivy illustrates the relationship between light intensity and the difference in shapes of leaves on one plant, while the bramble shows a link between age of shoot and number of leaflets on each compound leaf.

Although we don't keep animals in school, a large variety is easily found. Spiders and insects of all kinds and in all stages shelter in the dense cypress trees. Ants make homes under the loose paving stones, birds nest in shrubs, air bricks and on ledges under the eaves. A bath of water contains a thriving community of cyclops and daphnia and heaps of damp leaf litter keep us constantly supplied with worms, slugs, tiny snails, etc., all of which are returned back to their niche once we have finished looking at them. Other animals are brought in for a short spell only – toads, tadpoles, caterpillars, etc. Sometimes an animal just arrives, such as the field mouse which fell into the empty footbath of the swimming pool and couldn't climb up the slippery sides without our help, or the tiny hedgehog we found struggling to get through the iron railings which we needed to prise open before he could get free and scuttle across the playground and into the safety of the shrubbery.

Inside school we always have a supply of visual aids relating to the animal world which can be kept without fear of deterioration – fossils of all kinds from different types of rocks, discarded birds and wasps nests, pieces of bark showing the larvae galleries of the bark beetle and cones stripped by squirrels or torn by woodpeckers. The mature marble galls on oak twigs will keep indefinitely and children can see for themselves the tiny hole showing how the causer got away or the larger uneven cavity made by a predator who has broken in the gall and devoured the occupants before they fully developed and escaped. Simple aids such as these from the natural world never fail to attract the children's attention, stimulate them to ask questions and set them off problem-solving and finding out for themselves. Perhaps encouraging a lively interest in the world around them is the key factor in helping all middle school children to learn about science.

21   Resources for Primary School Science

Margaret Collis

Editorial Introduction. *Underlying the work described by the other contributors to this section lies sound organization of resources. Margaret Collis provides detailed guidance in this chapter on how resources might be organized at school and class levels so that children can collect and return materials without constant recourse to the teacher, thereby freeing him to teach rather than act as a storekeeper. Her suggested approach is very much in line with the approach to school policy-making discussed by Roy Richards (Chapter 15) and illustrated by Arthur Ashton (Chapter 18).*

Introduction

Science 'is essentially a practical way of finding out about the environment' (Wastnedge, 1967). It is a way that is appropriate for children, for they are naturally curious and enjoy doing something to find out. Children carrying out practical investigations explore, ask questions, collect and study many living and non-living things, make comparisons by measuring and testing, learn skills, sort and arrange finds according to differences and similarities and build up a series of observations that may provide them with evidence of patterns and relationships.

For such activities they need a wide range of resources. At secondary school level this has long been recognized. In the majority of these schools we find laboratories equipped with apparatus, materials and services and often good facilities in the school grounds. In primary schools, as recently as 1978, HM Inspectors found situations much less satisfactory. 'Although four fifths of all classes had access to some resources for their work in science, the provision was generally inadequate' and 'older children were only maginally better catered for than the younger children in this respect' (DES, 1975). Yet in primary schools the need is greater. Children in the earlier stages of intellectual development must examine real things and become involved in actual situations. It is through such concrete experience that they acquire memories to compare with other objects and new situations. Abstract thought about things they have never seen or experienced is not possible.

Improvements in primary schools will not be achieved by imitation of secondary school resources and organization. Younger children do not need commercial glassware, a wide variety of chemicals or sophisticated measuring devices. We know already that they can gain valuable experience of problem-solving by trying to improvise equipment from scrap material. Time and imagination are commodities required for assembling collections of such useful junk. A smaller number of items need to be made or purchased.

The majority of primary school children work for most of their time in class bases with their own teachers so day-to-day organization can be flexible and varied. Sometimes it may be appropriate for all members of a class to do science at the same time, but often children work in small groups, or even individually, at different times and for different lengths of time. It follows that they will need resources at different times too, so they must be able to collect and return them without constant recourse to the teacher.

Clearly, the work of improving resources will involve more than increasing supplies. If the equipment and materials are to be appropriate for the kind of work envisaged, and a firm pattern of organization for their use established, many decisions must be made. This is when the headteacher's leadership becomes vitally important – in bringing members of staff together – in convincing them that a team effort is required. When the staff, through discussion, reach agreement on a course of action they have their *own* policy. All will be fully aware of its details and have an interest in making it work.

Places for Resources

Resources used for scientific activities fall into two categories. Different kinds of papers and card, graph paper, rulers, painting and writing materials will be in continuous use for recording varied experiences, scientific or otherwise, and for many other purposes. Some collections of resources will be needed for certain scientific investigations, but not others. The pond explorers will set out with nets, shallow dishes, strainers and small corked tubes. When these children become weather recorders, they will make demands on supplies of balsa wood, plasticine, off-cuts of hardboard, miscellaneous containers, funnels and mirrors to construct their wind speed and direction indicators, rain gauges and cloud reflectors. When their teacher thinks the time is right for arousing their interest in electricity bulbs, batteries, wires, crocodile clips, an old torch and bits and pieces of junk will make their appearance in the classroom.

These changing demands create problems for teachers working separate-ly. There is little or no space in classrooms for items out of use for considerable periods. These then become dispersed and teacher enthusiasm wanes when a time-consuming search for resources must precede every change of scientific theme. The problem can be tackled if staff retain resources in constant demand in all their class bases and agree to set up a central bank or library for all the other scientific equipment. This would enable teachers and children to draw from the central supply whatever they need for their various enquiries and to return it for safe keeping when their work is completed. Smooth working of these arrangements will depend on good organization and responsible use of the equipment by all concerned.

Class-Based Resources

Arrangement of furniture in classrooms must allow individual children and small groups to move freely from one working area to another and to supplies of resources. Definite places must be found for these supplies and for items of equipment that belong permanently to practical areas like infant home bays. When all children know where to find what they need, collection and return of it after use becomes a straightforward matter. There must also be decisions about whether this equipment should be placed on open shelving, mobile trolleys on the floor or in cupboards, large boxes on castors, small boxes or trays. Further information concerning classroom layout, shelving, containers for equipment and names and addresses of suppliers can be obtained from a practical handbook produced by the Schools Council Learning through Science Project team, *Science Resources – for Primary and Middle Schools* (Richards, R. *et al.*, 1982).

Shared Resources

In addition to equipment and material stored in a central bank within the school building, resources essential for science exist in school grounds, the immediate neighbourhood and the countryside. The indoor-based resources will be accumulated by collecting, constructing and purchasing; those out of doors may need enrichment or selective use. Children will often move in and out of doors in the course of an investigation but here, for clarity, each kind of resource will be considered separately.

The Indoor Resources Bank

Before a central bank can be established there must be agreement on where it should be set up followed by erection of shelving in the place selected. In schools where rolls are falling there may be empty classrooms which can be used for storage, even if they cannot be heated. Sometimes wall space can be found in medical rooms or alcoves. In other situations it may be possible to create space at one end of a cloakroom by replacing a fixed row of pegs with one or two mobile coat trolleys that can then stand between remaining fixtures. In some primary schools teachers may prefer to establish a collection for the infant children and a second one near junior work bases. Special circumstances must also be taken into account, for example, when school premises consist of a permanent building and a collection of huts on the school field – two collections could eliminate much toing and froing with awkward burdens.

Experience has shown that shelving 30 cm in depth is very suitable. Individual shelves can be adjustable but often, in practice, a distance of 26 cm

Photograph 1 View of Resources Centre

between them is sufficient for accommodation of boxes, trays and single items varying in size while leaving little unused space (see Photograph 1).

Boxes or trays will be required for small collections of things that need to be kept together. Cartons of different sizes obtainable from supermarkets are suitable for this purpose. Plastic trays supplied by equipment dealers are also widely used.

1 A Retrieval System

Some of the most important decisions required will be those concerned with a method for sharing the resources available. Arrangements need to be as straightforward as possible. Just as each book in a public library is allocated its own place so each box, tray or single item must be given its own position on the shelving. This could be achieved in the following way:

(i)   Decide on the main groupings into which the total collection of resources should be divided and allocate a colour to each group.

(ii) Give each section of shelving a colour to correspond to this grouping (see Figure 1).

(iii) Number each shelf in each section (see Figure 1).

(iv) Give each container and single item its place in its appropriate section (see Figure 3).

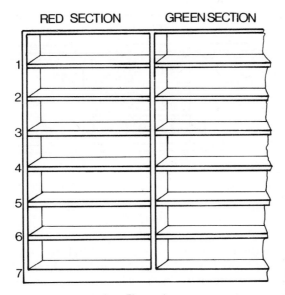

RED SECTION   GREEN SECTION

Figure 1

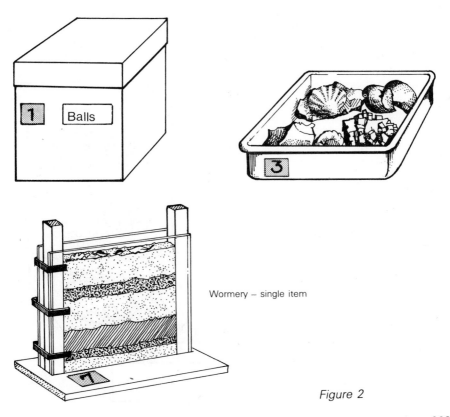

Balls

Wormery – single item

Figure 2

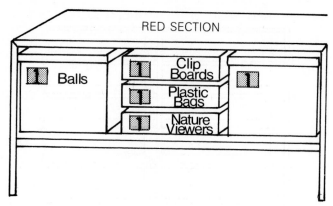

RED SECTION

Balls

Clip Boards

Plastic Bags

Nature Viewers

Figure 3

(v) Indicate these positions by attaching labels to containers and single items appropriately colour coded and numbered. (See Figure 2) It does not matter if positions of boxes on the same shelf alter, say to top or bottom of a pile. What is essential is that only items with red labels 1 can go on shelf 1, in the red section (see Figure 3).

(vi) Reduce risk of loss when equipment is in use by attaching a list of contents to each container. Add instructions regarding any action required to maintain the equipment in good condition (see Figure 4).

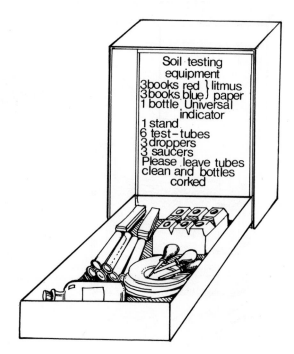

Soil testing equipment
3 books red } litmus
3 books blue } paper
1 bottle Universal indicator
1 stand
6 test–tubes
3 droppers
3 saucers
Please leave tubes clean and bottles corked

Figure 4

When children require something from a box or tray they should collect the whole container and return it with contents complete after use.

(vii) Prepare clearly visible cards in stands for indicating whereabouts of equpiment taken to class bases. These should be placed in positions usually occupied by absent resources. (see Figure 5).

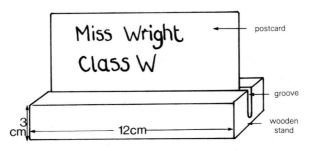

Figure 5

(viii) Keep two trays in the resources area labelled 'FOR BREAKAGES' and 'FOR REPAIRS'.

(ix) Attach a notebook to the shelving, so that names of usable materials needing replacement and suggestions for requistioning can be noted.

Figure 6

Stock List

I RED SECTION – Resources for arousing and
developing curiosity

Shelf 1   Box of balls
          Box of plastic bags
          Box of small containers
          Box of clip boards
          Box of nature viewers

Shelf 2   ....
          ....
          ....

7   ....

II GREEN SECTION – Resources for maintaining
living things in good condition

Shelf 1   ....
          ....

(x) Before the resources bank is opened for use make a complete list of its contents (see Figure 6).

(xi) Duplicate copies of this list for all members of staff.

(xii) Each member of staff should allocate time to explaining to children the organization to be followed and their responsibilities for maintenance when the resources bank is in use.

2   Team Work for Maintenance

Many people can contribute to the work of maintaining the resources in good condition. Table 1 provides some suggestions for division of labour.

Table 1

Helpers	Frequency of contribution	Nature of service
Headteacher	At any time	Encourage staff and children through interest Make a reasonable sum from the school allowance available for upkeep and improvement
Class teachers	As seems necessary	Remind children to: – check contents of containers after use – return items to correct shelves in central store – report breakages promptly – avoid wasteful use of perishable materials
Older children (in pairs)	Daily (five minutes at end of afternoon)	Dust shelves and check that appropriate boxes or indicator cards are in position
Older children	At any time	Help younger children to find and return resources
Parents two or three from a rota	Monthly, or more frequently if necessary	Deal with minor repairs and replacement of perishable materials
Parents two or three	Termly	Check labelling on boxes and replace or renew where necessary
Staff assisted by parents and children	Annually	Spring cleaning and stocktaking

| LEA advisers and/or advisory teachers | At any time | Facilitate exchange of ideas between schools |
| | | Respond to requests for guidance and help |

Team work involved in the establishment and maintenance of a resources bank for science must be coordinated. The obvious person for this responsibility is the holder of a scale post for science. In schools where such a post does not exist, the deputy headteacher or another senior member of staff, preferably with enthusiasm for science, might be invited to accept this important role.

Duties should cover:

> chairmanship of planning groups;
> convening and oversight of working parties for construction of apparatus, major repair work, spring cleaning and stocktaking;
> establishment of a system by which older children working in pairs assist with daily maintenance of the resources bank;
> supplying members of staff with updated stock lists and ensuring that teachers joining the staff become fully informed;
> recruitment of parental help and organization of their activities;
> forging links with LEA advisers, teachers in science, craft and education departments of secondary schools, technical colleges and colleges of education, for mutual help and interchange of ideas;
> organization of supplies of scrap materials through contact with parents, shopkeepers and local industrial concerns;
> keeping in touch with developments through attendance at courses and exhibitions of equipment and books (or arranging for a school representative to attend);
> collecting and coordinating teachers' suggestions for increasing resources;
> advising the headteacher on 'good buys' and purchases deserving priority.

The holder of the post of responsibility will find useful guidance on the development of this coordinating role in a paper published by the Association for Science Education in its Science and Primary Education Series entitled 'A Post of Responsibility' (ASE, 1981).

Grouping Resources on Shelving

Resources can be arranged on shelving in many different ways. When teachers discuss this matter they will need to remember that colour coding and shelf numbering are mainly important as a convenient method for locating and returning items correctly. In class bases the same equipment is likely to be used in different ways by children at different stages of development. Therefore, the criteria used for allocating boxes and single pieces of equipment to groups should provide a framework of organization within which flexibility is possible (for example, see Figure 7).

Figure 7

RED SECTION	GREEN SECTION	YELLOW SECTION	BLUE SECTION	WHITE SECTION
Resources for arousing and developing curiosity	Resources for maintaining living things in good condition	Resources aiding the practice of enquiry skills	Useful collections of objects and materials for testing	Resources for aiding communication

1 RED SECTION (Figure 7): Resources for arousing and developing curiosity

Children's natural curiosity is a potent educational tool for it drives them to question and make efforts to find answers – good ways of beginning science. Many infant teachers are already expert in equipping practical areas within their working bases with resources that can arouse curiosity and, so often, serve as starters to science. Therefore, their next course of action should be to work together listing possible further developments that could stem from use of their water trolleys and practical areas like home bays, music corners and craft areas. For example, here is a list of some activities children could be encouraged to carry out in the 'home corner,' when initial provision of dolls and their clothing has aroused interest:

> make measurements of various parts of the dolls' bodies;
> suggest reasons for people differing in size;
> consider which of their dolls could be members of the same family and offer reasons for these opinions;
> match clothing to dolls for size weather conditions and occupations;
> arrange clothes in sequence corresponding to dressing and undressing;
> make a wardrobe from cartons that will hold all the dolls clothes; relate its size to the largest garments to be stored (experience of relative size);
> paint surfaces of wardrobe after discussion on quantities that must be prepared to cover them (experience of area, volume and the way water affects a material);
> investigate the fabrics from which the clothing is made for patterns that may provide examples of repetition, alternation and rotation; arrangement of threads (woven); strength of unravelled threads; springiness of strips of the material cut diagonally (on the cross); their capacity for soaking up water; the rate at which water runs through them;

consider the value of clean clothing;

organize a wash day;

devise a washing machine from a carton;

compare experience of washing with (i) cold and hot water; (ii) with and without soap powder;

investigate drying rates of clothing consisting of (i) different materials; (ii) similar material but placed in different environmental conditions;

consider whether the drying tests were fair.

After making such a list it would be necessary to decide on resources that should be accumulated in the central bank to enable these suggestions to be carried out. Infant teachers will find a very comprehensive list of scientific investigations using water, together with the appropriate resources required in *Science Resources* (Richards *et al.*, 1982 pp. 16–22).

This could be used as a guide to the construction of similar lists related to

cooking;

scientific use of the musical instruments and other things that make sounds;

work with materials (sand, soil, clay, papers, paint and fabrics);

building with large blocks and constructional apparatus;

the classroom shop.

'Investigation' tables containing challenging displays of objects and materials such as wheels, bottles, wooden things or moving things can provide both infant and junior children with incentives to investigation. Working parties of teachers and parents will find interesting suggestions for making evocative collections in Richards *et al.*, *ibid.*, pp. 22–3. All is grist to the mill and some enjoyable outings could be arranged as interest in 'treasure seeking' escalates.

Children will certainly benefit from a constantly changing supply of these collections to measure, compare and test, but they will also need their teacher's challenging questions to lead them on. The same collection can be used in different ways by different children and the teacher's conversation must also vary to provide the kind of impetus required. A good example of how a collection of shapes can be used with children at different stages of development is described in Richards *et al, ibid.*, pp. 23–5.

Growing interest in the collections provided indoors will often encourage children to move out-of-doors in search of their own material. After some initial reconnaissance they will probably find things they would like to study more thoroughly. Then they will need collecting gear such as trowels, fine paint brushes or pooters, sweep nets and a pair of secateurs and resources for transporting their finds to the classroom – bags for moist soil or plants, and small boxes to serve as separate compartments for invertebrate animals. Numerous things of interest like rare plants, trees, wind and clouds cannot be brought indoors but information about them can be collected and recorded if children are armed with tape measures, clinometers, cloud reflectors and clip boards. Places in the resources area must, therefore, be found for these items too.

2   GREEN SECTION (Figure 7): Resources for maintaining living
    things in good condition

'There is hardly any material more suitable for study by young children than
living forms' (CAC, 1967), so there must be equipment enabling living things
brought into the classroom to be maintained in good condition. Children gain
first-hand experience of conservation through caring for their specimens.

Much of the usual biological equipment belongs to this group of resources
– insect cages, aquaria, vivaria, plant pots and propagators. Again very
effective use can be made of scrap material (see Figure 8).

If certain other items are well made they will last indefinitely – a
wormery is a good example. This useful piece of equipment need not be
limited to studies of earthworms. If a seed, say a broad bean, is planted against
its glass, children can observe its root system in relation to surrounding soil
and the shoot tip bent over at the top to protect delicate leaves as the shoot
grows upward through the soil. Working groups of fathers are often willing to
help with apparatus construction if materials can be provided. They need
precise instructions through clear working drawings on which dimensions are
marked. Such drawings can be found on numerous pages of Richards *et al.*,
ibid. When equipment needs to be purchased teachers should consider what
constitutes a 'good buy'. Something that can be put to a number of uses is one
criterion, for example, a seed propagator (see Figure 9).

Figure 8

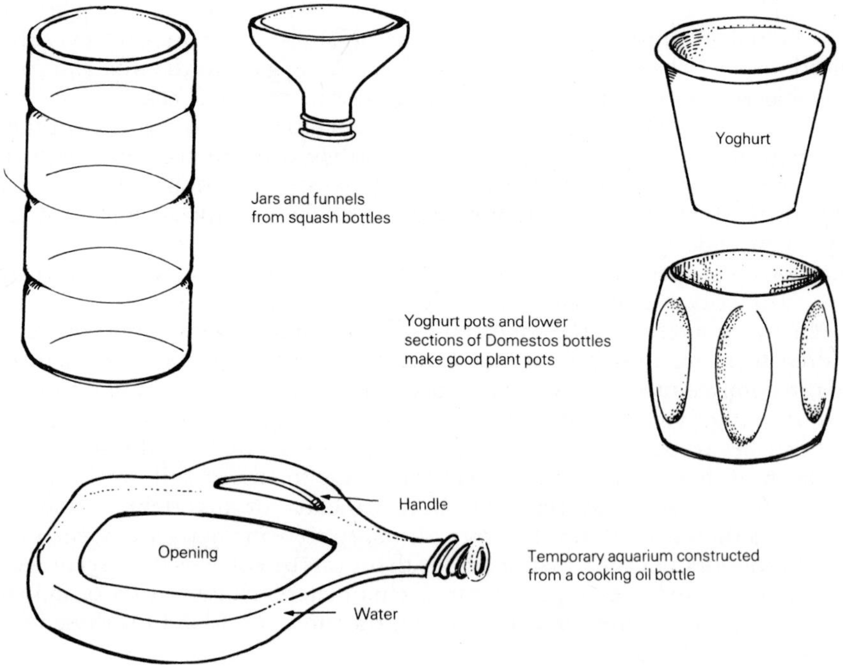

Jars and funnels
from squash bottles

Yoghurt

Yoghurt pots and lower
sections of Domestos bottles
make good plant pots

Handle

Opening

Temporary aquarium constructed
from a cooking oil bottle

Water

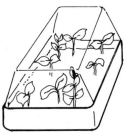

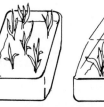

Studies of growth,
germination tests, sequence
of events, water cycle in
miniature as an
environmental influence

Container for soils
under investigation

Making comparisons:
same number of seeds,
same type of soil;
one set grown in open,
one in cool greenhouse conditions

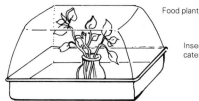

Food plant

Insect cage for rearing
caterpillars or stick insects

Figure 9   Uses of a Seed Propagator

3   YELLOW SECTION (Figure 7): Resources aiding the practice of enquiry skills

When curious children have explored, found something of interest to collect for further study, and provided this, if alive, with good living conditions, they come to the heart of primary school science – making investigations in depth.

Therefore, this next section of the bank should contain resources for aiding the enquiry skills of observation, making comparisons, measuring and testing. Children must be encouraged to make use of resources they cannot store on the shelves – their own senses.

Sensory information may not be sufficiently precise when comparisons have to be made. By holding up one object after another against the pull of gravity it is usually possible to decide which object is heavier, but not *how much* heavier. Measurements must be made and the appropriate devices for doing so provided. Eyes alone are inadequate for collecting information about very small things like pollen grains, root hairs or pollen baskets on a bee's legs. The help of magnifying instruments is required.

A number of arbitary measuring devices can be made from scrap material – a useful undertaking bringing children in contact with some of the general ideas involved in measuring. Previous mention has also been made of classroom equipment such as rulers and, of course, there will be classroom thermomenters and clocks. If children are to entend their work as fully as possible, there must also be provision in the resources bank as shown in Table 2.

Table 2

Quantity	Measuring instruments
Distance	Trundle wheel, surveyor's tape, calipers, clinometer
Mass	Compression scales (domestic type with pan with capacity for holding an object like a small mammal); bathroom scales; balance for small quantities such as postal type or diabetes' scales; Slotted masses on a wire
Force exerted by pushes and pulls	Newton meter
Volume	Measuring cylinders: 100 ml, 250 ml and 500 ml capacity
Temperature	Stirring thermometer, soil thermometer, maximum and minimum thermometer
Time	Seconds timer (stop-watch)
Direction	Compass

Equipment should be provided for magnifying: nature viewers (for outdoor use); hand magnifiers; magnifier on stand or fixed to flexible arm (see Figure 10).

One long-term aim might be possession of a stereomicroscope of good quality. (This can take children into new worlds.)

Some of this equipment will already be in the school, in use for mathematics, possibly geography and for other occasional purposes. The information these instruments help children to obtain is so essential that the purchase of any still required should be given priority when money becomes available.

One observation, however thoroughly made, can only be of limited value. Comparisons and searches for patterns are only possible when a number of observations have been recorded. Weather-recording instruments will

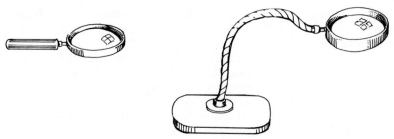

Figure 10

prove very useful when such data is required. Children should be encouraged to construct their own wind and direction indicators and set up home–made rain gauges. In doing so and in trying to get the apparatus to work, they will encounter many problems: 'What can be used to make parts stick together?'; 'What can we use for a firm base?'; 'How can we get the arrow to balance?'; 'What must be done to get it to spin round?'

When one arrangement does not work they must think again of others to try. This experience provides so many opportunities for improving upon first ideas, so plenty of material must be available to ensure that this becomes possible. Examples are *materials*: balsa wood, plasticine, cotton reels, poly-styrene tiles, adhesives, card, off-cuts of wood, squeezy bottles, squash bottles, yoghurt pots, clothes pegs, knitting needles; and *tools*: scissors, paring knife, hammer, tenon saw, nails and screws.

Children find many good reasons for developing the skill of testing when they study properties of materials and wish to find those which are most suitable for particular purposes. They soon become ingenious in thinking of things to do to discover whether a specimen is hard, soft, readily soaks up water, stretches, bends or breaks, burns or fades. There are certain pieces of equipment that can be generally useful for this type of work. Some examples are: a mechanical type of hammer that can strike with the same force each time; an all purpose stand from which pendulums and pulleys can be suspended (see Figure 11); an adjustable ramp (see Figure 12). This kind of apparatus does not need to be devised each time it is required. It does need to be large and strongly made, for it will receive a great deal of hard use. Again, it is something a working party of parents can contribute.

Figure 11

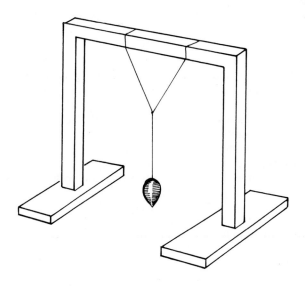

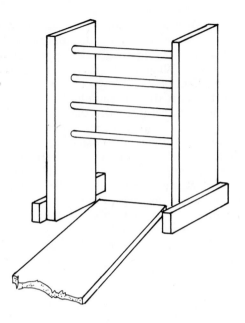

Figure 12

4 BLUE SECTION (Figure 7): Useful collections of objects and materials for testing

In primary schools science can be a very worthwhile part of broader studies generally referred to as 'topic work'. Unfortunately, this approach is some-times criticized because opportunities for doing science afforded by the themes are not sufficiently exploited. This may be due to inadequate resources.

In the course of topic work children often raise interesting questions: What is the best roofing material for a house?; What kind of litter lying about the countryside will not be destroyed by weather? Some excellent science could result from attempts to find answers to such questions, but children can only make these attempts if suitable collections of materials for testing are at hand. When a week or two has to elapse while requirements are being assembled, enthusiasm is likely to evaporate. It is not very difficult to imagine what might be required and placed in the resources bank – floor-covering materials, fabrics, rocks, soils, roofing materials, bricks, foodstuffs to name a few. Additional suggestions can be found in Richards *et al.*, *ibid.* During testing the outcome may be affected by altering certain conditions – a fact important to bear in mind.

Collections can also be assembled that enable children to discover which of a number of variable conditions will affect the issue and which will not matter. For example, a good parachute, when open, will fall slowly. In making parachutes for testing children could alter:

materials from which they are made;
their shape;
their size;

positions of attachment of strings;
length of strings;
number of strings;
material of strings.

If a box containing fabrics (such as nylon, terylene, cheesecloth, calico, muslin and silk) and string, ribbon, nylon thread, elastic, scissors and some bobs to represent the airman could be provided, a group of children could spend time very profitably discovering which of the variable conditions affect the parachute's descent.

When the question is 'What affects the time of the pendulum's swing?', there would be need for a box containing bobs varying in size, shape, mass and type of material and suspensors of string, twine, catapult elastic, tape, thin dowel rod, springs and metal corset bones.

This work has bearing on the devising of fair tests, for it encourages children to consider which conditions must remain constant and which can be permitted to vary.

5 WHITE SECTION (Figure 7): Resources for aiding communication

When children work as explorers and investigators they soon find themselves in possession of interesting information which they wish to share. Resources for communication through speech, drawing, writing of charts, tables and descriptions or for graphical representation will be in all class bases, ready for use at any time. There is, however, another effective way of sharing experience that has not been mentioned – by children setting up displays of their own 'finds' together with results of follow-up studies. This activity gives children opportunities for sorting and grouping specimens in ways that draw attention to their differences and similarities. They can point out what is significant in other ways by displaying things at different levels, marking them with coloured map pins or connecting them with coloured tape. What we are considering here has often been referred to as the 'nature table'. It is a resource that many regard with disfavour because it has often become a neglected classroom dump instead of an effective, interesting means of communication. It may fulfil its purpose more satisfactorily if it is set up by children rather than the teacher (or infants and teacher together); if children make use of it *when* they have something to communicate; and if resources for mounting an effective display are available. Resources required for this activity are what one would expect to find in the school bank. Suggestions regarding what is required and from where requirements can be obtained are given in Table 3.

Table 3

Resource	Source
Pegboard screen (see Figure 13)	Construction by working party
Pegboard fittings	Purchase

Container for specimens – polythene
          bottles
          jars
          pots
          yoghurt
          pots
	From scrap material

Small trays often divided into sections	From scrap material
Stands and holders	From scrap material such as egg boxes or made from wood by working party
Map pins,	From school stock

Photograph 2   Pegboard Screen

When children have worked in groups on aspects of a common theme they can coordinate their efforts by bringing their displays together to form one exhibition. Groups can also be encouraged to comment critically on each other's efforts and then opportunities should be given for adjustment to be made if exhibitors think they will result in improvements. Teachers stocking the various sections of their resources bank are advised to consult lists in the very comprehensive appendix to Richards *et al.*, *ibid.*

Outdoor Resources: School Grounds[1]

In outdoor surroundings children will find some of their most profitable investigations and problems. Something so close at hand as school grounds can be visited daily to make the regular observations so necessary for in-depth studies. Although any outdoor place can offer a wealth of starting-points for scientific investigation, they are not all equally obvious and attractive to young children. Since teachers can exercise a certain amount of control over their school premises, it may be profitable for them to review the opportunities their school grounds already offer 'explorers' and consider whether more could be done to increase their value as an educational resource.

The earliest decisions about grounds of new schools are made by administrators and architects so their cooperation should be sought in retaining valuable natural features that may already exist on the site, for example, a hedgerow, an interesting old wall or stream. Before staff are appointed, LEA advisers and advisory teachers are the people who can contact the developers. They can also provide guidance when teachers reach the stage of wishing to enrich outdoor areas.

Some valuable facilities that working parties of teachers and parents might try to create are:

1 Variety in plants

Children using their senses will find discoveries of different colours, patterns, shapes, sizes and scents rewarding. These features in both wild and cultivated plants are an incentive to sorting activities.

2 Variety in living conditions for animals

Animals settle in places with environmental conditions that happen to suit them. Therefore, children are likely to find different creatures if they can search in places that are shady, sunny, trampled, exposed, sheltered, damp, dry, sloping, flat, warm or cold. Provision of small mounds, rotting logs, unmown patches of grass, a few broken flower pots or tiles and some damp sacking can increase the number of habitats (living places) and so give children more varied opportunities for studying animal numbers and behaviour in relation to their different surroundings. Frequently, too, these investigations will give children practical experience of the important biological concept of interdependence (one thing affecting another).

3 Adventure facilities

These include rough ground, facilities for climbing and scrambling, places and materials for devising large constructions like tree houses and hides, an old car or boat immobilized and firmly anchored and even a swimming pool. In such places children can collect weeds, search under stones or swing on low branches without fear of doing damage. They can try out their own ideas, discover more about their own strength and capacity for movement on land and in water and make discoveries about shapes, sizes and different materials.

Photograph 3 View of Primary School Chequerboard Garden

4 *Provision for carrying out comparisons and tests*

A chequerboard garden makes a fine outdoor laboratory. Paving slabs alternating with garden plots give children plenty of standing room while they work. Unwanted growth in the small plots can easily be controlled leaving children time to compare the growth of different plants, observe the work of animal friends and foes, test the effects of planting seeds in different ways, test soil and the effects of using fertilizer or lime.

5 *Facilities for long-term investigations*

Discovering evidence of patterns and relationships in records is an important scientific process and observations collected through long-term studies in school grounds are an important source of records needed. Some resources for long term work are:

- a cleared square metre plot for study of plant colonization and succession; trellis for climbing plants;
- a bird table and nesting boxes for studies of feeding and nesting behaviour;
- a large movable run for grazing animals like rabbits or guinea pigs (see Figure 13) (effects on lawns of their feeding can be studied);
- some pitfall traps for making comparisons of numbers and types of animals captured at different seasons;
- a weather station.

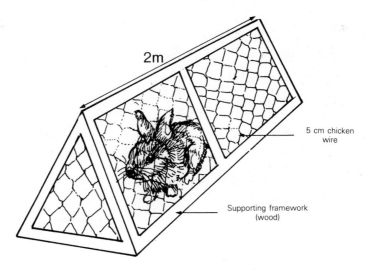

2m

5 cm chicken wire

Supporting framework (wood)

Figure 13

6 Special provision

Scientific enquiries in primary schools can often form part of broader thematic studies. Herbs, for example, have interesting connections with country lore and human behaviour when the value of hygienic habits was less well known. The craftsman can make use of plants that yield vegetable dyes, while the scientist can study their growth and the process of dyeing. Farmers and scientists share an interest in grasses. These plants make interesting crops for chequerboard plots, especially when in flower.

7 Limited premises

Teachers with outdoor premises consisting of no more than an asphalt surface and iron railings need not despair. It is worth remembering that 'small is beautiful' and small areas are often more suitable for young children to cultivate, maintain and weed. Figure 14 provides some suggestions for creating small places to explore.

Much has been written about development of school grounds as an educational resource (see Note 1). Also the Council for Environmental Education offers a resource sheet entitled 'School Grounds and Gardens' designed to help teachers to select source books, children's books, charts and slides. It can be obtained by sending a stamped addressed envelope to:

The Council for Environmental Information Service,
School of Education,
University of Reading,
London Road,
Reading RG15 AQ.

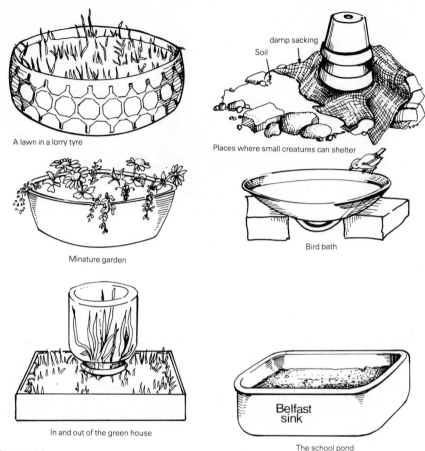

A lawn in a lorry tyre

Places where small creatures can shelter

damp sacking

Soil

Minature garden

Bird bath

In and out of the green house

Belfast sink

The school pond

Figure 14

Outdoor Resources: Beyond the School Site

As children develop and become increasingly experienced investigators, their teachers, looking for opportunities to lead them on, may make use of resources beyond the school site. At day and residential field centres, educational centres such as that provided at the Severn Wild Fowl Trust and some local museums (for example, Haslemere) there are outdoor and indoor facilities where children can carry out their own investigations and make records for comparison with earlier studies made near home.

Children out and about in urban areas may follow town trails. Then teachers need to make sure that children do not limit themselves to treating their surroundings as animated visual aids, by simply walking round looking at things mentioned in trail notes. If such notes are designed to promote scientific enquiry, they should not give the answers but they should offer children many suggestions about what they can actively do themselves to discover answers, or partial answers, to the questions posed.

Visits to places like the local railway station, bakery or shopping centre can equip children with many good ideas for further enquiries. If use of this resource is to result in science, in-depth follow-up practical investigations must be carried out on return to school. For example, after an interesting visit to the docks children could undertake practical investigations concerned with water, shape of boats, floating and sinking and the work of cranes. A pack of audio-visual material produced by the Learning through Science Project team in association with ASE, and designed for in-service education, contains a tape-slide sequence on 'Science from the Building Site' (Richards *et al.*, 1983) that teachers will find helpful.

Visits can be exciting for both children and teachers but when resources are at a distance certain more mundane administrative matters require attention in order to ensure success. Conversation with adults helps children to think about their experience so organization which provides each small group (of, say, six) with an adult companion will be beneficial, both educationally and for promotion of safety. Helpers might be parents, or students from a college of education. The membership of County Trusts for Nature Conservation often contains retired naturalists, biologists and teachers who will respond to invitations to assist.

Further matters for the teacher to consider are:

the necessity of making a preliminary visit to the site;
arrangements for access to the site (if in private ownership);
briefing needed by helpers;
explanatory note to parents;
preliminary information required by children;
procedure on arrival at the site;
promotion of responsible attitudes with regard to use of both urban and
    rural places;
safety precautions.

Books As a Resource for Science

Doing science and *reading about* science are two very different ways of working. Neither is wrong, but the second should not be allowed to replace the first. Neither should children be allowed to believe they are doing science when they are simply reading a book about something scientific. How can books be helpful to those doing science? Children are always anxious to name their finds: books dealing with identification of plants, animals and rocks can provide valuable help. Young children use them by trying to match finds to named pictures, so books containing accurately coloured illustrations and single specimens, or a few well spaced, on their pages will be the most suitable to provide. Older juniors should be encouraged to use simple identification keys such as those contained in the 'Clue' Books by Allen and Denslow. *Science Resources* (Richards *et al.*, 1982) contains a very comprehensive list of books aiding identification from which teachers could obtain guidance about specimen copies they might try to examine.

The best time for making use of a book should also be considered. When children come into the classroom with specimens they should begin investigations by recording information that their own senses, aided by measurement and magnification, can provide. This may cause them to wonder about something, to try testing and to accept their teacher's advice about other useful courses of action. *After* all this they could continue by comparing their own findings with those of somebody who has studied the same kind of material has described in a book. Discrepancies between the two accounts could lead to further examination to see if something has been missed, checking with accounts in other books and testing to find out whether mistakes have been made – all useful scientific practice. On the other hand, living things of the same type are not identical and two similar things, correctly examined, could show differences. Consequently, work of this nature may help children to think about the important biological concept of *variation*. Statements in books unsupported by evidence can also provide incentives to further checking and testing.

Resources to Aid Independent Learning

It is essential that some ways of working should enable teachers to develop conversations with individual children and small groups. This stimulates the children concerned to think about what they are doing and helps forward their understanding of concepts. Anything that can help children to deal with a certain amount of their work independently will free the teacher to circulate and assume a consultant role.

Much material designed to aid independent learning in the form of sets of assignment cards is now appearing so this is another resource teachers must examine, know how to evaluate and consider whether it should be used. When children work with cards that are too prescriptive they simply follow directions then wait for the next orders from whoever is doing the thinking. This way of working has little connection with science. Materials that consist of little more than gap-filling exercises should certainly be avoided, for children increase their own depth of understanding when they try to express their thoughts and findings in their *own* language.

What can we expect from pupil material that does deserve consideration? We can expect this material to be about the environment, since science is a practical investigation of influences that make places as they are, at any time. Apart from this, the material should stimulate children to carry out the activities (that is, processes) that enable them to acquire scientific knowledge. Teachers could check this when they examine cards by asking the following questions. Do the assignments encourage children:

> to use a variety of senses in making their observations?
> to do something in attempts to answer questions that have been posed?
> to collect series of observations and look for patterns in this data?
> to make comparisons by measuring and testing?
> to make sure the tests they carry out are fair?
> to check results by repeating tests?
> to suggest possible answers to questions and then test to find out which
>   suggestions appear to be on the right track?

Obviously all these processes will not be included in single assignments. Also the number of actions on the list that children perform will depend on the level of intellectual development they have reached. In order to give children scope for carrying out the actions just listed, cards must be written in a way that stimulate children to add their own ideas to the work suggested. When children do progress to using their own ideas they will abandon the card material for a time. This is desirable as it brings about a change of approach. Science should provide more than repeated experience of working through one card after another.

Although pupil material should aid independent learning, it should not make teachers redundant. It should bring children in contact with problems that cause them to seek their teacher's help. Such help, given through discussion, will encourage children to think in ways which help their understanding of concepts to develop. Notes for teachers relating to each pupil assignment should draw attention to leading questions that should be asked, and ideas that should be emphasized, when children seek help.

Many teachers comment on the value of some assignments as aids to language development. The subject-matter and practical work arising certainly encourage children to talk and write about many things. Groups of children also talk and argue among themselves as they cooperate over tasks. The need for tests to be fair promotes some of the most vigorous argument and, therefore, some of the most lively thinking.

Assignments also have a very important role to play in extending children's language development. If the practical work these resources promote is interesting and enjoyable, children feel it is worthwhile to read carefully in order to join in with what is going on. The text should also include some words that are probably unknown because they can be learnt within the context of the experience in progress. Many teachers welcome suggestions about different ways in which children should record their investigations, so the assignments should provide this help. In asking for labelling of displays, lists of observations and recording of data on charts the teaching material will encourage children to collect words. At other times it should ask for clear descriptions, explanations of ways in which processes have been carried out and for evidence in support of statements.

The teacher's organization should not be limited by the way the material on cards is presented. Variety of organization is required to suit varied tasks. It should be possible for teachers to select work from the material that can be done by large numbers of children at the same time. For another occasion it should provide a variety of tasks relating to the same topic that different groups could work on and then bring together to illustrate the range of work covered. Cards should contain small tasks for the children who need the satisfaction of completing a job quickly and ideas that encourage the most able children to tackle work demanding persistent effort over a period of time.

Implementing Suggestions

When the range of resources for science in primary schools is considered, it is obvious that providing them will involve thought, planning, imagination, skill and much hard work. Teachers concerned with every area of the curriculum may well ask how the demands can be met. The first answer is, 'Not all at the same time.' Many school staffs have given staff meeting time to planning and providing resources for language development and mathematics. Why not devote a year to concentrating on science? Other aspects of the curriculum in turn should also receive attention in due course. Secondly, cooperate with colleagues: decision-making in isolation can be a worrying business; much of the anxiety goes when people decide on a course of action through cooperative discussion. Then no one person can be held responsible for unsuccessful results. Also, many people are prepared to help with the physical work of setting up a resources bank. Make efforts to find and involve them. Thirdly, make a start for, as soon as that is done, it is possible to see how improvements can be achieved. Non-starters are the sinners who make no progress.

Conclusion

Well selected resources make a wide range of practical work in science possible and, through this, children can be helped to increase their knowledge of their surroundings; to gain experience of scientific ways of working; to learn and practise certain skills; to develop increased understanding of some scientific concepts. Above all, what has been described is an exercise in cooperation: cooperation between the headteacher and staff, between staff and parents, staff and advisers and colleagues in other schools, between staff and children and between the children themselves.

When this is achieved the rewards are great, not only in higher standards of work and the satisfaction of knowing that children are receiving well prepared teaching. Attitudes are also fostered – attitudes of willingness to work for the community; respect for the ideas and skills of others; willingness to share; willingness to use facilities responsibly and with consideration towards others (conservation). In putting hard work into this effort, staff will save themselves work in the long run, but they will also gain the satisfaction of creating something which can help them towards achievement of the aims of teaching science.

Note

1 For materials on the school grounds as an educational resource, see (1973) *Project Environment: The School Outdoor Resource Area*, Longmans; (1975) *Science 5/13 – Using the Environment 4 – Ways and Means*, Macdonald Educational; Durham Country Conservation Trust, *Wildlife Areas for Schools*, (from SPNC, 22 The Green, Nettleham, Linc.); Arnold, N. (1976) *Wildlife Conservation by Young People*, Ward Lock; *The Built Environment* (Book List), from The Council for Environmental Education; *RSPB Teachers Guides*, one of the series deals with bird studies using school grounds from RSPB Education Department, The Lodge, Sandy, Beds, SG19 2DL.

Reference

ASE (1981) *A Post of Responsibility in Science*, Science and Primary Education Paper No 3, Association for Science Education.

CENTRAL ADVISORY COUNCIL FOR EDUCATION (England) (1967) *Children and Their Primary Schools*, HMSO.

DES (1978) *Primary Education in England: A Survey by HM Inspectors*, London, HMSO; see Chapter 4 in this book.

RICHARDS, R. *et al.* (1982) *Science Resources for Primary and Middle Schools*, Macdonald Educational pp. 8–12: Classroom layout, shelving, containers and names and addresses of suppliers; pp. 16–22: Work with water in infant schools; pp. 22–3: Collections for arousing curiosity; pp. 23–5: Using a collection to develop curiosity; pp. 49–51: Ideas for collections for topic work; pp. 63–71: Index – equipment lists; pp. 78–80: Books for identification; also many line drawings of apparatus.

RICHARDS, R. *et al.* (1983) *A Tape/Slide Sequence on Science from the Building Site*, from 'Ways Forward', Learning Through Science, Macdonald Education.

PART VII

Recent Developments in In-service Education

Introduction

As the chapters in Part V demonstrate, curriculum development projects were the favoured strategy for developing primary science (as well as most other areas of the curriculum) during the sixties and early seventies. In an evaluation of their impact on policy and practice in primary schools, the HMI Primary Survey (1978) commented:

> During the past few years considerable efforts have been made to stimulate and support science teaching in primary schools. There have been curriculum development projects at national level and in some areas local authority advisers and teachers' centres have been very active.... Yet the progress of science teaching in primary schools has been disappointing; the ideas and materials produced by curriculum development projects have had little impact in the majority of schools (Chapter 4 of this book, p. 37).

The Inspectorate's professional evaluation of the state of primary science, reiterated two years later in the Scottish context (DES, 1980), was not challenged.

Why did the projects have so little impact, except in a small number of schools such as those featured in Part VI of this book? Many reasons have been advanced. Some concern the nature and assumptions of project-based strategies of curriculum development, whether in science or in other subjects (see, for example, Richards, 1974 and Prescott, 1976); others are related to the particular problems of primary science (for example, Chapter 3). One key factor appears to have been the insecurity of primary teachers arising from their lack of knowledge of science, itself the result of their own school experience and/or of shortcomings in their initial training (see Chapter 5). This factor is highlighted by HMI themselves (Chapter 4), Redman (Chapter 12), by Parker-Jelly (Chapter 14) and by Allsop and Whittaker in their contributions to this section of the book (Chapter 24.1 and 24.2). A second very significant factor, almost entirely unacknowledged in the literature of primary science, was the marked difference between the exploratory, 'child-centred' approach advocated by all the project teams and the more pragmatic, directive approach favoured by very many primary teachers. In her contribution Whittaker acknowledges a failure by curriculum developers and in-service providers to begin where the teachers were; Parker-Jelly also reports Science 5–13's inappropriately high expectations of teachers, given the wide range of their abilities, interests and aptitudes. Too often, project teams assumed the existence of adaptable 'child-centred' teachers able and willing to learn science 'alongside' their children, and did not realize that the population of primary teachers was highly heterogeneous in terms of outlook, attitudes and capabilities.

The HMI Survey of 1978 and the Scottish equivalent of 1980 have been very significant in the development of primary science. They have given it an impetus far more powerful and more authoritative than any offered previously. Both have placed their weight behind improvements in in-service education (and, to a lesser extent, in pre-service education), both on and off school sites, in an attempt to provide the sustained support required if science is to become a firmly established part of the curriculum in every primary school.

Judging from the accounts by Wastnedge and Macleod (Chapters 22 and 23), there are differences in approach to in-service development north and south of the Border. The Scots seem to be placing greater faith on central initiatives through schools' participation in trials associated with the Learning through Science project, through involvement in the recently established Primary Science Development Project and through the production of national policy documents for science and environmental studies by the Committee on Primary Education. In addition, many of the regional educational authorities are producing guidelines for primary science. Unlike the English, the Scots are not developing the role of consultants for science at school level.

In his contribution Wastnedge reviews developments in England since 1978. The role of HMI in 'consciousness-raising' is noted, as are their attempts to disseminate their ideas through conferences, a film, a pamphlet* and the sponsoring of a small number of local initiatives. He places particular emphasis on the role of local advisers and colleges in fostering in-service work tailored to the needs of the locality – a theme taken up and developed by Allsop and Whittaker (Chapter 24.1 and 24.2.) The importance of starting where the teachers are, of sponsoring in-school in-service activities, of tailoring more initiatives to school staffs rather than to individuals and of training teachers to take responsibility for policy formulation and/or the day-to-day development of the work are discussed. As Allsop's and Whittaker's contributions well illustrate, the agencies providing courses have had to be sufficiently flexible to seek out different audiences over time, and to respond to their differing needs. Typically, a teacher's concerns might be how to group children for science activities and how to store the equipment used; a head's concerns might be with developing a school policy for science and schemes of work for each year group taught. Dealing with a clientele often inexpert in science, advisers and college tutors are often required to use the individual school as base for their in-service work for despite unease about the labour-intensiveness of such a stategy, it is only then that teachers can get the help pertinent to their particular setting to ease them through their early implementation problems.

It is too early to evaluate the result of such initiatives. A follow-up to the

---

* Now published as *Science in Primary Schools* (DES, 1983).

HMI Primary Survey could provide such an evaluation. Certainly, recent in-service developments are based on a fairly realistic appreciation of the difficulties facing teachers, individually or collectively, in taking up primary science. Wastnedge, one of the pioneers of science in the early sixties, should perhaps have the last word: 'What is needed is great patience, recognition of the magnitude of the problem and of the time scale involved. . . . There are no easy answers and those who seek a philosopher's stone in the form of work cards or any other promises of instant success will undoubtedly be disappointed (Chapter 22, p. 241).

References

DES (1978) *Primary Education in England: A Survey by HM Inspectors of Schools*, London, HMSO.

DES (1980) *Learning and Teaching in Primary 4 and Primary 7*, Edinburgh, HMSO.

DES (1983) *Science in Primary Schools*, London, HMSO.

PRESCOTT, W. (1976) *Innovation at the National Level*, E. 203, *Curriculum Design and Development*, Unit 24, Open University Press.

RICHARDS, C. (1974) 'The Schools Council: A critical examination', in *Universities Quarterly*, 28, 3.

22 Primary Science in England and Wales: Developments in Retrospect and Prospect

Ron Wastnedge

The Inspectorate's Primary Survey Report in 1978 marked a significant point in the development of science education in the nation's primary schools (see Chapter 4). Before then, there seems to have been a steady regression from the high levels achieved in the sixties. In the seventies it became increasingly difficult to find children learning through practical enquiry, and that was true even of mathematics, that long-standing centrepiece of primary education. The work card and work book had taken over, a sure indication that teachers were feeling under pressure, insecure and ready to grab any support that offered itself. More and more teachers were asking for help with classroom organization. Apprehensive teachers, lacking in confidence, were apparently less willing to embark on practical science, especially the exciting kind that begins with observation of the environment and follows children's own questions. Where practical work did go on, it often took the form of investigations dictated and prescribed by commercially-produced cards and had little to do with the general work of the class or the immediate interests of the children. Frequently, science consisted of no more than copying information from books.

In case all this sounds too depressing, let it be said at once that there were individuals and groups of teachers all over the country who were doing exciting work in science. Much of it was based on the excellent programmes on radio and television, or on the 5/13 books. But, somehow, much of the sparkle and exhilaration had gone and the overall picture was, to say the least of it, distinctly patchy. The reasons for the fall-off were not hard to find. Teachers whose own science education had never included learning to observe, finding patterns or devising experiments could hardly be expected to be brimming with confidence and enthusiasm over teaching those same 'processes' to children (see Chapter 24). Their difficulties were often compounded by the fact that they had not clearly understood the subject-matter either. To make matters worse, teachers were also being put under pressure to raise standards in the so-called 'basics' and the response was all too often an increase in the time spent on hearing children read, along with more and more pages filled with computation and comprehension exercises. It seems that teachers and parents gained reassurance from books filled with words and figures, even though the HMI Primary Survey told us that children who were educated through a broadly-based curriculum were likely to do better in the 'basics' than those whose schools had concentrated narrowly on maths and language.

To some extent, teachers had been their own worst enemies. Too many had jumped too readily and uncritically onto the bandwagon of so-called 'progressive' education. Too often the expression, 'children learning through practical exploration', was interpreted as 'fill the room with things and then turn them loose to teach themselves.' 'Let the children learn by following their own interests', for some teachers meant opting out of teaching. How well I remember saying to groups of teachers, 'At this stage, I am more concerned with *how* they learn than with *what* they learn.' And how clearly I remember the headmaster who, ten years later, asked me if I still thought it didn't matter if children didn't learn anything. It was as though people read the headlines and ignored the detailed explanation. Such uncritical approaches made it easy for people to find horror stories. Add a few half-truths and the back-to-basics movement was in full swing, and many teachers were deterred from teaching any science at all.

So the Primary Survey Report came at an opportune moment, drawing attention as it did to science's lowly standing in the curriculum and to the strong case which can be made for its inclusion. The Inspectorate itself decided to give a lead. It did this in several ways. It made a film showing teachers making a start on science and turning the spotlight on all the agencies they drew upon for support. (This is available on free loan either as a film or on videotape.) HMI also organized a series of one-day conferences at which teachers, advisers, college lecturers, administrators and HM Inspectors discussed the problem and how it might be solved. Out of the fourteen conferences emerged a consensus on the nature of primary science, with a series of suggestions for suitable actions to promote it. A general summarizing statement was sent to everyone who had attended a conference. It stated clearly the views of teachers, advisers and teacher trainers, together with an analysis of the difficulties they face.

The conferences, I believe, gave encouragement, support and a degree of unity to those who were seeking to establish science in their schools. They reaffirmed the principle of placing the emphasis on 'processes' but also made it clear that thought should be given to the problems of choosing appropriate content and ensuring continuity and progression of both content and process (see Chapter 1). They also made it clear that the amount of time available in BEd and PGCE courses, especially with the present emphasis on academic 'respectability', is quite inadequate to rectify the problems faced by students, thus giving a feeling of vindication to those who, for some years, had been saying that we shall never get primary science right until we have changed the nature of secondary school science.

Other Inspectorate initatives included a new pamphlet on science (DES, 1983) and support in a few authorities for groups of schools where total staffs agreed to commit themselves for at least a year to developing a policy for science. The results over two years have been most gratifying and it seems that the combination of factors – the head's belief in science, the staff's communal commitment and the knowledge that practical support is available – produces results. The supporting techniques varied from area to area and included courses, seminars, links with colleges or secondary science departments, and the production of 'swop packs' by teachers in the scheme. There is little doubt that the strategy of involving whole school staffs is one which needs to be examined and taken much more seriously than heretofore.

But it would be wrong to suggest that all the running was made by the Inspectorate, however important that may have been. Science advisers exploited the new climate of opinion, running courses, persuading groups of teachers to produce teaching materials and generally devoting a high proportion of their professional time to primary schools. It seemed that more than ever before they were working in close collaboration with teachers, and many of their strategies show imagination and ingenuity. Nor should we ignore the contribution of primary advisers, especially when primary and science advisers worked together and gave support to one other. One group of advisers established a working party of heads and teachers to examine the problem and their deliberations led them to invite a college to join them in planning a year-long course tailored to the needs of *their* schools. It included workshops, tutorials and supportive visits by tutors. It also involved a commitment by the authority to release teachers for several weeks at a time, and evaluation was a continuing process performed by a teacher who attended the course and sounded the opinions of the other teachers who were involved.

Of course, many colleges have played an important part in the overall plan. There are tutors who run courses, who work in schools, and who give support in any ways that teachers want and need (see Chapters 24.1 and 24.2). And there are the teachers themselves. Never let us forget them and what they have to offer to their colleagues directly from their experience in the classroom. From outside the profession came more offerings. One national industrial concern is producing videotapes on science teaching, and the very first is about primary schools which are developing science policies. Another has produced teacher support booklets and is working on materials related to the Science Museum.

The energy and enthusiasm being put into the system is reminiscent of the sixties. The goodwill and expertise available are tremendous. What is needed is great patience, recognition of the magnitude of the problem and of the time scale involved. The danger is that people will expect too much too quickly and that the schools will lose their nerve again. Most important, we have a renewed recognition of the importance of science in the primary curriculum and a general agreement about its nature. Now we must harness the energy and enthusiasm and try to ensure that all those involved move steadily in the right direction. So, where should they be going?

First, there are the tried and trusted techniques. Short courses run by the Inspectorate, by local authorities and by colleges have an important part to play in helping teachers to understand and use the processes of science for, if there is to be any success, teachers must know how to plan and carry out scientific enquiry. But what we should not forget is that they also need to know what kinds of questions can be answered by employing the processes of science. To operate a system based on scientific processes, they must also know how to explore and question the environment. In other words, we should be running an increasing number of courses on environmental studies so that teachers can learn (i) how to explore and observe; (ii) how to ask pertinent questions; (iii) how to recognize which of those questions can be answered by applying the disciplinary skills of science, or history, or geography, or art, or mathematics; and (iv) how to apply the disciplinary skills to the problem in hand. This is no small order and it could never be achieved through one course per teacher. In fact, it will probably need intermittent courses with intermediate supporting work in the schools.

Along with these courses it will also be necessary to teach most teachers as much of the content of science as possible so that they will know how to help children through their investigations, how to ask appropriate questions, how to involve them in pertinent discussion, and how to build up a supply of relevant materials with which the children can work. Not a great deal of work has been done in this area and there is a need for, say, science and primary advisers to try a variety of approaches, and pool their experiences.

Another important line of development is the involvement of a whole school staff in developing a policy for science (see Chapter 15). This is already happening and some of the results are promising. But, again, it is a long-term process in which educational aims and objectives have to be thought out clearly and examined critically. Once a staff has decided on the role of science within the total curriculum they then have to examine a number of very important detailed questions (see Chapter 1). For instance, are there some scientific ideas which are so important that all children should meet them by the time they reach the age of eleven – energy? the perpetuation of life? chance? Teachers will need help with this kind of problem and will probably have to draw on the expertise of secondary teachers or college tutors. Once the important scientific ideas have been identified, at what stage of a child's development would they be appropriate? Would you teach something about energy to 5-year-olds as well as to 10 year-olds? If so, how? Is it possible to build up a range of experiences between the ages of 5 and 11 which will reveal to children the great variety and richness of living things, the patterns of movement of animals or of life cycles of organisms? How do you ensure progress in the processes, making sure, for example, that observation becomes more acute and experimenting becomes more rigorous? Having reached some – albeit provisional – decisions how does a school ensure that there is no repetition of experience, only extension and development, and that the enthusiasms, fears and expertise of individual teachers can be accommodated within the overall plan? For it is just as useless to ask Miss Jones to teach about pulleys if she does not understand them as it is wasteful not to ask her to study life in a hedgerow about which she knows a great deal.

If all these momentous developments are to be achieved, where will the leadership within a staff come from? Again, progress is being made on this front by the training of science 'specialists' or 'consultants', or 'co-ordinators'. Primary teachers have a long-standing reluctance to accept the idea of subject specialists but, in this case, experience is proving that their fears are unfounded. Those schools which have taken up the idea are finding it extremely helpful. One member of the staff takes on a degree of responsibility for science just as, for many years, individuals have been responsible for mathematics or language. The job of this 'coordinator' is then determined by the staff, the head, the adviser and the coordinator him or herself. Basically, it means learning some science, producing papers for discussion at staff meetings, preparing a scheme of work for consideration and modification, being informed about books and equipment, perhaps giving practical help to colleagues and supporting and advising by example. To produce coordinators, there have to be more courses, seminars and discussions. For such a post the 'job description' grows with experience; so does the job satisfaction.

This short chapter has tried to set out the areas which are already being explored and which need to be developed further and more fully. The task is huge. There are no easy answers and those who seek a philosopher's stone in the form of work cards or any other promises of instant success will undoubtedly be disappointed. But that is no reason for despondency. There are many people who have the experience and expertise to give support. Let me repeat what I have said many times in the past: not only have we grossly underestimated our children, we have also grossly underestimated our teachers. When you believe that, how can you fail?

Reference

DES (1983) *Science in Primary Schools*, London, HMSO.

23 Primary Science: Developments in Scotland

Sinclair Macleod

The Scottish Education Department (SED) report on primary education was published in 1980. Its findings were similar to those of the DES two years earlier and identified science as a priority area for curriculum development. However, even before the survey was carried out and the report written, initiatives were being taken both at national and regional level.

At the national level, the SED agreed to help fund the Schools Council's Learning through Science Project (see Chapter 15). The Committee on Primary Education (COPE) allocated the funds and one of its sub-committees – the Scottish Committee on Environmental Studies (SCES) – was asked to oversee the work. A steering committee was set up and three study groups were formed to discuss the draft document, 'Towards a policy for science in Primary and Middle Schools'. In addition, the discussion document was sent to every education authority in Scotland, to every college of education in Scotland and to the SED, along with a request for comment. The reports were collated by the steering committee and sent to the project team in London. As a result of the comments received, the steering committee decided to produce a shorter version more relevant to Scotland. The document (SCES, 1980) was published by COPE and distributed to every school and college of education in Scotland.

When the trials of Learning through Science pupil materials started in the autumn term of 1979 the schools used were those of the headteachers involved in the study groups. Since only twelve sets of cards on 'Ourselves' and twelve sets on 'Colour' were available and since the steering committee was of the view that it was better to have two teachers per school working on trials, it was decided that the cards would be tried in half of the schools, with the others using the corresponding Science 5–13 units only. This arrangement of trial and control schools proved to be very successful. Immediately after the trials the schools exchanged cards and tried the other set. The experience gained by the schools resulted in their incorporating science into their curricula as a matter of policy.

As the trials of further pupil cards continued, more schools from the original regions were used and some schools tried more than one set of cards. In the spring term of 1981 Grampian Region in association with Aberdeen College of Education become involved in the trial of pupil cards. Scotland has been involved in the trials of every set of Learning through Science cards and more than 200 schools have been involved. The recent involvement of Grampian Region illustrates the significance of these trials as a means to curriculum development. The schools involved sent their teachers to meetings run by the college in collaboration with the region. At the same time the promoted staffs were meeting in order to discuss the policy documents (*Towards a Policy for Science in Scottish Primary Schools* (SCES, 1980) and *Environmental Studies in the Primary School – The Development of a Policy* (SCES, 1980).

Apart from Learning through Science, other developments have been taking place. Fife and Tayside were involved in the British Association Project Award Pilot Exercise. In the Glasgow Division of Strathclyde a research project is involving the use of engineering apprentices as demonstrators and advisers in the use of the Craigie science kit. Also in Glasgow a joint approach by the education authority and Jordanhill College of Education is developing the use of science materials throughout all stages of about eighty schools. Glasgow is now producing guidelines on a science policy for schools. Central Region has also produced guidelines for a science policy, together with copies of specimen projects on 'Time' and 'Structures and Forces'. The Ayr Division of Strathclyde has set up a group of schools which, after a short in-service course to be led by the London-based Learning through Science Project team, will follow a scheme based on these work cards. Many schools, some in organized groups, are following 'Science Workshop', the new BBC TV series on primary science, and preliminary reports indicate that this could be very fruitful. There is renewed interest in the Starting Science series produced by ITV.

The way forward looks exciting as more regions recognize the need for policy statements on primary science. To date there has been a wide spectrum of approaches. At one end there are those, fortunately a dwindling band, who think that no science is good science – leave it all to the secondary school. At the other are those who would teach formal lessons from the infant stages. A similar diversity exists among those who believe science has a place in the primary school, those who think science should only appear within the area known as environmental studies and those who believe that science should have a place of its own, equal in emphasis with any subject in the curriculum. The SED publication *Primary Education in Scotland* (1965) placed science within the environmental studies component of the curriculum. In 1980 SCES produced a policy guide based on a skills and concepts approach and including science as one of the subject areas (SCES, 1980). Another divergence exists – between the followers of a process approach and those of a structured content approach. Fortunately, there are indications that these two groups are coming together. All agree that processes are important, that there are certain fundamental broad areas of content and that processes cannot be taught without content.

As a result of the HMI findings (SED, 1980), the SED decided to fund a Primary Science Development Project. This project, based in Moray House College of Education, was established in November 1981 to run for the three years. The project team believes that there are sufficient pupil resources on the market or in production. What is needed is something to help teachers make the most of these resources in the classroom and to assist promoted staff in the production of school policies. It is hoped to produce a multi-media package that can be used by individual schools or groups of schools. The particular needs of the remote school will also be taken into account. The project also intends to examine the links between science and health education and investigate topics where science and mathematics can reinforce each other. Early work at the infant level will not be neglected.

In July 1982 a national course provided participants with an overview of current developments in Scotland and enabled them to discuss ways in which a wide range of resource material could best be utilized to create and support a balanced programme of primary school science. With the existing enthusiasm among the representatives of the advisory services and colleges of education, and the goodwill of the teachers, the scientific education of young children is likely, in the future, to play an increasingly important part in their total primary school experience.

References

SCES (1980) *Environmental Studies in the Primary School – The Development of a Policy*, COPE.
SCES (1980) *Towards a Policy for Science in Scottish Primary Schools*, COPE.
SED (1965) *Primary Education in Scotland*, HMSO.
SED (1980) *Learning and Teaching in Primary 4 and Primary 7*, HMSO.

24   In-Service Teacher Education: Possible Approaches

24.1   The Development of In-Service Courses in Primary Science: One College's Approach

Leo Allsop

For many years initial training students at Newman College opting to train as primary specialists have been able to follow a course designed to help them introduce science into their teaching programmes. Although these courses were optional, they were always over-subscribed indicating that they were seen by the students as a valuable and worthwhile component of their primary training. As a result of the expertise acquired and developed in this work, the science department began to provide in-service courses for primary teachers in 1975. At that time we believed that the reason many primary teachers were not prepared to tackle science was due to a lack of confidence and that this was primarily due to their own poor scientific background. Consequently the courses provided were designed to familiarize teachers with the nature of science in the primary area through a study of selected topics. The courses included a blend of content and method in an attempt to develop the teachers' own scientific knowledge of the topic and also to demonstrate those practical applications of it, relevant to the classroom. Each course was heavily over-subscribed and selection of course members was done on the basis of LEA representation. Most courses included teachers from five to six LEAs and this original recruiting policy has been maintained throughout. Each course lasted a term with teachers attending college for one evening a week from 1600–1800 hours. Forty-five teachers were taken as three groups of fifteen, and two or three weeks devoted to each topic. Some element of choice was provided. The format of each session included a lecture/demonstration in which the underlying scientific theory was outlined, followed by practical work consisting of a range of investigations which used almost exclusively home-made apparatus. Evaluation was largely subjective, being conducted on the basis of discussions with course members and between course tutors. In general, teachers were pleased to receive clarification of what was meant by 'primary science' and to see and try out for themselves appropriate practical investigations. Course tutors, however, were left with the impression of the existence of an enormous void in teachers' awareness of the place of science in primary work and the realization that courses of this sort were probably not significantly contributing to an improvement of this situation. Many teachers, for example, had not encountered important curriculum development projects such as the 5–13 project and still fewer had actually used such material.

We were only too aware that even when teachers knew of the existence of the 5–13 project, many were unable to translate the ideas provided into suitable practical activities and investigations for their pupils. Hence in the next stage of our in-service programme we became involved in DES/Regional Courses. We based the courses on selected 5–13 topics and included formal workshop/discussion sessions. In the latter, course members were required to adapt published material for their own classroom use and more attention was given to methods of originating science work in the school curriculum, to maintaining the original impetus and to developing progression. This was achieved by firstly identifying starting points and then by drawing up flow diagrams to illustrate how the topic might develop. The work also involved identifying suitable investigations relevant to the development of part of the flow diagram, to performing and evaluating these investigations and finally to designing work cards based on the latter. Opportunity was provided for course members to assess suggestions made by others. These DES courses required more active participation and response from course members than was demanded of teachers on our early in-service courses. Most of the participants were highly motivated but a few had obviously been sent by the headteacher to 'learn some science' and were rather less motivated. The general impression of course tutors, advisers and HMIs was that, despite the provision of many such courses throughout the country, there was a disappointing lack of dissemination of ideas and progress in science in primary schools. Science was still not happening in the classroom to the extent and in a form which might counteract the type of criticism outlined in the 1978 HMI Primary Survey (see Chapter 4).

The third phase of our in-service programme attempted to tackle this problem by involving the entire staffs of two local schools where the headteachers had asked their local adviser for help, in one case to initiate science and in the other to help the staff make the transition from observational to experimental science. These teachers came to college on six occasions for instruction and advice on a chosen topic. College tutors then followed this up by going into the schools to offer continuing support and practical help. This modest experiment proved to be reasonably successful – the headteachers, advisers and tutors were, in general, pleased with the progress made, even by those teachers who orginially had insisted that science activities were not suitable or appropriate for their particular children. The success of this small-scale pilot scheme was deemed to be due to the mutual support teachers gained from one another, particularly during the regular staff meetings that were held, to the concentration of the whole staff on 'matters scientific' and to the high degree of involvement of the two headteachers. On the basis of this venture, college tutors were invited by the DES to contribute to an instructional film on resources in primary science, in collaboration with the staffs of these two schools. (This film, 'Primary School Science: Support for the Teacher', is now available from the Central Film Library.)

Consolidation of the real gains being made was achieved by extending the programme to include local school consortia. Schools within a consortium were visited by science tutors to discuss suitable topics which could be developed in the following term by the teachers in their classrooms. Once these topics had been chosen, flow diagrams were constructed by the teachers and forwarded to college for comment and modification. Areas common to most of the flow charts were selected by tutors for further development with the teachers who visited college for two input sessions. These busy sessions included some background theory, suggestions for suitable school-based practical work, displays of reference material and discussions of how the work might develop, once initiated. Science tutors then began a regular programme of school visits to follow up these 'awareness' sessions. Each school within the consortium was visited once a week for ten weeks. The post-holder for science or the deputy head of each school provided the liaison between the school staff and the college tutor and by directing the tutor to those staff with specific queries or problems, maximum use was made of available time. In most cases, teachers were consulted in their own classrooms on each of three visits. We were thus able to provide first-hand help with difficulties, suggestions for future activities and were often able to provide support in the form of apparatus for investigations. This provided excellent monitoring and discussion facilities and threw into sharp focus the real nature of the problems encountered by teachers in this area of their work. It now became quite clear that much of the reluctance of teachers to become involved with science was in fact due to their basic lack of knowledge of the subject. Assessment of this consortium work was achieved at a plenary session in which progress reports were made by individual teachers, problems were discussed and possible future developments outlined. College tutors, in particular, felt that this had proved to be a valuable experience. The advantages of working closely with teachers in the classroom were obvious but unfortunately the disadvantages were equally real. These mainly concerned not only the heavy demands made on the time of college tutors but also the fact that the system did not really tackle the root of the problem: the basic insecurity of teachers arising from lack of knowledge of science.

It was in an attempt to focus on this latter problem that our in-service programme entered a new and significant phase with the approval by the DES in 1981 of a Diploma in Primary Science, validated by the University of Birmingham. In the first year of this two-year part-time diploma we recruited eighteen teachers who attended college for some five and a half hours each week. The course has been designed to provide knowledge in science to about 0-level standard, running concurrently with primary applications of the theory. All aspects of planning, resource provision, philosophy, etc. have been included. We have great hopes that this will prove an effective way of ensuring that science becomes a more permanent feature of primary work but it is too early yet to make any kind of assessment.

Meanwhile, our DES-sponsored short course in-service provision is continuing alongside the diploma. However, in recognition of the crucial role of the headteacher in instigating, supporting and maintaining a school science policy, (see Chapter 15), the emphasis of these courses has changed. We now recruit heads and deputy heads only and, although some practical work is still included to give the 'feel' of what we mean by a practical investigation in primary science, much more emphasis is given to planning, assessment of performance and the role of the headteacher in policy-making and in the initiation of science activities in the school. There is generous provision of time for discussion and 'think-tank' sessions which have proved very useful. Our impression is that these courses are a very necessary and important form of in-service provision.

Our overall assessment of the variety of courses offered so far is that each is fulfilling a different aspect of the same purpose, some more successfully than others. Short awareness-courses for class teachers should be judged on how effectively they motivate teachers to introduce, develop and maintain some science activities in their classrooms. The effectiveness of courses for head-teachers obviously depends on the individual, and how successfully he can motivate his staff and maintain any impetus which may be achieved. However, in the long term both these approaches may still lead to a lack of progress in our schools due to the teacher's inability to recognize the science inherent in an everyday situation. It *is* clear, however, that the continual assessment of the success or otherwise of in-service courses in science, on the basis of what happens in the classroom, cannot be part of the job of a college of education lecturer. For this we must work to improve the feedback from appropriate HMIs and advisers.

24.2 *Whom Are We Trying to Help?:*
In-School Work in Primary Science

Muriel Whittaker

Primary teachers, mostly not science specialists, pressed to include science in their teaching programme, will bring to the task ideas about, and attitudes to, the subject, derived from their own educational and social experience. If resource materials and in-service provision are to be usable by a teacher, they must be capable of assimilation to that teacher's frames of reference. If it is desired to modify attitudes or frames of reference, it is essential to be clear about the position from which one starts, as well as the final goal, and to provide steps and resting places along the way. Very few people are capable of deliberately making radical changes in their view of the world; most can modify it gradually, if they are convinced of the value of doing so. It is my contention that, too often, we veer widely between demanding that teachers radically change their ideas, and then, under their protests, pandering too completely to their views (see Chapter 14). Neither is profitable.

Considerable attention has been paid to the need to match science teaching to children's developmental levels (Harlen, 1977; Gagné, 1965; Shayer and Adey, 1981). Some careful thought has been given, for instance, by the West Sussex 5–14 scheme and the Leeds Middle School Project, to the need for a hierarchical progression of ideas within a topic, if full understanding is to be reached.

Too little attention has been paid to helping teachers to identify their own levels of understanding in science, although there has been some work on, for instance, concept levels of students and of the adult population (Kuhn, 1979; Lovell, 1974; Lawson, 1979). At one end of the spectrum of curriculum provision for primary science, there seems to be an assumption that all teachers have, or can somehow magically attain, advanced understanding of the nature and processes of science. Such an assumption makes it difficult for a teacher to examine his or her own understanding critically, in case threatening deficiencies become apparent. On the other hand, one hears a lot about 'the ordinary classroom teacher', whose attainments in science seem to be rated almost insultingly low. This offers little encouragement to the teacher whose self-esteem in the subject is already poor, and encourages a comfortable laziness of mind which results in lack of challenge to children working in science.

Primary science, in the view of most curriculum developers now working in the field, should be essentially exploratory, involving children in active investigation, observation and experiment at their own level, and strongly related to their own interests (see Chapter 6). According to the survey by HMI 1978, science should teach children skills such as observing, formulating hypotheses, experimenting, recording, identifying significant patterns, studying mechanical artefacts and carrying out constructional activities. The Match and Mismatch Project's publication, *Raising Questions*, has an important page, 'Is Science being learned here?', setting out criteria for identifying classroom situations which facilitate science learning. Such an approach to science, with its emphasis on the process and developmental stage, is, as I shall show below, not within the experience of most primary teachers, in their own education.

Enthusiasm for process in primary science work was at its height in the late 1960s. The desire to enthuse teachers who claimed not to know any science led, at its extreme, to the claim that 'content is unimportant'. Sad experience of the potential of this principle, uncritically applied, for producing a mass of unfocussed work, impossible to evaluate, led to some rethinking. Attempts were made to outline basic scientific ideas that could be developed in primary school (see Chapter 7, and various local schemes.) However, the emphasis continues to be on an investigative, exploratory approach, based on concrete experience, not a didactic, theoretical one. Such an approach places great reliance on the teacher's questioning, observational and improvisatory skills. If teachers cannot observe critically and devise clear problem-posing questions and experiments to solve some of them, they can hardly help children to develop these skills; nor will they recognize their beginnings in a child's tentative speculations.

I have argued elsewhere (Whittaker, 1980) that a large majority of primary teachers now in post will have had very limited experience of science, especially the physical sciences, in their own schooling. Data in HMI survey show that 80 per cent of all primary teachers are women, and 75 per cent of all primary teachers in 1978 had five years' experience or more. Thus their own schooling will have taken place at a period when we know that girls' science education was often very limited (see Kelly, 1981). There is, in any case, plenty of evidence that girls have not been expected to be good at science.

On the other hand, the 20 per cent of primary teachers who are men are somewhat more likely to have had a more extended science education, and will certainly not have been socially discouraged from it. Indeed, they may complain that they are expected to be able to teach science, with no better formal background than their female colleagues. Their problems in approaching primary science will be different from those of women.

Teachers who did have science education at least to 0-level will not necessarily be better equipped thereby to tackle primary science. The HMI Secondary Survey (1979) states that, in many cases, science teaching 'offered few opportunities for pupils to show initative or develop speculative thinking'. Pupils recorded what they and the teacher?) thought they knew; opportunity to make appropriate selections from sets of observations was not provided. My own initial training students, writing for me about their science education, frequently report that they disliked science because only right answers were accepted ... and they kept getting wrong ones, which were simply disregarded. Or, if they had liked science, it was because they did get their answers right, and they felt uneasy in a situation where the answer was not 'known'. Only a tiny minority had ever been encouraged to speculate in science.

Tests of students' science concepts, using a simple list such as that of Harlen (1977). reveal many examples of misconceptions, held often in total disregard of actual experience. 'The sun is overhead at midday' ... in England on a sunny November morning! 'Air pressure holds things down on the Earth's surface'; 'Things stop moving because they run out of momentum'; 'Heavy things fall faster than light ones'; and the endless confusions between 'heavier than' and 'more dense than' and dissolving and melting are just a few. Such learning is characteristic of Ausubel's (1963) 'rote learning', which, he points out, is often developed because of chronic experience of failure in a subject. Barnes (1976) contrasts 'school knowledge', with little relation to life outside the classroom, and 'action knowledge', which is incorporated by the learner into his map of reality. It seems clear that, for a teacher to operate effectively in primary science, he or she needs action knowledge. It is equally clear that many students lack it.

Have these deficiencies been addressed in the initial training of teachers? All too often the answer must be 'No'. A survey in 1981 of 655 primary teachers in Derbyshire found that 257 had no curriculum science in their initial training. Of those who had, 187 said it was adequate, a number saying they had taken science as a main study, and doubting whether the course would have been adequate for non–scientists; 205 said it was inadequate, complaining specifically that it was too content orientated, with a secondary bias and lacking relevance to the primary schools. Interestingly, a survey in 1974 of a smaller sample, 273 teachers, produced responses in much the same proportions (Whittaker, 1976).

The target population for in-service work in primary science is obviously highly heterogeneous. A competent teacher, faced with a class of children of such varied background, would surely resort to some form of individualized or small-group learning; yet much in-service provision seems to ignore the customers' background, and much resource material seems to assume that, while the children will be at different stages, the teachers will not be. That the providers may have been abetted in this by the teachers themselves is really little excuse.

Unless effort is spent on identifying a teacher's stage of understanding of science as a process and a human activity, suggestions for content will be treated as a syllabus, to be 'done'. Even worse, we shall find offered in the primary school 'experiments' which 'prove' something only when they 'work', the so-called proof being often an argument of perfect circularity, or at least very dubious logic.

If a proper match is to be achieved between what is provided and the teacher's needs, tutors and providers of resources must work hard and critically to evaluate their expertise in science in terms of the real teachers who are looking for help. One teacher wrote of her initial training, 'In designing a science course we need to determine what is being taught, and what children enjoy learning about. Lecturers with pure science backgrounds have little to offer teachers.' While not sharing her pessimism, I would strongly agree that we science specialists must respect the teaching expertise of non-scientists, and present our discipline in ways to which they can relate, if we wish to help them, and thus their children, to grow in understanding. What follows is a, necessarily personal, account of an exploration of ways of doing this.

Like most college tutors, I became involved in courses for teachers at teachers' centres. Anyone who does this, sooner or later meets the response, 'It's all very well, but you couldn't do that with my children.' (This often means that one has failed to communicate the emphasis on process, and the teacher is concerned about 'right answers'.) My answer, whenever possible, was, 'Lend me your children, and we'll see.' When this offer was accepted, I found the rewards were great. I increased my own experience of children's responses to the material I was offering. The teacher, if not won over, was able to criticize from a more informed standpoint, and I made contact and often worked with other teachers at the same school. I was sometimes able to arrange for students to share the work, and their response was always favourable. At least, it helped with the problem of credibility of the tutor on initial training and in-service courses!

I felt the advantages of working in this way lay in the reciprocity involved. The teachers and I recognized and valued each other's expertise, and the children told us clearly, by their effort and involvement, if we were getting it right. We achieved much more together than we might have separately, and the school benefitted more than is sometimes the case when a teacher simply attends a course. I have attempted to illustrate the differences I see in the patterns of working in Figures 1 and 2.

I was fortunate in being offered the chance to test my ideas on in-school in-service work in a more structured way by taking part in a DES-initiated project. This would not have been possible without the support and back-up assistance of my college, and the interest and help of the Derbyshire LEA advisory service. The project ran for two years, following essentially the same pattern in both years.

In each year, I worked with a linked groups of schools, covering the full

Figure 1
Course Run from a College or Teachers' Centre

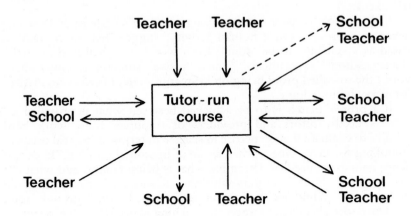

Some teachers successfully apply the work in school – solid outward arrow

Some teachers do not succeed with the work in school – broken outward arrow

Some teachers do not use the work at all – no outward arrow

Figure 2
In-School In-Service

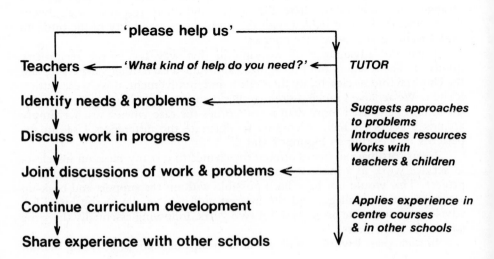

nursery, infant and junior age-range. The enthusiasm and involvement of the heads was, of course, vital. The schools were offered a total of one and a half days of my time and a small sum of money for equipment. In return, they were asked to ensure that as a many teachers as possible took part in the project. I explained to staff meetings that my function was to help to develop science work in the schools, in cooperation with the teachers. I was available for consultation, to help teach classes, to advise on books and resources, or to help in any other way that seemed useful. I explained my approach to primary science, especially the emphasis on practical investigation and on children's ideas and interests, with written work arising only when the children felt they had something to record.

The schools in the first year of the project were a nursery, an infant and a junior school, linked but in separate buildings. In these schools, I eventually worked at least once with nearly all the classes, having had extensive consultations beforehand with the teachers about the topic they were following, and where a contribution from me might fit. I emphasized that what I did would be just one of several possibilities, and that I would use my personal judgement on how to proceed as an in-comer with an unknown class. It was not to be seen as a demonstration lesson. In these sessions, some teachers asked me to deal with or extend a part of a topic they felt the children should cover, but of which they themselves were not sure. Others, more confident, valued most the specimens and equipment I could bring in. In either case, one of my main aims was to allow the teacher to stand back and watch their children, whether or not they approved my particular teaching style.

I hoped through the project to encourage the teachers to think about children's progression in science throughout the primary age-range. To this end, we held three joint staff meetings, covering the staffs of the three schools, at which the work in progress was outlined. I hoped that the teachers would be able to relate the work being done at other stages to their own planning. These meetings were only partially successful. Some teachers, mostly of the younger children, did feel that sharing experience was valuable. However, others shared the view expressed by one senior teacher, 'As far as I'm concerned, when they come to me they know nothing' – hardly encouraging in a joint meeting, and important only as illustrating a common, and very limited, view of 'knowing'.

Some really good work was done by the children, and the schools decided, jointly with the local teachers' centre, to hold an exhibition of the work done for other teachers to visit. I felt ambivalent about this, fearing that concentration on the production of exhibitable material might prove an impediment to, and an excuse for avoiding, real thought about the process of science. To some extent these fears were justified, but against this must be set the fact that the exhibition was visited by over 100 teachers, as well as by many parents and local people whose interest had been caught by children's enthusiastic accounts of what they had been doing. There is no doubt that the social benefits were very great, and there was in-service benefit as well, both in increasing the involvement of some teachers within the schools, and in catching the interest of those from other schools. Those teachers already well advanced in their understanding of primary science used the exhibition to extend their children's work, with great skill. The nursery teachers also produced a booklet on the science work they had done, which has been most valuable in in-service courses elsewhere in the LEA.

The second year of the project involved linked junior and infant schools, the infant school having a nursery unit. I aimed to build on the previous year's experience while remaining broadly responsive to the wishes of the schools. The pattern of work was somewhat less structured than the previous year.

In the junior school, I worked through the teacher with responsibility for science, and through the deputy head, and had most contact with their classes and that of a probationer. Other teachers consulted me over topics and resources. In the infant school, we had a number of lunch-time consultancy sessions, with the whole staff and with individuals. Again, I worked with several classes.

I did not specifically design joint meetings this time, but the teachers soon asked for sessions after school on particular topics. These were well attended, by both junior and infant teachers, and provided a means of developing the ideas about progression which I had tried, but failed, to do in the first year's schools. Some teachers who had felt unfavourably towards the project were won over to the idea of primary science by these sessions, as they came to see that the concrete, exploratory approach was not 'stealing the secondaries' thunder'. The session were also valuable in letting the teachers see one another's strengths and limitations in science – in my opinion an essential preliminary to devising a school scheme.

The junior school, whose science planning had originally been for specific, clearly defined science lessons, began to look for science possibilities in relation to the rest of the curriculum, and we specifically examined their history and geography schemes with this in mind. The infant school developed its work in science into an exhibit for the local science fair in the summer term.

At the end of the second year, we held a meeting of the teachers with science responsibility to discuss our views on the project. In general, they felt it had been of considerable value. Benefits generally mentioned were:

Taking place in school made it easier for more teachers to take part, and helped to increase confidence because it was 'home ground';

The project could be used in different ways, according to the teachers' perceived needs, initial level of expertise and preferred way of working;

Having the consultant tutor available to work with the children helped the teacher because it was possible to stand back and observe the children's response; this was felt to improve the teacher's planning for science work;

Ideas about the nature of science and its place in the primary school were changed and extended; some became more favourable, no one became less favourable towards it;

The project catalyzed discussionof the whole curriculum, especially in the junior schools; these discussions had continued, at a more analytical level than had been achieved previously.

Disadvantages mentioned were more specific to events at particular schools, particularly involving conflicts over the tutor's role. It was felt that problems which arose were due to inexperience in this way of working, not inherent in the project. It was interesting to hear that some teachers had been dubious about the open-ended approach, feeling that they would prefer to be told what to do, but they had later agreed that this style had helped them to think for themselves.

From the tutor's point of view, this way of working is demanding, because it cannot be wholly planned. However, colleges encourage students to work this way with children, so we should at least remind ourselves of the demands of the style. There may also be administrative problems over timetabling and 'student numbers'. Nevertheless, a total of forty teachers was reached by the project, some of whom have already moved on promotion to other schools.

In-school work must be related to the network of other in-service provision (see Chapter 22). This project benefitted from the strong provision for primary science within the LEA and was able to feed back into it. Whatever the problems, I believe the advantages are such that it should be seen as an important part of in-service provision in this field.

References

Ausubel, D. (1963) *The Psychology of Meaningful Verbal Learning*, Greene and Stratton.

Barnes, D. (1976) *From Communication to Curriculum*, Penguin Educational.

Des (1978) *Primary Education in England: A Survey by HM Inspectors of Schools*, London, HMSO.

Des (1979) *Aspects of Secondary Education in England*, London, HMSO.

Gagné, R. (1977) *The Conditions of Learning*, Holt, Rinehart and Winston.

Harlen, W. (1978) 'Does content matter in primary science?', in *School Science Review*, 59. (Chapter 7 in this book)

Harlen, W. *et al.* (1977) *Raising Questions, Finding Answers*, Match and Mismatch, Oliver and Boyd.

Kelly, A. (Ed.) (1981) *The Missing Half: Girls and Science Education*, Manchester University Press.

Kuhn, D. and Capon, N. (1979) 'Logical reasoning in the supermarket: Adult females' use of a propositional reasoning strategy in an everyday context', in *Developmental Psychology*, 15.

Lawson, A. (1979) 'The developmental learning paradigm', in *Journal of Research in Science Teaching*, 16, 6.

Lovell, K. (1974) 'Intellectual growth and understanding science', in *Studies in Science Education*, 1.

Shayer, M. and Adey, P. (1981) *Towards a Science of Science Teaching*, Heinemann Educational.

Whittaker, M. (1976) 'An investigation into teachers' attitudes to objectives for primary science teaching', in *School Science Review*, 58.

Whittaker, M. (1980) ' "They're only playing": The problem of primary science', in *School Science Review*, 61.

The Teaching of Primary Science: An Introductory Annotated Bibliography

Compiled by Robert England

This annotated bibliography provides brief descriptions of published material in addition to that found in this book. The bibliography is very selective, but in the opinion of the compiler and the editors it refers to most of the important British books and articles published in the area of primary science since 1958.

Allen, G. *et al.* (1958) *Scientific Interests in the Primary School,* National Froebel Foundation.

> Science is viewed mainly as an extension of nature study, but including all natural phenomena in its field of exploration. The role of the teacher and the place of children's questions are explained, along with practical suggestions as to how to develop children's scientific interests. Evaluative questions for teachers at the end of the book indicate the general approach advocated, for example, 'Am I in touch with the children's real interests? ... Have I resisted the temptation to generalise ...?'

APU (1977) *Science Progress Report 1977–78 Appendix: List of Science Concepts and Knowledge*

> Contains a list of over forty generalizations ('concept statements') which, it is argued, form an appropriate content base for the assessment of pupil performance in science at the age of 11.

ASE (1971) *Science for the Under-13s*

> Discusses science for the 8–13s in relation to knowledge about child development, curriculum planning, suitability of various teaching methods, accommodation, staffing and teacher-training.

ASE (1974a) *Science and Primary Education Papers, No. 1: The Present Situation – A Review*

> The first paper produced to elaborate some of the suggestions and recommendations of 'Science for the Under-13s'. Contains a summary of

teachers' opinions as to what sort of science is appropriate for primary school children.

ASE (1974b) *Science and Primary Education Papers, No. 2: The Role of the Headteacher*

The paper attempts to demonstrate to headteachers the importance and place of science in the school curriculum. It gives examples of how scientific experience may develop from aspects of curriculum which should already exist. Organization, communication, resources and staffing are also discussed.

ASE (1976) *Science and Primary Education Papers, No. 3: A Post of Responsibility*

Discusses the importance of staff and pupil working relationships and suggests how to get science started in the school. Gives useful guidelines for the selection and organization of resources. Describes the way in which science activities should be developed and provides many practical hints and tips along with useful lists of resources.

ASE (1981) *Education through Science: Policy Statement*

Contains a number of important recommendations for the teaching of primary science and the training of primary teachers. An orthodox view of primary science is presented, laying stress on 'first-hand experience' and 'the exploration of the immediate environment'. Stresses that 'the Association remains firmly committed to the development of effective provision of science education in the early years of schooling.'

ATCDE et al. (1959) *Science in the Primary School*, John Murray.

Provides guidance for those endeavouring to extend nature study to include physical science. Gives examples of how 'scientific exploration' with young children may proceed, and sets out some areas of content thought to be appropriate. Telling children answers to scientific questions, and the attitude of 'Science on Thursdays, from 2.30 to 3.00', are strongly discouraged in favour of children's active involvement with questions which they can solve or part-solve.

Bainbridge, J.W. et al. (1970) *Junior Science Source Book*, Collins.

A reference book of scientific information, derived from, and related to, the environment, and appropriate for children of primary and middle school ages. To be dipped into by those who wish to get their facts straight before setting the children to work, and also by those with scientific or non-scientific backgrounds who wish to gain useful ideas and suggestions. The emphasis is on children's enquiries backed by teacher's knowledge of where they may usefully lead.

Bingham, C.D. (1976) 'The New Nuffield Combined Science themes for the middle years', in *Education in Science*, September, pp. 15–18.

Explains how the themes arose, describes their content and format, and points out how the materials and approach may match the various forms of organization in schools catering for children in the 'middle years'. (See Chapter 16 in this book.)

Booth, N. (1971) 'Middle school science', in *Trends in Education*, 24, October, pp. 13–16.

Discusses the variability of approaches to science teaching in the middle years in the context of major curriculum development projects. Proposes that 'no-one has yet produced a nationally acceptable core of material suitable for young children, capable of being soundly taught by class teachers without specialist qualifications in science and acceptable as a foundation for what comes later.' The case for such a core is outlined.

Booth, N. (1978) 'Science in the middle years', in *Education 3–13*, 6, 2, October, pp. 37–41.

Describes the author's view of the nature and purpose of science in the middle years, and notes some approaches that should be used. It points to some 'areas of experience' from which a common syllabus could be drawn, briefly discusses 'pupil differences' and the identification of outstanding potential in pupils.

Bradley, H. (1979) 'Strategies for INSET in primary science', in *Cambridge Journal of Education*, 9, 2 and 3, Michaelmas term, pp. 112–15.

A short article, drawing on the author's previous work, and indicating reasons for poor responses to INSET in this area. The importance of providing science semi-specialists and the need for school-based INSET are highlighted.

Brown, C.A. (1980) 'Planning for primary science: An investigation into the difficulties faced by primary teachers in this area of the curriculum', in *British Journal of In-Service Education* 6, 3, summer, pp. 148–52.

Reports a study of attempts to improve INSET effectiveness by developing teachers' science skills. Improvements in general scientific ability are noted. Concentrates on teachers' ability to plan science topics.

Central Advisory Council for Education (England) (1967) *Children and Their Primary Schools*, HMSO, Chapter 17 (G), pp. 240–7.

The essential elements of 'the new approach' (learning by discovery) are discussed with respect to science in the context of the 'increasing variety of subject matter' in primary schools. Examples from infant and junior classrooms briefly illustrate the general approach which is commended.

Clegg, A. (1977) 'Science and environmental studies', in *Trends in Education*, winter, pp. 20–5.

Should science be integrated, or just associated with other aspects of environmental studies, such as history and geography? This problem is examined and illustrated with some useful examples of junior and middle school practice.

Conran, R.J. (1980) 'Nature study: Its rehabilitation', in *Education 3–13*, 8, 2, pp. 12–18.

Maintains that nature study should not be neglected in the primary curriculum since it provides a good introduction to the fostering of scientific skills of enquiry. Discusses the importance of children's familiarization with scientific concepts by multiple experiences, and considers the nature of inferences children might draw from these.

Crossland, R.W. (1972) 'An individual study of the Nuffield Foundation Primary Science Project', in *School Science Review*, 53, March, pp. 628–38.

A study of teachers' responses to the project, based on interviews and questionnaires during 1966/67, and including comments on pupils' scientific and non-scientific gains. Responses from 'progressive' and 'conventional' teachers are compared. The further training of 'conventional' teachers is discussed and the importance of teachers' scientific knowledge considered.

Department of Education and Science (1983) *Science in Primary Schools*, HMSO.

A discussion paper produced by the HMI Science Committee which squarely faces the difficulties involved in initiating science in primary schools and which suggests ways forward. Discusses scientific processes and ideas, and stresses the importance of continuity and progression. Has a useful section on organization and staffing and concludes with implications and recommendations for schools and local education authorities. A realistic appraisal and agenda for action.

Diamond, D. (1978) *Introduction and Guide to Teaching Primary Science*, Macdonald.

Introduces a series of books aimed to help class teachers and students in training to provide children with a wide variety of 'small, practical experiences'. The aim is that the pupils will be able to generalize from their own discoveries. Suggests skills that should be fostered by the various activities, and gives many practical suggestions for using easy to hand, cheap resources, as well as suggesting activities involving children in 'making and doing'. No scientific background is assumed of the teacher.

Elliott, J. and Harlen, W. (1980) *Portrait of a Project*, Schools Council.

Reviews strategies used by the Progress in Learning Science Project during its dissemination through in-service teacher education. The project aimed to help teachers of 5–13-year-olds gather information about their children's abilities, concepts and attitudes, and make decisions about learning activities and teaching strategies based on this information. It offers portrayal of the project through consideration of its history and its ideas at the point of their reception by the intended clientele. In doing so, it provides a reflective study of the process of dissemination.

Ennever, L. and Harlen, W. (1972) *With Objectives in Mind: Guide to Science 5–13*, Macdonald Educational.

Explains the philosophy of the Science 5–13 project. Exemplary objectives are listed and are related to eight broad aims and Piagetian stages of development. The overall theme is to 'develop an enquiring mind and a scientific approach to problems'. (See Chapter 14 in this book.)

Evans, P. (1977) *Technology in the Primary School,* ASE (also in *School Science Review*, 58, 205, pp. 635–57).

The creative potential of science education when approached through technology is illustrated with examples of how children in a Devon primary school identified and solved problems by designing, building and using apparatus.

Harlen, W. (1975) *Science 5–13: A Formative Evaluation*, Schools Council Research Studies, Macmillan Education.

Discusses the aims and methods of Science 5–13, outlines the role of evaluation in the project, and details the various attempts made to evaluate four sets of units. Last chapter draws out some lessons from the variety of evaluation methods used.

Harlen, W. (1977) 'Science and scientific thinking across the curriculum', in *Cambridge Journal of Education*, 7, 3, Michaelmas term, pp. 130–4.

A theoretical discussion of science in relation to different models of the curriculum. The questions of science as a subject and its links with other areas of the curriculum are examined. This is the introductory article of a special issue of the *Cambridge Journal of Education* on the above title.

Harlen, W. (1980) 'Selecting content in primary science', in *Education 3–13*, 8, 2, pp. 19–23.

Based on theoretical and practical considerations, three criteria are set out for the selection of content. Who should set guidelines, and at what level, is discussed along with whether these should be used for planning or evaluation. A major theme is that processes, attitudes and concepts are interpenetrating strands in the nature of children's development in science.

Harlen, W. *et al.* (1977a) *Raising Questions*, Match and Mismatch, Oliver and Boyd.

Examines ways of determining children's level of development in relation to particular skills, concepts and attitudes. Three major themes are discussed: making and recording observations about children; children's development and learning; and making decisions about the learning environment. Contains checklists of items related to earlier and later development in science.

Harlen, W. *et al.* (1977b) *Finding Answers*, Match and Mismatch, Oliver and Boyd.

Discusses the meaning of each item in the checklists in *Raising Questions*, discusses the kind of development which can be expected, and suggests experiences which are likely to help children's learning.

Hitchfield, E. (1980) 'Early scientific trends in children – a tribute to the work of Nathan Isaacs', in *Education 3–13*, 8, 2, pp. 24–7.

Reviews the contribution of Nathan Isaacs to thought about how children's initial interests and 'proto-scientific thinking' provide a basis from which to work. Outlines and explains two of his pieces of work: 'Early Scientific Trends in Children', and 'Children Learning through Scientific Interests'.

Isaacs, N. (1958) *Early Scientific Trends in Children*, National Froebel Foundation.

Discusses the place of young children's natural curiosity and interest in finding out, as well as their quest for reasons and explanations, in relation to the nature of science itself. The goal to be sought is seen as one of concurrent organic growth from children's proto-scientific interests towards science, both as ordered knowledge and as method.

Leeds University Institute of Education (1973), *The Objectives of Teacher Education*, NFER.

Identifies specific needs of pupils in the middle years of schooling. From that suggests four spheres of activity for the middle school curriculum to embrace, including exploration and learning about the physical environment through science studies. The kinds of opportunities science studies should provide are mapped out separately for the early (3–9), middle (9–13) and later years at school in terms of pupils' needs and the professional needs of teachers.

Ministry of Education (1959) *Primary Education: Suggestions for the Consideration of Teachers and Others Concerned with the Work of Primary Schools*, HMSO, Chapter 17.

Considers the common ground between geography and natural history. Discusses the growth of physical science from natural history and explains the teacher's role in this. Success is viewed in the extent to which 'children have come to regard ignorance as a challenge to inquiry'.

Ministry of Education (1961) *Science in Primary Schools,* Pamphlet No. 42, HMSO.

Emphasizes the value of science as direct experience of the environment and discusses starting-points, syllabus construction, organization and development. Briefly comments on the relationship between primary school science and secondary school science.

National Froebel Foundation (1966) *Children Learning through Scientific Interests.*

Basic premises as to how children learn most effectively are illustrated by using, and commenting upon, teachers' accounts of children's interests which developed in their classrooms. Issues discussed include children's variable reactions to making records of their discoveries and also the sustaining and reviving of children's interest.

Norwood, D. and Bonner, I. (1981) 'Developing primary science through IT-INSET', in *Education 3–13,* 9, 4, spring, pp. 32–7.

Describes how school-focussed in-service education was combined with the initial training of student teachers to aid the review and development of one school's science curriculum.

Nuffield Junior Science (1967) *Teacher's Guide I* and *Teacher's Guide II*, Collins.

Teacher's Guide I deals with the principles of child-centred education as related to primary science under such headings as 'Children Learning', 'Children in the Classroom', and 'Problems of Classroom Organisation'. Teacher's Guide II contains a large number of case studies. A basic premise of the approach is that 'Children are people. They grow into tomorrow only as they live today.' (See Chapter 13 in this book.)

Perkins, W.H. (Ed.) (1962) *The Place of Science in Primary Education*, British Association for the Advancement of Science.

Proceedings of a BAAS/ATCDE conference, with papers by Nathan Isaacs, Jack Kerr, headmasters of schools and directors and inspectors of education in different parts of the country. Discusses problems and solutions in introducing 'science' into the primary school, rather than 'just nature study'. (See Chapter 10 in this book.)

Prestt, B. (1976a) 'Science education: A reappraisal, part I', in *School Science Review*, 57, June, pp. 628–34.

Prestt, B. (1976b) 'Science education: A reappraisal, part II', in *School Science Review*, 58, December, pp. 203–9.

This two-part study suggests a two-stage (primary/secondary) framework for science education. Each stage is explained in part II.

Redman, S. *et al.* (1969) *An Approach to Primary Science*, Macmillan.

> Science is discussed within a framework of four major concepts: energy, structure, life and chance. Each of these areas, along with subordinate concepts, is discussed in relation to teaching approaches and content appropriate in school. No particular method or style of teaching is emphasized. (See Chapter 12 in this book.)

Richards, R. *et al.* (1980) *Learning through Science: Formulating a School Policy with an Index to Science 5–13*, MacDonald Educational.

> Provides a five-stage strategy for formulating a school policy in science. Contains a very detailed index to the twenty-six source books of Science 5–13 (See Chapter 15 of this book.)

Scottish Committee on Environmental Studies in the Primary School (1980a) *Environmental Studies in the Primary School: The Development of a Policy*, Committee on Primary Education.

> Discusses and illustrates how a school policy in environmental studies can be designed to develop six basic skills and nine basic concepts by means of an appropriate balance of content topics involving science, health education, history and geography.

Scottish Committee on Environmental Studies in the Primary School (1980b) *Towards a Policy for Science in Scottish Primary Schools*, Committee on Primary Education.

> Discusses the nature of primary science and argues the case for its inclusion in the primary curriculum. Provides a classification of attitudes, skills and concepts which scientific activities foster. Outlines how a school policy might be formulated and implemented.

Shayer, M. and Adey, P. (1981) *Towards a Science of Science Teaching*, Heinemann Educational.

> Based on findings of the Concepts in Secondary Mathematics and Science Project, the book explains the methods and results of the research programme. It describes testing instruments (Science Reasoning Tasks) which teachers can use to assess the cognitive levels of their pupils, and gives details of a Curriculum Analysis Taxonomy for analyzing the level of difficulty of any science activity. The authors' finding that the average age at which each Piagetian stage is attained is far higher than is usually quoted has direct implications for the choice and structuring of primary science activities.

Squires, A. (1976) *A.S.E. Study Series No. 6: Science in the Middle Years*, ASE.

> Carefully explains theoretical issues in the philosophy of science, educational psychology and curriculum development. These are discussed in relation to existing resources, organization and course design.

Squires, A. (1980) *Core Intentions for Science in the Middle Years,* The Middle Years Science Curriculum Project, Leeds City Council Department of Education.

> Maps the concept of core science in terms of three parameters: scientific ways of working, scientific ideas and making use of these scientific skills and ideas. Core science is then briefly set within the whole curriculum. A detailed mapping of core science suitable for the middle years follows, based on seventeen areas of content such as 'growth', 'heat', 'rocks and minerals'. Finally, this mapping of core science provides the basis for an example of a four-year programme for science activities and of a topic-centred teaching approach.

Ward, A. (1980a) 'Thoughts on the style of primary science', in *School Science Review*, 61, 216, pp. 418–26.

> Gives examples of how primary science can be spontaneous or integrated with other subjects and can 'awaken a sense of wondering open-mindedness in young children'. Simple examples of 'instant science' are given and the 'magical' quality of science discussed. The process of science is seen as an approach to problem-solving which is largely 'applied commonsense'.

Ward, A. (1980b) 'Questions of primary science: Important questions which have been asked by teachers, with some practical answers', in *School Science Review*, 61, 217, June, pp. 639–47.

> Intended to persuade any teacher that he or she *can* teach primary science. Important questions answered include, 'Why attempt scientific activities with infants and juniors?'; '. . . how do I start organising lessons . . .?'; 'I don't think I could teach *real* science'; 'How do I know whether the result of a child's experiment is correct?' Practical advice is given about work cards, attitudes, questioning, the class lesson and investigations. It emphasizes the process of science throughout.

Contributors

Leo Allsop is Principal Lecturer and Head of Science at Newman College.

Arthur Ashton is Headteacher of Elaine Junior School, Kent.

Paul Black is Professor of Science Education and Director of the Centre for Science and Mathematics Education at Chelsea College, University of London.

Margaret Collis was formerly an Inspector of Education in Kent and a member of the Learning through Science Project team.

Jean Conran is Principal Lecturer, Science Education Centre, Froebel College, Roehampton Institute of Higher Education.

Barry Davis is a primary school teacher who was seconded as an advisory teacher to help develop primary science in Oxfordshire.

Elizabeth Engel is a research officer for the National Foundation for Educational Research.

Robert England is Year Leader and Mathematics Coordinator, Stanton Middle School, Milton Keynes.

Peter Evans is Headteacher of the primary school in Holsworthy, Devon.

Wynne Harlen is Senior Research Fellow at Chelsea College, University of London.

Derek Holford is Lecturer in Education, University of Leicester.

Nathan Isaacs was a businessman, philosopher and important contributor to the scientific education of young children.

Jack Kerr was Emeritus Professor of Education at the University of Leicester.

Sinclair MacLeod is Lecturer in Biology at Moray House College of Education.

Gerry McClelland is Lecturer in Education concerned with curriculum studies at the University of Sheffield.

Sheila Parker-Jelly is Director of Studies, Department of Professional Studies in Education, Bristol Polytechnic.

Stewart Redman was Director of the Oxford Primary Science Project.

Colin Richards was formerly Lecturer in Education at the University of Leicester and is now a member of Her Majesty's Inspectorate of Schools.

Roy Richards is Principal Lecturer in Education at Goldsmiths College and was Director of the Learning through Science Project.

Anne Squires was until recently the Organizer of the Leeds Middle Years Science Curriculum Project.

Bill Thornley is Headteacher of St Cleophas C. of E. Primary School, Liverpool.

Ron Wastnedge was Organizer of the Nuffield Junior Science Project and a member of Her Majesty's Inspectorate of Schools.

Molly Wetton was Headteacher of Heathcote Memorial Middle School, Surrey.

Muriel Whittaker was until recently a Senior Lecturer at Derby Lonsdale College of Higher Education.

Subject Index

BBC, 21, 22, 26, 139, 184, 244
Bristol, University of, 138
Britain
  see United Kingdom
British Association for the Advancement
  of Science, 140

Chelsea College, 85
Children's Centre (Natural History
  Museum), 21–2
Committee on Primary Education
  (COPE), 234, 243
content approach, 6, 14, 17–27, 40–1, 45,
  46–7, 54, 60–9, 76, 143–4, 169, 182,
  244
  see also process approach; primary sci-
    ence curriculum, content
curriculum
  consistency in, 9–10, 11
  content, 181, 187–99, 238, 259–67
  continuity in, 8–9, 11
  development, 14, 39, 125–9, 233, 243–
    5, 259–67
  evaluation, 10–11, 15, 39–40, 41–2,
    169
  range, 4–5, 11
  structure, 5–8, 9–10, 11
  see also primary science curriculum

Department of Education and Science
  (DES), 10, 26–7, 69, 75, 248–9
  see also author index

Education Act (1944), 3
Elementary Science Study (ESS), 140–1
England, 3, 11, 46, 83, 84, 175–80, 234,
  237–41, 252–6
  see also United Kingdom
ESN schools, 144, 145
evaluation

of children's progress, 40–2, 71–81,
  161
  see also curriculum evaluation; monitor-
    ing; recording

Froebel Institute, 17, 144
  see also Froebel Foundation (author
  index)

Her Majesty's Inspectorate (HMI), 42,
  125, 196, 198, 234, 237–41, 248, 250
[HMI] Primary Survey
  see Department of Education and Scien-
    ce (author index)

Impact and Take Up Project, 150, 156
in-service education, 51, 145, 151, 162,
  196, 199, 233–57, 261, 262, 265
  see also teacher training
Ireland, Northern, 11, 84
  see also United Kingdom

LEAs
  see local education authorities
learning process
  in children, 6–7, 20–1, 47, 101–23,
    126, 131–8, 139–46, 147–57, 162–4,
    167–72, 175, 182, 202–4, 205, 250–
    1, 263–5, 266
Learning through Science Project, 6, 8–9,
  26, 30, 51, 126–9, 151, 153, 159–65,
  207, 227, 234, 243–4
local education authorities (LEAs), 9, 10,
  11, 21, 26–7, 39, 40, 42, 135, 147, 149,
  150, 151, 154, 162, 213, 223, 247, 256–
  7
'Look' scheme, 41, 169

materials
  see teaching materials
Micro-Electronics in Education Program-

271

Author Index